THE GLOBAL INVESTOR

Opportunities, Risks and Realities for Insitutional Investors in the World's Markets

Gavin R. Dobson
Blairlogie Capital Management

Probus Publishing Company
Cambridge, England
Chicago, Illinois

First published in 1994 by
Probus Europe, 11 Millers Yard, Mill Lane, Cambridge CB2 1RQ, England

© 1994, Probus Europe

ALL RIGHTS RESERVED. No part of this publication may be reproduced, stored in a retrieval system, or transmitted in any form or by any means, electronic, photocopying, recording or otherwise, without the prior written permission of the publisher and the copyright holder.

This publication is designed to provide accurate and authoritative information in regard to the subject matter covered. It is sold with the understanding that the publisher is not engaged in rendering legal, accounting or other professional service.

Designed, illustrated and typeset by Nick Battley, London, England

ISBN 1 55738 556 4

Printed in the United Kingdom

Probus books are available at quantity discounts when purchased for business, educational, or sales promotional use. For more information, call the Managing Director on (0223) 322018, or write to:

Probus Europe
11 Millers Yard
Mill Lane
Cambridge CB2 1RQ
England

To Terrill for her enormous help, my mother for her editing suggestions, Henry, who was born in the middle of this project, and Alyssa, who told me to to keep my humour.

Acknowledgements

Thanks to all the people who have provided information and statistics used in this book. They include the research departments of James Capel, Goldman Sachs, Morgan Stanley, and Baring Securities, as well as the Financial Times, State Street Bank & Trust, the International Financial Corporation, The WM Company, Frank Russell, InterSec Research, Consensus Forecasts, IBES, Datastream, the Tokyo Stock Exchange, Chase Manhattan Bank, Global Custodian, Baker & Mackenzie, The Wall Street Journal, Pension Investment Research Consultants and Barron's. Data is attributed wherever possible. I have made every effort to be accurate but errors, omissions and the interpretation of data are my responsibility alone.

On a more general note, this is a great opportunity to thank all the people I have worked with over the years, who have provided support, amusement, wisdom and friendship along the way. There are simply so many that to list them all would make this book resemble a telephone directory. But I would single out David Hale at Kemper Financial Services for his particular friendship and the inspiration of his fertile and eccentric mind. David and his wife, Maureen, have been great friends since I touched down in Chicago in 1980, so my special thanks go to them.

G.R.D

Contents

Preface   xiii

PART I: Historical background

1. **Introduction: An historical perspective of international investing**   3
   State-sponsored international investing   3
   Infrastructure investing   5
   Private international investing   5
   Corporate investment   6
   International portfolio management   7
2. **Early protagonists of international portfolio management: three Scottish trusts**   9
   The Scottish American Investment Company (SAINTS)   10
   The Alliance Trust   13
   The Edinburgh Investment Trust   16

PART II — The case for international investing

3. **Background**   23
4. **The size of world stock markets**   27
   Developed markets   27
   Emerging markets   29
   Conclusion   32

5. Performance of stock markets: the MSCI World Index	33
Developed markets	*33*
Emerging markets	*34*
6. Risk diversification	**39**
Developed markets	*40*
Emerging markets and diversification	*45*
7. Particular opportunities in international investing	**49**
Large capitalized stocks	*50*
Cyclical turnaround stocks	*52*
Unique investments	*53*
Global sector themes	*58*
Conclusion	*65*
8. The weight of money	**67**
The strategic reallocation of institutional assets	*67*
The ageing of baby boomers	*70*
The shift out of cash equivalents in search of yield or capital appreciation	*74*
Summary	*75*

PART III: The practice of international investment management

9. Background	79
10. The top-down approach to international investing	81
Economically-related factors	*82*
Stock market related factors	*92*
Country ranking	*97*
The weighting decision	*98*
Conclusion on the top-down process	*101*

11. Portfolio construction	**105**
Rapid implementation by the use of futures	*105*
12. Stock selection	**109**
Stock options	*109*
Investing to replicate or approximate the index	*111*
Sector analysis within stock markets	*111*
Dollar-sensitive stock markets	*114*
Interest-rate sensitive stocks	*116*
Risk optimization in the stock selection process	*121*
International stock selection	*121*
Analytical tools in security analysis	*122*
Intrinsic value	*125*
Key ratios	*125*
Ratios commonly used for a quick assessment	*127*
Accounting differences	*130*
13. Currency	**139**
Controlling currency risk	*140*
Conclusion	*143*
The use of cash in international equity portfolios	*143*

PART IV: Some administrative considerations

14. Global custody	**147**
What is global custody?	*147*
Network management	*149*
Settlement	*151*
Safekeeping	*151*
Cash administration	*152*

Foreign exchange   *153*

Securities lending   *153*

Client servicing   *156*

Conclusion   *156*

15. Corporate governance and social screening   159

Aspirational screens   *161*

Avoidance screens   *162*

Social screening and international investing   *163*

Environmental investing   *163*

Portfolio consequences of social screening   *165*

16. International performance measurement   167

Benchmark   *167*

The peer group   *169*

Discretion   *171*

Carve-outs   *171*

How was performance achieved?   *172*

17. Investment vehicles   177

Multinational companies   *177*

Mutual funds   *179*

Closed-end funds/investment trusts   *184*

Investment trusts in the United Kingdom   *186*

American Depository Receipts (ADRs)   *186*

18. Technology and sources of information   189

Soft commissions   *192*

Glossary   195

Appendix A: Withholding tax rates   233

Appendix B: The Cadbury Code of Best Practice   249

Appendix C: Environmental Declaration	253
Appendix D: Representative indices in world markets	259
Appendix E: Some key data providers	261
Index	263

Preface

Over the years, like many people who have been in the front line of an exciting business, it has occurred to me to write a book. I didn't think the dream would necessarily be fulfilled but, in 1993, I decided to take up the challenge by accepting a request by Probus to write this publication. I have since learned that there is nothing like a deadline to concentrate the mind!

This book is about international equity investment. It is aimed at those who want to learn about a burgeoning branch of the investment business. It should appeal to the neophyte as well as the more seasoned practitioner and, to this end, I have broken the book into four parts:

- **Part I: Historical backgound**
  Particular reference is made to the development of Scottish investment trusts in the late 19th century.

- **Part II: The case for international investing**
  This is written mainly from an American perspective with examples in US dollars, to reflect the potential readership of the book. But since the investment principles described here are universal, this part should be just as relevant to a Swedish, British or Japanese reader.

- **Part III: The practice of international investment management**
  My experience has been in the field of international equity portfolios for American institutions, so there is a US slant to the book, with the dollar as base currency in most examples. Again the universality of investment principles is such that my use of the dollar as numeraire currency should not detract from the relevance of examples to readers outside the United States.

- **Part IV: Some administrative considerations**
  There is a lot more to international investing than the glamour of hitting a home run in the Malaysian stock market. This part is about the logistics of international investment management and discusses the operational framework in which an investment manager functions.

Hundreds of statistics in this book relate to the 1980s and 1990s. It is not designed to be an almanac of statistics for the current year, however, and my use of examples is intended to illustrate the case. A reader wanting real-time current data should subscribe to an on-line information service. Statistics will always date, and where they become obsolete, can be updated in subsequent editions of this book.

My own experience in this field has been varied. After qualifying as a Scottish lawyer, in 1977 I joined the International Corporate Finance department of Kleinwort Benson in London. I can safely admit after 17 years that I knew very little about eurobonds at the time, but I learned fast and enjoyed the experience.

In 1980, I moved to Murray Johnstone to set up a joint venture with Kemper Financial Services in Chicago. Arriving in the United States at the dawn of the Reagan Era to start a new international investment company was surely one of the great career breaks. Over the next 12 years I gave thousands of speeches from one end of the United States to the other, became president of Murray Johnstone International, launched three mutual funds (Kemper International Fund, Phoenix International Portfolio and the Calvert World Values Fund) and acted as portfolio strategist for a wide range of clients, from foundations and pension funds to insurance companies and partnerships of high net worth individuals. Over the years I have been involved in the international investment of over $1bn.

In 1992, I was approached by Steve Bailey of Pacific Financial Asset Management to start a new international investment firm from scratch. It seemed like a golden opportunity to build the dream investment team with people I had respected and liked for a long time. Blairlogie Capital Management was born in 1992. At the time of writing, we have 18 very bright, energetic people working at Blairlogie. I want to thank them for taking the risk to join The Great Adventure.

Blairlogie, Scotland, June 1994   *Gavin R. Dobson*

PART I

Historical background

Chapter 1

Introduction: An historical perspective of international investing

This book deals specifically with international equity investment, but before getting into the subject in detail, I would like to explore the roots from which international investment has grown over the years.

The word investment literally means 'to lay out money with the expectation of profit', and as defined, international investment must be one of the oldest professions.

For thousands of years, international investing has been practised by the nation state in many parts of the world for military, commercial and social reasons. It has been practised by entrepreneurs, merchants and corporations for as long as trade and commerce have flourished. Historically, equity investment is a new phenomenon, but its roots are deep in the soil of global commerce, which has been around for a very long time.

I suggest a few examples below which can be regarded as early forms of international investing.

State-sponsored international investing

Hadrian's Wall

When Hadrian became Roman Emperor in 117 AD, he immediately set out to consolidate and re-define the Roman Empire. This involved heavy spending on fortifications and public works in many countries. He came to Britain in 122 AD and ordered the construction of a wall in the north of England to defend against aggressive North British tribes.

Ten thousand men worked on the project between 123 and 126 AD, building a 45-mile wall, 16 feet high and 10 feet wide. It contained about 1.7m cubic yards of hewn rock and had watchtowers, granaries and fortresses at regular intervals. It was an expensive project, which can be estimated to have cost US$2.5bn in 1990s' terms to complete, or roughly the cost of building and equipping two aircraft carriers for the US Pacific Fleet. Much of Hadrian's Wall remains today, as it stretches from the Irish Sea to the North Sea, a monument to an ancient budget spent to protect Roman interests internationally.

The Boer War

Some wars can be seen as a form of investment to protect commercial interests. The Boer War, from 1899 to 1902, was fought by Britain to defend its economic interests in South Africa when The Orange Free State and Transvaal seceded from the British Empire. The war was expensive and was 'won' by the British militarily, but the value of the investment was questionable. Perhaps the greatest investment consequence was the adoption of khaki uniforms by British troops, which prevented even worse slaughter than was experienced in the First World War twelve years later.

The Belgian Congo

King Leopold II of Belgium financed Henry Stanley in 1882 with £60,000 a year—equivalent to about £6.7m in today's terms—to open up the Congo basin and plant the Belgian flag 'before anyone else notices.' At Belgium's peak of empire in the early 1950s there were nearly 100,000 Belgians living in the Congo, holding most of the skilled jobs in mining and government. Copper, diamonds, cobalt and chromium were found and great fortunes were made by some Belgian families from their Congo interests. On balance, it would appear that Belgium's investment in the Congo turned out profitably for the investor[1].

The Suez Canal

In 1854, the Frenchman Ferdinand de Lesseps was awarded a concession by the Khedive of Egypt, Mohammad Sa'id, to construct a canal across the Isthmus of Suez. Initially, the Compagnie Universelle du Canal Maritime de Suez was financed mainly by French interests (52 per cent) and the Khedive of Egypt (44 per cent). When the Khedive was forced to sell his shares in 1875, they were snapped up in a famous financial coup by the British government under Disraeli for 568 francs a share. They were worth 3600 francs a share in 1900—a six-fold increase in non-inflationary times—but proved to be an embarrassment to the British government when the canal was nationalized by Egypt's President Nasser in 1956.

---

[1] See 'The Scramble for Africa' by Thomas Pakenham.

Infrastructure investing

Infrastructure investing, formerly known as social investing, is not always done for an obvious or direct commercial return by the investor, but which usually has beneficial effects. Projects in this category would include an airport built by the French government in Noumea in New Caledonia or US aid financing a school in Panama. These fall into the category of state-sponsored investing. Some investments have enduring results, like the Indian government buildings in New Delhi designed by Sir Edwin Lutyens and the US embassy building in Grosvenor Square in London. Others do not, unfortunately, like the massive investment the Soviet Union made in Cuba, which yielded a little infrastructure but no lasting goodwill.

Private international investing

Entrepreneurial roots

The great trading cities of Alexandria, Constantinople, Samarkand and Beirut have their origins in pre-Christian times and became successful through international trade and commerce fostered by the investment of the merchant classes. In the 15th century, Genoese and Venetian businessmen helped the Flanders textile trade flourish: cities like Antwerp, Bruges and Ypres owed much of their wealth to Italian capital. In 1470, the Medicis from Florence had banking operations in London, Bruges, Lyons and Avignon. During this period merchants from the Italian city states invented double-entry bookkeeping. The 'Italian method' caught on world-wide, and it is to this influence that we owe many financial and accounting terms of today: the words bank, capital, folio, cash, debit and credit are but a few of Italian origin. In the 15th century, cartels of wealthy families banded together to regulate exchange rates and the price of commodities. The global reach of some families was impressive, even by today's standards. The German, Jacob Fugger of Augsburg, had thirteen offices around Europe, from the Baltic Coast (Danzig) to the Adriatic (Venice), the North Sea (Antwerp), Atlantic (Lisbon) and Mediterranean (Naples). He had the patronage of Charles V, the Holy Roman Emperor, and was granted the European monopoly on pricing copper and silver in the 1520s.

Until the invention of the joint stock company in late Elizabethan England, private merchants, sometimes with state sponsorship, had no choice but to make direct investments in foreign ventures. The attendant risks and rewards were sometimes astronomical. A Genoese merchant financing a ship with a cargo of spices from East Africa could make a princely fortune if the ship returned safely, or alternatively lose everything if it did not. Pirates, storms, and primitive navigational techniques were all hazards that accompanied international investing. These hazards were well described by Shakespeare in The Merchant of Venice:

> 'Have all his ventures failed? What! Not one hit? From Tripolis, from Mexico, and England; From Lisbon, Barbary and India? And not one vessel 'scape the dreadful touch of merchant-marring rocks?'
>
> 'Not one, my Lord'[1]

Typically, merchants would own part shares in ships that ventured abroad, or underwrite a fraction of the trip, then jointly share in the profits on the cloves, ivory, nutmegs, silks and precious stones that were unloaded when the ship eventually returned to its European port. As Shakespeare's quotation implies, the trick was to take shares in many ventures to spread the risk. The profits were so high on each venture, it was not uncommon for one success to wipe out a string of failures.

Corporate investment

Take-overs and direct investment

The equivalent today of foreign direct commercial investment is easily quantified. The 1993 *World Investment Report*, a United Nations publication, estimated the historic book value of the total world stock of foreign direct investment to be US$2 trillion. In 1990, US$234bn of direct foreign investment was recorded, followed by US$183bn in 1991 and US$150bn in 1992.

These investments were made mainly by public companies, either in acquiring companies overseas, or in setting up their own facilities. For example, Siemens of Germany announced in 1993 that it was spending the equivalent of US$38m to buy two telecommunication equipment producers in Poland—Zwut in Warsaw and Elvro in Wroclaw—and that it would be investing US$57m to upgrade facilities. This is on the heels of AT&T's US$28m and Alcatel's US$37.3m telecom equipment acquisitions in Poland in 1992.[2]

General Electric (GE), of the US, bought Tungsram, the Hungarian lightbulb manufacturer in 1990, and now has a significant share of the Eastern European light-bulb market. This was not without cost. Because of the primitive state of the Hungarian telephone system, GE has had to invest a

---

[1] *William Shakespeare, 'The Merchant of Venice', Act III, Scene II.*
[2] *Financial Times, 24 September 1992.*

large sum installing microwave telecommunication links in its Nagykaniszi plant in western Hungary.

Company takeovers are a common form of international investing. For example, in the 1980s, there were many highly-publicized multi-billion dollar foreign take-overs of US corporations, such as Beecham buying Smith Kline Beckman Corporation and BAT Industries buying the Farmers Insurance Group.

As well as predatory corporate actions, many companies have invested in new sites and built factories from scratch, such as IBM in Scotland, Ford in Spain and Coca Cola in Poland. In many cases, such investments are inspired by incentives from local governments like cheap utilities, tax holidays, construction grants and job incentives.

In 1993, Goodyear Tire & Rubber announced plans to build a US$150m joint venture factory on a green-field site in India. The plant is being constructed at Aurangabad, in Maharashtra, Western India, and is a 50/50 joint venture with CEAT, the Indian tyre company. The target is to produce 3m tyres a year within 3 years.[1]

In 1990, it was estimated that nearly 4 per cent of US corporate assets were owned by foreigners, and that some 2m US workers worked for British interests. Ironically, that was more than the entire population of 1.8m colonial Americans who seceded from Britain in 1776. But in case Americans worry that King George III has taken his revenge from the grave, they should know that over 5 per cent of Britain's working population toils for American interests.

International direct investment is not a modern phenomenon. If statistics were available, we would see huge foreign investments in the New World as early as the 16th century. The economies of Peru, Mexico and Brazil were heavily influenced by Iberian interests, and the non-native economies of North America were similarly controlled by British, French and Dutch interests.

International portfolio management

Statesmen, entrepreneurs, merchants and soldiers have thought in global terms for thousands of years. More recently, multinational companies have internationalized many industries, from fast food to electronics. It is consistent with these trends that investing should be taken in a global context as well. While a small-time entrepreneur may still take the risk of setting up

---

[1] *Financial Times, September 1993.*

the corner shop and limit his or her future to one location, portfolio investors no longer have to act locally. The explosion of information, opportunity, availability and choice means that all equity investors can take advantage of choices and opportunities around the world.

The next chapter is a profile of three Scottish investment trusts. Even though portfolio investing has been around in various forms since the invention of the joint stock company in Elizabethan times, my starting point is the phenomenon of investment trusts in the 1870s. This is because of the variety of trusts, controlled risk-taking, different styles, and the natural way in which Scots managers sought and managed their investment overseas.

Indeed, such was the flow of Scottish capital overseas that by the 1890s, an English commentator wrote: 'For a small country like Scotland to be able to spare even for a time, tens of millions sterling, is one of the most striking paradoxes in the history of commerce. The Scots, of all people in the world, are supposed to be best able to take care of themselves and of their money. Wherever an honest penny can be earned they will not be far to seek. And yet it has come to this with them, that they will face almost any risk for the sake of the difference between 4 per cent at home and 4½ per cent across the Atlantic.'[1]

[1] *Intermarket magazine, March 1986.*

Chapter 2

Early protagonists of international portfolio management: three Scottish trusts

Some argue that international investment management was invented in Scotland, but the purpose of this chapter is not to debate that particular issue. What is indisputable is the proliferation of global investing that took place from Scotland from the 1870s. It was a function of many concurrent factors. First, by the 1870s, Scotland was consistently generating more wealth than it could invest or save profitably at home. The Industrial Revolution benefited Scotland considerably: many of the ships and locomotives that plied the Empire were built in Scotland, and great fortunes were made from jute milling, coal mining, tobacco and textiles.

Second, the Scots had always been world travellers, whether from a lack of opportunity at home or just an adventurous spirit. They saw opportunities abroad and made fortunes in many countries, from trading in Hong Kong (Jardine Matheson) to early telecommunications in North America (Alexander Graham Bell), steel in Pittsburgh (Carnegie) or trading grain in the Midwest (Cargills).

Third, Scottish education at that time was excellent. Literacy and numeracy rates were among the highest in the world, which gave Scots an edge in identifying and exploiting opportunities on their travels. It has often been observed that for hundreds of years, there were four universities in Scotland (Aberdeen, Edinburgh, Glasgow and St. Andrews), but only two in England (Oxford and Cambridge). Higher education was democratic and widely available to those with the intellectual wherewithal.

Fourth, the 'Presbyterian work ethic'. The single-mindedness with which many Scots approached their calling was a distinct advantage in an unresolved world. Many entrepreneurs were as evangelical and altruistic as they were pragmatic and materialistic. Hence, Andrew Carnegie's zeal in setting up educational trusts and financing libraries throughout the English-speaking world with the fortune he made. As he put it: 'the secret of happiness is in renunciation'.

Fifth, and a great deal more mundane, the yields available on British government debt were low. It is testimony to the financial stability of Great Britain that between 1830 and 1914—a period of 84 years—the yield on consols did not exceed 3.4 per cent. Banks seldom offered more than 4.5 per cent to their depositors, and there was a general perception that yields above 4 per cent were risky—the Victorian equivalent to junk yields. So when investment trusts were created with secured debentures yielding 5.5 per cent, backed by a diversified income stream from rural mortgages and railroads in America, they attracted local investor attention.

This chapter describes the origin of three Scottish investment trusts and traces their evolution from the entrepreneurial risk takers of late Victorian Scotland to the sophisticated global portfolio managers of today.

The Scottish American Investment Company (SAINTS)

'Such depressions serve an excellent purpose.'

It may sound odd in today's world, but in the 1870s one of the most important functions of a Scottish lawyer was to act as financial advisor and wealth custodian to his clients. In 1873, one such lawyer, William Menzies, formed the Scottish American Investment Company with its aim, described in the prospectus, to provide 'the opportunity of investing capital in the United States and British America; (1) upon well selected railroad mortgages, government, state and municipal stocks, and (2) upon mortgages over improved city or country lots.'

This was an investment trust, a structure invented so that, as a limited liability company, it could manage the funds of the shareholders and borrow against the investments. Today, it would be termed a 'closed-end' fund as opposed to an open-ended, or mutual, fund.

The prospectus waxed joyfully about the 'wonderful fertility of the virgin soil' and 'the development of almost illimitable resources and the creation of material wealth' in America. And since the demand for capital was likely 'for many years to come' to 'be greater than the supply', it argued that the rate of return was likely to be higher than at home.

By June 1873, the shares were fully subscribed, mostly by people from the Edinburgh area, and were 'taken up on the merits of the concern itself without our having resorted to any pushing such as is common in London.'

There was also a keen subscription to the debentures at 5.5 per cent, and by March 1874, the company had reached the limit of its borrowing powers. The company's next challenge was to put the money to work with a certain urgency, because with its debentures paying 5.5 per cent, the managers could not leave the money on deposit with an Edinburgh bank at 4.5 per cent.

An investment board was assembled in New York consisting of three Scots-Americans, Messrs. Kennedy, Stewart and Denny, and one Dutch-

American, James Roosevelt. There was £250,000 to invest, or about US$40m in today's terms, in 'the very highest class of securities.'

Since the end of the American Civil War, the gold price had been rising in dollar terms. The managers bought gold in the summer of 1873 then sold it for a significant cash profit. In September, as luck would have it, there was a stock market crash in New York accompanied by the collapse of 58 broking firms. Cash in hand, the Scots moved in and a portfolio of high grade railroad debentures was assembled. For instance, New York Central Railroad 6 per cent debentures had fallen from US$100 to US$78 and now yielded 7.7 per cent. The managers believed that the 'Panic of 1873' was a short-term crisis, caused by 'temporary overproduction in farming and manufacturing', and that the secular outlook for the United States was pretty bright.

Flushed with its initial coup, the company decided to stay in railroad bonds as an investment policy, provided that 'not more than one-tenth part of the capital of the company was to be invested in any one security.' Other guidelines for railroad investment were drawn up:

- The line was to be a trunk line serving important towns, not a branch line.

- Debt on the line was to be 'reasonable and less than the value of the property.'

- 'The net revenue of the company should be more than sufficient to pay the interest on the mortgage, that the mortgage itself is in proper terms and sufficiently constituted and, not least, that the management is in the hands of competent and honest men.'

This last paragraph is as important and fresh in the 1990s as when it was written in 1873. Here is the kernel of good security analysis: know the management of companies you are dealing with, study the terms of the securities and ensure that there is more-than-adequate debt-service cover. In today's terms, that means: stay hard-headed in the face of corporate and stock broking hype. 'Knowing your company' meant in 1873 what it means today: a rigorous due diligence process that involves a lot of tyre-kicking. Today, a British analyst of American companies might accumulate 35,000 miles a year towards frequent flier bonuses. By the time William Menzies retired in 1904, he calculated that he had spent a year of his life afloat on the Atlantic.

What was the investment performance of SAINTS, as it had become known?

Bearing in mind that the objective was to give its shareholders a dividend over what was available from British government debt (3.4 per cent) or bank deposits (4.5 per cent), the company got off to a flying start. In 1874, a 10 per cent dividend was paid, and it never fell below 10 per cent for the next fifty years. It was often much higher, such as between 1881 and 1884, when it was 15 per cent and between 1912 and 1923, when it was at 18 per cent.

During the first fifty years of SAINTS' existence, as in any such period in history, there were wild economic and political swings that the managers had to contend with. The 1873 crash, near war between Great Britain and America over a British Guyana boundary dispute, the depression of the 1890s, the Boer War and the First World War were some of the 'exogenous variables' that tested their mettle. These gave rise to memorable observations, such as at the 1910 board meeting, reporting on slow business conditions in the United States: 'Such depressions serve an excellent purpose, because during their currency, the resources of the country are accumulating, economy is being practised and new ventures are being discouraged. Sooner or later confidence revives and fresh developments take place, but these occasional breathing times are beneficial.' There is a coolness and poise in this assessment that today's impatient portfolio manager could benefit from. This has an echo in William Jennings Bryan's comment that 'depression restores wealth to its rightful owners.'

One feature of SAINTS in the early 20th century was the gradual inclusion of equities in the portfolio. In 1913, the ratio of equities to fixed income securities was 20:80. By 1929, 72 per cent of total assets were in equities—partly, it must be assumed, due to the tremendous stock market run-up relative to bonds in the late 1920s. The stock market was approaching such a pitch that in late 1928, the fund's manager Charles Munro, visited the United States to see for himself what was going on. His observation anticipated trouble ahead, 'I have put forward some suggestions, especially the rails. These seem to me to be neglected because the brokers cannot get the public interested in sound investments when gambles only are wanted... By increasing our railroad list we are in the best position to face a readjustment in values however drastic it may be whenever it comes.' He concluded in October 1928 that 'profits are a grand thing to take right now.' By July 1929, a substantial part of the American portfolio had been 'turned over'—30 per cent into cash and the balance into bonds and less frothy parts of the market.

Having substantially side-stepped the crash in October 1929, the managers reinvested in the United States market too soon, and subsequently suffered a serious dent in total assets. By 1933, the value of the total fund was down 39 per cent from its peak in late 1928, and the value of assets attributable to ordinary shareholders was down 91 per cent. However, owing to bonus issues of ordinary and preference shares in the late 1920s, a long-term ordinary shareholders would 'only' have seen the market value of their holdings fall by 47 per cent and their income by 34 per cent.

The management of SAINTS had a shrewd approach to investing assets. It was an early example of geographically-specific international investing, with well-defined income objectives set at a time when British inflation was low. Its shareholders garnered 6 per cent to 8 per cent real income returns for the best part of fifty years. In this respect, it was a highly successful vehicle.

By the 1990s, SAINTS had had to react to some major exogenous shocks with creative solutions. The imposition of capital gains taxes in Britain in 1965, the introduction and then abolition of the dollar premium in the 1970s, the creation of favourable tax-savings schemes for people to invest in investment trusts in the 1980s, have led to a restructuring and evolution of the aims of the fund to tailor itself to 1990s investor requirements.[1]

At the end of 1992, the net valuation of SAINTS' investments was £402,542,000 or approximately US$600m. Only 11.5 per cent of the quoted securities were invested in North America, in the equities of conservatively-managed companies like Archer Daniels Midland, Illinois Tool Works and Southwestern Bell. Some 74.6 per cent was invested in Europe, of which the lion's share was in the United Kingdom, and 13.7 per cent was invested in the Pacific Rim, from Chile and the Philippines to Japan and Hong Kong. Altogether, 18 countries were represented in the quoted part of the portfolio.

Evidence of evolution from the aims of the founders in 1873, is that 6.7 per cent of shareholders' funds in late 1992 was held in unquoted companies, from Japanese venture capital vehicles, to a successful investment in Noble Grossart Holdings, the merchant bank, which was valued at over 28 times SAINTS' acquisition cost. Despite the long-term capital appreciation element represented by equities in the portfolio, SAINTS has never lost sight of its original aim, to provide income to its shareholders. In 1992, the dividend was 4.35 pence per share, and for the previous five years, it had been increased at an annual compound rate of 15.2 per cent.

The Alliance Trust

'Look after the income and the capital will take care of itself.'

The Scottish city of Dundee was a wealthy place in the 1870s. Its industrialists had prospered mightily during the American Civil War by selling can-

---

[1] *The Scottish American Investment Company plc. Annual Report 1992.*

vas for tents and jute for sandbags to both sides. After the war, the use of canvas for covered wagons was in demand, and Scottish jute manufacturers began setting up agents at the starting points of the great Western trails in America, to sell the canvas.

In 1873, a group of wealthy Dundee businessmen formed the Oregon and Washington Investment Company (O&WT), to lend money to immigrant farmers in the State of Oregon and Washington Territory. It may seem an unlikely venture today, but it was not clear in 1873 that more money might have been made in California. What was clear was the annual departure for the 'West' by tens of thousands of hopefuls in Wagon-Trains. One of the company's directors visited the Willamette Valley in Oregon in 1876, and reported, 'drought is unknown and a harvest is never lost.'

The lending policy of the company was strict:

- Lending had to be on improved farmland close to a railway or township.

- No loan should exceed 40 per cent of the appraised value of the property and title deeds had to be retained in Dundee until the loan was repaid. Every mortgage had to be repaid in gold coin.

- No loan should be made to any religious or charitable body, to prevent unpleasantness in the event of a foreclosure.

A local board was set up in Portland to supervise the operation of the company.

By 1876, the company had 263 outstanding mortgages and was paying a 10 per cent dividend. By 1879, the Oregon & Washington Trust was merged into the larger Dundee Mortgage & Trust Company, which was able to lend to a broader geographical area: basically, all of the United States and the British Empire. To lessen the company's dependency on land mortgages, a reserve fund was created for the investment of retained profits, mainly invested in US railroad bonds. The reserve fund was the origin of the trust's future investment management expertise, and as it grew, it was invested in a wider selection of portfolio investments world-wide.

Large land loans were soon made. In 1882, the 800,000-acre Matador Land and Cattle Company on the Pease River in Texas was bought by Dundee interests. (It was sold in 1951 for more than 30 times the original investment.) A loan of US$200,000 on 594,000 acres of the Tierra Amarilla grant in New Mexico was made, of which two-thirds of the capital was syndicated to Edinburgh interests.

The Alliance Trust was formed out of a variety of Dundee trust companies in 1888. By 1905, there were 3500 mortgages outstanding on 2m acres in the United States and the revenues generated by the mortgages led to surpluses being invested in other securities. These were mainly invested in railroad bonds and, for the first time, investments were made in Central and South America and Japan. At that time, Hokkaido Colliery and Railway Company securities appeared in the portfolio. To those foreigners who proudly claim to have discovered Japanese investment in the 1960s, we would refer them to the Alliance Trust half a century earlier.

In 1918, management of The Western and Hawaiian Investment Company was taken over by the Alliance Trust, and it was renamed The Second Alliance Trust. During the 1920s the companies moved away from their mortgage roots and became increasingly involved in traded instruments, mainly fixed-income securities. By 1940, 60 per cent of investments were in the United Kingdom, 26 per cent in 'colonial and other' stock markets and a mere 14 per cent in the United States. Income was still a prerequisite for the trust's investors, and the manager, W.O. MacDougall, coined the memorable phrase: 'look after the income and the capital will take care of itself.'

By 1940, the company owned 1300 investments and approached its analysis in a way that is recognizable today. There were 70 transactions a month and portfolios were well diversified according to industry, commodity and geographical location. A bi-product of the trust's North American mortgage business was that, as the mortgages expired, the Alliance Trust kept mineral rights over much of the land. In 1932, oil was discovered on the 6000 acre Cormier Plantation, a Louisiana cotton farm that had been repossessed in 1923 by the Trust, and produced substantial annual royalty payments until it was sold in 1958.

The Second World War forced the sale of American assets by the Trust as part of the British government's policy to raise dollars to pay for the war effort. The careful nurturing of wealth by a group of Dundee businessmen over several generations led to realizable assets at a crucial time in British history.

After 1945, the firm reorganized and began to take the shape of a modern investment house, with security and economic analysis being performed in a rigorous manner. Investment assets rose eight-fold, the net asset value of the ordinary shares rose 12 times and the increase in dividends rose 8 times, in the twenty years to 1968.

Today, the combined Alliance and Second Alliance Trusts manage over £1200m (US$1845m). It is company policy not to take on business outside the trust, so that the managers can devote all their energies to the trust's affairs.

In the 1993 *Report and Accounts*, the Alliance Trust had a geographical breakdown of funds as follows:

UK:	52.7 per cent
Europe:	10.9 per cent
N. America:	30.2 per cent
Far East:	6.2 per cent

The largest single category was 39.1 per cent in consumer goods, of which 10.5 per cent was invested in stores, such as Wal-Mart in the US and Marks and Spencers in the UK. There was a faint echo of the past in its 11 per cent holding in public utilities, such as Pacific Telesis, Bell South and Northwest Water—but these were equity holdings, not 6 per cent railroad debentures.

The fund only held 2.8 per cent in convertibles and 1 per cent under the heading of preference and loan stocks. The trust's ten-year dividend record continues to move steadily ahead of the British retail price index, and total assets rose from £355m to £901m during that period. A good illustration of the adage, 'take care of the income, and the capital will take care of itself.'

The Edinburgh Investment Trust

'The railroads appear to offer the least hope of recovery with competition growing from the trucking industry as well as the airlines.'

The Edinburgh Investment Trust was the brainchild of an Edinburgh lawyer and a stockbroker and was launched in March 1889.[1] The first issue was fixed at 30,000 shares of £10 each, which were split into £180,000 of 4.5 per cent preferred stock and £120,000 of deferred stock. Debenture stock could then be issued in an amount equalling two-thirds of the nominal amount of the subscribed capital.

By the end of March 1889, £57,000 had been invested in a 'balanced' portfolio of equities and bonds yielding between 5 per cent and 6 per cent. Equities included the Hong Kong & Shanghai Bank, the North British Rubber Company and Dalmeny Oil. The bonds were mainly railroad bonds, in Argentina, Brazil, Costa Rica, Cuba, Greece, Mexico, Philippines, Spain, Uruguay, and the United States. It is interesting to observe that five of these countries are today regarded as 'emerging markets' and subject to much analytical commentary and journalistic hype, whereas over 100 years ago they were the destination of the first tranche of money invested for Scottish lawyers, doctors and farmers.

---

[1] W.G. Cochrane, 'A History of the Edinburgh Trust, 1889-1989'.

The Edinburgh Investment Trust differed from many other Scottish trusts in that it did not invest in mortgages, as a matter of policy. The nearest it got to a mortgage was to take a secured one-eighth interest in a ship. By April 1889, the trust allocated £6000 to Germany, and had invested in the British North Borneo Tobacco Company, as well as the Sumatra Tobacco Plantation Company. A sum of £5000 was invested in a Canadian mortgage company. De Beers Diamond Mining and Broken Hill Proprietary were added shortly afterwards. After a year, there were 209 securities, split 52 per cent into equities and 48 per cent into bonds. The securities of at least 18 countries were in the portfolio—from the United States and Great Britain at one end of the scale, to Costa Rica and Borneo at the other. Even in the 1990s, it is a fair bet that a US registered mutual fund being launched with this degree of geographical spread and illiquidity would be regarded as exotic, and would command a lot of journalistic attention, not to mention enquiries from the Securities and Exchange Commission (SEC) during its registration process.

During the First World War, as with so much British wealth, the trust was obliged to liquidate its US portfolio. The money was repatriated and invested in British securities, but by 1925, the United States again represented 16 per cent of the total and the portfolio was benefiting from the US stock market boom.

Until the arrival of 'comptometers' (adding machines) in the late 1920s, it could typically take up to three days to value a portfolio, and the company had to build a large strong-room to physically store the portfolios' securities. The days of electronic switching of securities and a network of global sub-custodians were still far in the future.

In March 1932, the first published breakdown of the portfolio was in the annual accounts, as shown in Figure 2.1.

The portfolio contained 549 holdings and its total valuation was approximately £1.6m. On-site economic and company research by the managers was being performed regularly by the 1930s. For a firm that started fifty years earlier by investing heavily in railroad bonds, the passing of the railroad era was marked in 1935, when a director observed on a visit to the United States 'the railroads appear to offer the least hope of recovery with competition growing from the trucking industry as well as the airlines. The journey from Chicago to New York by plane occupies only five to six hours while the best train takes 17 hours. Tracks, locomotives and freight cars are in need of repair.' While, sixty years later, there is still a handful of profitable private US railroads like Union Pacific or Norfolk and Southern, the era when the portfolios of Scottish trusts were underpinned by income from the debentures of exotic-sounding railway companies was over. Ironically, with the global trend to privatization in the 1990s, it is possible that

	Fixed interest	Equities	Total
Great Britain	20	34	54
Other British Empire	6	8	14
USA	8	9	17
Latin America	4	2	6
Far East	2	3	5
International	0	3	3
Europe	1	0	1
	41	59	100

Figure 2.1 Edinburgh Investment Trust March 1932 portfolio breakdown
Source: W.G. Cochrane 'A History of the Edinburgh Investment Trust'.

we could re-enter the era of private railroad debentures with regional British railway companies taking the lead.

By the 1950s, the trust's investments were substantially more invested in equities than in fixed income. The balance sheet in March 1950 showed equity investments totalling £18m and debentures totalling £3.6m. Since the 1930s, the philosophy of investing had switched in favour of equities. This was partly due to the default of so many interest-producers during the Depression, partly due to the systemic inflation creeping into the world economy from the 1940s which made bonds less attractive, and partly due to the philosophical shift of investor preference towards capital appreciation. People wanted an equity—literally, a share—in the explosion of world-wide economic growth taking place after the Second World War.

In the 1990s, the Edinburgh Investment Trust invests on a thoroughly global basis. In March 1992, the geographical breakdown was as follows:

UK:	60.3 per cent
North America:	10.3 per cent
Japan:	9.8 per cent
Other Pacific Basin:	5.6 per cent
Continental Europe:	14.0 per cent

At the beginning of 1993, the managers significantly shifted assets to the United Kingdom, to benefit from the early recovery of the UK economy ahead of other major European economies. By March 1993, the UK portion of the portfolio had risen to 88.8 per cent, with the largest holdings being in British Gas, Lloyds Bank, Shell Transport and Grand Metropolitan. The fund retained 5.2 per cent in North America, 2.5 per cent in Japan, 2.7 per cent in Continental Europe and 0.8 per cent in the rest of the Pacific Basin.

By historical standards, this is surprisingly concentrated in one market—the United Kingdom only represented 54 per cent of the portfolio in 1932—and certainly does not reflect the general perception that an investment trust should be diversified across a wide range of countries. But the managers evidently took the view that the United Kingdom had some unique investment characteristics and adjusted the portfolio accordingly.

It is interesting to peruse the portfolio and find small amounts invested in very long-term holdings such as the Kleinwort Benson Mezzanine Fund for US smaller companies, the Brazil fund, and Arjo Mezzanine Debt in Europe. There are still traces of the risk-capital that Scottish investment trusts were famous for a hundred years ago. Today the fund stands at about £1.1bn, or nearly US$1.7bn and has seen its net asset value per share rise from 109.3 pence in March 1983 to 300.8 pence ten years later. It is clearly well positioned to take on the world in its second century of business.

PART II

The case for international investing

Chapter 3

Background

There are many reasons for investing internationally and the purpose of this section is to give the case convincingly enough to persuade equity investors to consider investing a portion of their equity assets overseas.

The facts behind the 'case' have not changed in essence for 20 years, although the details have steadily moved in its favour.

As described in the first section, for thousands of years, it has been a powerful instinct for mankind to invest overseas—whether in the form of Hadrian building a wall to define the Roman Empire, the Medicis setting up shop in Bruges, a Frenchman building a canal in Egypt or a Scottish schoolteacher looking for income in New Mexico railroad bonds in 1875.

Since the 19th century, the British have probably been the most persistent international investors. This is partly because fifty years ago, about one-third of the globe was under British hegemony, partly because Britain is an island and the people have naturally looked outwards for opportunities, and partly because industrial and fiscal decline at home forced British money into more certain growth elsewhere. It is estimated today that 25 per cent of the assets of British pensions are invested overseas.

Other countries have had varying degrees of regulation that has limited international portfolio investment, but this is changing. The watershed in the United States was the combination of the Employee Retirement Income Security of 1974 (ERISA) and the abolition of interest equalization tax in 1974. Although it was not specifically aimed at international investing, ERISA stipulated a standard of prudent investing by diversification that had to be applied by pension fund managers. The days when a pension fund could be invested solely in the stock of its own company shares were numbered. As recently as 1981, I came across a Fortune 500 company in Texas whose entire pension assets were 'invested' in fast food franchises. They may have done well, but at high potential risk to its pensioners. Today, such concentration of pension assets would be actionable by the plan's beneficiaries.

In 1974, the share of the world market capitalization represented by the United States was over 65 per cent. Apart from occasional investments in Royal Dutch Shell or 'British Pete' (BP), it was quite rare to find pension funds approving specific asset tranches for dedication to international investing. In the late 1970s, some managers ventured to buy inflation-hedge stocks or natural resource plays in Canada, Australia or the UK market, but they were usually American Depository Receipts (ADRs), and usually part of a sector preference play as a small part of a much larger US equity portfolio.

Spectacular investment returns in foreign markets in the late 1970s and early 1980s had two effects: they attracted the attention of US investors and they reduced the percentage of the US market capitalization in the Morgan Stanley Capital International World Index (MSCIWI). By the early 1980s, the US share of world capitalization had fallen to 40 per cent, and by the late 1980s, to 32 per cent of the total market capitalization of the world. Indeed, there was a mad, anomalous period from 1986 to 1990 when the Japanese stock market capitalization exceeded that of the United States. In September 1989, Japanese stock market capitalization stood at 39.9 per cent of the world total, against 31.6 per cent for the United States. The Japanese market price/earnings ratio (P/E) at 51 times prospective earnings was the most expensive in the world. Japanese investors were convinced that it was 'different this time', and that the web of cross-holdings between Japanese enterprises cemented the market fabric tightly. It had worked during the Crash of 1987 while the rest of the world fell apart. It would work again, as Japan became the new economic superpower: high multiples meant nothing if the economy predictably grew at between 5 per cent and 7 per cent each year. Earnings were expected to rapidly catch up with high stock prices.

Between 1990 and 1992, the Nikkei Index proceeded to fall from 39000 to 16000 and the stock markets of the United States replaced Japan as the world's largest. By the end of August 1993, US stock market capitalization had risen to 36.97 per cent of the Morgan Stanley Capital International World Index, and Japan stood at 28.67 per cent.

During this period (between 1970 and 1989) other markets were growing too. Sweden rose from 0.5 per cent to 1.1 per cent of the total, Hong Kong from 0.2 per cent to 0.7 per cent, Singapore from 0.2 per cent to 0.6 per cent, Denmark from 0.1 per cent to 0.3 per cent, Norway from 0.1 per cent to 0.2 per cent, France from 2.5 per cent to 4 per cent, and Germany from 3 per cent to 4 per cent.

During the 1980s, there was a series of take-overs of American companies by foreigners that drove home to Americans that significant financial muscle existed overseas: Sohio was sold to BP, Pillsbury to Grand Metropolitan, Texasgulf to Elf Aquitaine, Farmers Insurance to BATUS, the Rockefeller Center to Mitsubishi Estate. It was becoming difficult to ignore overseas investing, and pension plan beneficiaries increasingly wanted exposure to foreign markets.

Many international, global and regional mutual funds were launched for retail investors in the United States in this period. In 1980, there was a handful of international funds managed by the larger mutual fund groups, such as Putnam, T. Rowe-Price, Templeton and IDS. By 1989, there were few mutual fund companies that did not offer an international fund. In many cases, these were managed by international sub-advisors to the mutual fund company, such as Stewart Ivory for DL Babson and Robert Fleming for the T. Rowe-Price Funds. These alliances allowed domestic fund groups to offer the services of experienced international managers without having to build their own track records slowly.

Specialist international funds also proliferated in the United States, such as the Spain Fund, the Korea Fund, the Taiwan Fund, and the Templeton Emerging Markets Fund. These tended to be closed-ended and often traded at a premium to their asset value. They were often launched by the most powerful investment institutions in the United States, and underwritten by syndicates of regional brokerage firms. It was not unusual for US investors to invest thousands of dollars in a single-country European closed-end fund, before many of them even had a well-constructed portfolio of US securities.

The remainder of Part II will deal with five broad reasons for investing overseas:

1) size of markets;
2) performance of markets;
3) risk diversification;
4) particular opportunities, and;
5) weight of money.

Chapter 4

The size of world stock markets

Developed markets

In the 1970s, the Capital International Company in Geneva, Switzerland worked on developing a global equity index to act as a suitable benchmark against which international investors could measure themselves. Today, it is known as the Morgan Stanley Capital International World Index (MSCIWI). It comprises the developed stock markets of the world. The company also offers permutations of the index, such as the EAFE Index (Europe, Australia, Far East), as well as Europe-only, Asia excluding Japan, Australia and New Zealand benchmarks. With the depth of their data base, MSCI can design virtually any benchmark against which speciality portfolios can be measured. They have recently brought out an emerging markets index.

There is also an emerging markets index compiled by the International Financial Corporation (IFC), a subsidiary of the World Bank. The index covers Asia, Latin America and Europe/Middle East/Africa. IFC also has permutations of its main index, offering IFCL (Latin America) and IFCA (Asia).

The value of these indices is that an investor or portfolio manager can know—on a daily basis, if required—how a portfolio is doing against its relevant benchmark.

Figure 4.1 sets out the dollar capitalization of each market in the MSCI World Index at the end of 1980, and in late 1993. The significance of these dates is to show the phenomenal growth in market capitalization over a short historical period. A near-tripling of world market capitalizations in less than 13 years in a relatively low inflation environment is worthy of note. The percentage of each market's share of the index is noted at each date.

What is evident in Figure 4.1 is the sea-change that occurred in world financial markets between 1980 and 1993. For example, the US market moved from being 53.6 per cent of the World Index in 1980, to 36.96 per cent in 1993. Japan rose from 15.6 per cent in 1980 to 28.67 per cent of the index in 1993. This is despite the drop in Japanese share values from the Nikkei Index level of 39,000 in early 1990 to 20,000 in December 1993.

The British share of the index edged up from 8.4 per cent to 9.98 per cent over the period, and all European markets except Italy have gained since 1980.

Australia and Canada have seen relative decline, partly because they are perceived to be 'mineral markets', and the inflationary forces that pushed up mineral and commodity prices in the 1970s, reaching an apex in 1980,

	Billions of dollars		Percentage of index	
Country	December 1980	December 1993	December 1980	December 1993
EUROPE				
Austria	2	28	0.1	0.2
Belgium	10	68	0.4	0.6
Denmark	4	37	0.2	0.3
Finland	-	20	-	0.2
France	53	428	2.5	3.6
Germany	71	421	3.3	3.5
Ireland	-	19	-	0.2
Italy	25	126	1.1	1.1
Netherlands	25	189	1.1	1.6
Norway	3	17	0.1	0.1
Spain	16	118	0.8	1.0
Sweden	12	68	0.5	0.6
Switzerland	46	163	2.0	1.4
United Kingdom	190	1126	8.4	9.4
Total Europe	457	2828	20.5	23.8
ASIA				
Australia	60	188	2.7	1.6
Hong Kong	38	308	1.6	2.6
Japan	357	3345	15.6	28.1
Malaysia*	24	135	1.1	1.1
New Zealand	-	24	-	0.2
Singapore*	-	118	-	1.0
Total Asia	479	4118	21.0	34.6
OTHER				
Canada	113	224	4.9	1.6
South Africa	-	-	-	-
United States	1240	4726	53.6	40.0
Total Other	1353	4950	58.5	41.6
TOTAL WORLD	2289	11,896	100.0	100.0

Figure 4.1 The dollar size and percentage weighting of developed markets

*In 1980, Singapore and Malaysia were stated as one market; in 1993 they are separate. The total Singapore/Malaysia figure for 1980 has been put against Malaysia ($24.3 billion).

Note: All figures have been rounded to the nearest whole number.

Sources: MSCI (1980); IBES (1993).

have been in abeyance since then. They have striven to diversify their economies from natural resources, but new enterprises have not yet made a significant impact on overall market capitalizations. Extractive economies used to be beneficiaries of the early stages of industrialization. Today's advanced industrial economies need fewer raw materials to fuel economic growth, per unit of gross national product (GNP), than before the Second World War.

Once stock markets attain a certain market capitalization and are deemed by MSCI to be worthy of inclusion, they are added to the index. Singapore/Malaysia used to be treated as a single market, but were separated in 1993. Now, both Singapore and Malaysia are separately listed on the EAFE Index.

The purpose of including Figure 4.1 is not to show specifically how Japan has grown relative to the United States or the United Kingdom relative to Canada, but to demonstrate the enormous size of many markets outside the United States. When the United States represented 66.3 per cent of the world's capitalization in 1970, a US plan sponsor with billions of dollars to invest might legitimately worry about the ability of foreign markets to absorb a major overseas allocation of the pension fund. Today that is not a problem; a well-diversified EAFE portfolio of hundreds of millions of dollars can be absorbed easily by the markets in which it is invested.

Emerging markets

The financial club of the last decade has been gate-crashed recently by some brash newcomers: emerging markets. Just as there was a great shift of relative economic and financial muscle between the United States and the rest of the world, as reflected in the MSCI World Index since 1980, we may see a possibly greater shift to parts of the world loosely termed as emerging markets.

Since the 1980s, the International Financial Corporation (IFC) has been developing indices for emerging markets. It is worth describing IFC's methodology briefly here, because emerging markets are such a rapidly moving target.

The IFC Global Index was based at the end of 1984. The base for the Investable Indices was the end of 1988. Each was set at 100. The indices are calculated in local currencies and also in US dollars. The IFC uses exchange rates taken either from the Wall Street Journal or Financial Times, to ensure predictable sourcing. If these newspapers do not carry a country's exchange rate, the IFC uses the equivalent 'free market' rate, or the rate which would apply to the repatriation of capital and income on a particular date. As stock markets become eligible for inclusion they are added to the indices. To illustrate the dynamism of these indices, the list below shows when various countries joined the index:

Colombia	February 1991*
India	November 1992
Indonesia	September 1990
Korea	January 1992
Pakistan	March 1991
Taiwan, China	January 1991
Turkey	August 1989
Venezuela	January 1990

* Each country index was set at 100 on these dates.

Just as the EAFE Index includes countries as they become eligible, so the IFC Index is likely to expand. Poland and Hungary joined the index in April 1993. Other Eastern European countries including Russia, as well as more Asian, Africa and South American countries, are likely to be included. Vietnam, Morocco, Kenya and Ecuador are likely to be new names on the IFC Index in years to come.

In October 1993, Sri Lanka and Peru joined the index, as will a host of currently unlikely countries in the next five years.

In 1987, Sri Lanka's total stock market turnover was $4m. By 1993, that figure had risen 75-fold to $300m. In June 1990, the government abolished a 100 per cent transfer tax levied on foreigners. By mid-1993, 60 per cent of market turnover was foreign-originated. In the late 1980s, the government embarked on a privatization programme that boosted share ownership from 10,000 people in 1990 to over 60,000 in 1993. Although equity investing in Sri Lanka competes with 18 per cent interest rates from bank deposits, a political commitment to 'peoplization' of the economy will further encourage equity ownership in the 1990s. A state-of-the-art scripless central depository system funded by US AID was installed in 1991, which gives confidence to foreign investors that Sri Lanka means business. But just to put Sri Lanka in perspective, its total investable market capitalization is about the same of a mid-sized Hong Kong company like Cathay Pacific Airways.

It is testimony to the venturesome spirit of the Edinburgh Investment Trust that it was investing in Costa Rica in 1890, and that country was not yet on a recognizable investable index a hundred years later.

The distinction between the IFC Global and IFC Investable Indices (see Figure 4.2) is that not all the stock capitalization represented in the global indices is investable by foreigners. As countries open for investment, it is common for governments to limit the percentage of 'strategic' companies that can be owned by foreigners. This typically includes banks, insurance companies, telecommunications and local mining operations. The IFC

	IFC Global Indices			**IFC Investable Indices**		
Market	No. of stocks	Market capitalization (US$ millions)	Weight in IFC composite	No. of stocks	Market capitalization (US$ millions)	Weight in IFC composite
Latin America						
Argentina	31	31,499.4	3.8	11	28,926.3	7.5
Brazil	70	60,849.1	7.4	42	34,238.4	8.9
Chile	35	28,594.8	3.5	20	6134.4	1.6
Colombia	20	6953.0	0.8	8	5874.2	1.5
Mexico	69	123,813.0	15.0	56	109,833.6	28.6
Peru	18	2351.3		7	2201.6	
Venezuela	17	4840.2	0.6	8	2390.6	0.6
East Asia						
China	81	19,177.4		16	2274.5	
Korea	134	91,443.8	11.1	130	8758.4	2.3
Philippines	37	23,796.7	2.9	11	11,973.5	3.1
Taiwan, China	78	124,646.8	15.1	76	8177.3	2.1
South Asia						
India	108	49,261.1	6.0	61	9933.9	2.6
Indonesia	41	18,231.5	2.2	31	8660.2	2.3
Malaysia	66	135,431.5	16.4	61	92,310.1	24.0
Pakistan	64	7944.6	1.0	8	2711.0	0.7
Sri Lanka	30	1465.5		5	543.5	
Thailand	58	74,594.6	9.0	52	21,049.8	5.5
Europe/Mid-East/Africa						
Greece	35	6987.5	0.8	17	5500.1	1.4
Jordan	29	2545.6	0.3	5	847.4	0.2
Nigeria	24				5	
Portugal	33	8749.8	1.1	16	5123.5	1.3
Turkey	36	23,742.0	2.9	31	22,050.5	5.7
Zimbabwe	21	890.0	0.1	5	127.3	
Regions						
Composite (a)	1006	824,707.0	100.0	649	384,493.2	100.0
Latin America (b)	242	256,549.5	31.1	145	187,397.5	48.7
Asia (c)	586	525,242.6	63.7	430	163,574.2	42.5
EMEA	133	42,024.9	5.1	69	33,521.5	8.7

Figure 4.2 December 1993: Country weights in IFC indices

Notes: (a) Peru and Sri Lanka not included; (b) Peru not included; (c) Sri Lanka not included

analyses markets for their 'foreign availability factor'. Only that portion is included in the investable indices.

Some markets are more open than others. Mexico, for instance, had a total market capitalization of US$123,813m in December 1993 and its weight in the Global Index was 15.0 per cent of the total. But because Mexico is more liberalized economically than many emerging markets, its share of the IFC Investable Index rises to 28.6 per cent, with an available capitalization of US$109,833.6m.

India was the opposite: its market capitalization of US$49,261.1m represented 6.0 per cent of the Global Index, but because of investment restrictions, only US$9933.9m is available for investment by foreigners. This is only 2.6 per cent of the Investable Index.

In December 1993, the total size of the IFC Global Composite Index was US$824,707m. The capitalization of the Investable Index was US$384,493.2m, or 46.6 per cent of the total. Larger pension funds have the same problem with the IFC Index as they had in the early 1980s with the EAFE Index. That is, the inability of smaller countries to absorb the investment flows that international diversification entails.

InterSec Research of Stamford, Connecticut, estimated that in the first half of 1993, US$18bn flowed internationally from US institutions, of which US$2bn was destined for emerging markets. That is the equivalent of investing in only eight of the top ten capitalized stocks in the rest of the world. The combined market capitalizations of AT&T, Exxon, General Electric, Toyota, Fuji Bank, Sumitomo Bank, Royal Dutch Shell and the Industrial Bank of Japan amounted to US$551bn, or US$6bn greater than the combined IFC Investable capitalization of 20 countries. The market capitalization of General Electric is larger than the entire Mexican stock market.

Conclusion

The size of stock markets is only one component of the case for international investing. What size demonstrates, however, is that the United States today represents 36.96 per cent of the MSCI World Index. If the Investable component of the IFC Index is added, the United States represents 34.19 per cent of the total. This is a far cry from representing 53.6 per cent of the World in 1980, 66.3 per cent in 1970, and 75 per cent in 1960. The trend of faster economic growth by smaller countries is inexorable. As they grow, their stock markets will expand and the pool of capitalization will correspondingly increase for foreign investment. In time we will see a blurring of the distinction between emerging and mainstream stock markets. For example, Colombia today has nearly twice the market capitalization that Norway had in 1980, yet is regarded as a greater risk today than Norway was then.

Chapter 5

Performance of stock markets — MSCI World Index

Developed markets

The purpose of this chapter is to make the case for international investing by showing historical performance data.

Recent history shows that there have been powerful performance reasons for investing internationally. The case is as strong for investors from the United States as from Great Britain, Australia, Sweden or Japan. No stock market remains the best performer in the world for long, so investors everywhere must seek opportunities everywhere. How this is done will be covered in subsequent chapters.

Figure 5.1 shows performance, in dollars, over various periods from 1960 to 1992, of the markets in the Capital International World Index. The performance shown demonstrates that despite periods of strong performance in a particular market, no market remains the leader for ever. For example, in the 1960s, Spain had a compound annual return of 11.11 per cent, followed by a negative 5.83 per cent annual return in the 1970s. Denmark was the opposite. In the 1960s, it had negative annual returns of 0.17 per cent, but positive returns of 5.62 per cent in the 1970s.

Currency is covered fully in a later chapter of this book, but Figure 5.2 shows a snapshot of local-currency and dollar-adjusted market returns and demonstrates the impact of currency on international portfolios managed from a US dollar base.

In 1993, the dollar rose sharply against the major European currencies. The reason was economic decline in Europe, high unemployment and a shambolic realignment of the European monetary system in late 1992. Some European interest rates also fell sharply, which led to currency declines versus the US dollar. Falling interest rates also triggered bullish action in European stock markets, and even after the dollar's strength was factored in, all 14 markets beat the US index. A hedged European portfolio would have benefited a US investor even more. For example, a local investor in the Belgian market index would have had a return of 34.4 per cent, but an American dollar-based investor there would have seen a return of 23.5 per cent. A local investor in the Finnish stock market index would have had 96.8 per cent return, but an American dollar-based investor there would

	1960-1969 (%)	1970-1979 (%)	1980-1989 (%)	1988-1992 (%)
Europe				
Austria	3.84	10.75	13.58	37.56
Belgium	0.56	6.91	13.30	29.76
Denmark	(0.17)	5.62	17.67	81.56
Finland	n/a	n/a	n/a	(61.07)
France	(0.65)	4.62	13.25	80.17
Germany	1.25	6.13	13.07	44.38
Italy	(1.59)	(8.29)	19.96	(29.46)
Netherlands	2.09	4.76	14.79	53.62
Norway	5.43	14.39	8.94	84.42
Spain	11.11	(5.83)	11.23	(8.55)
Sweden	2.43	1.93	25.53	39.34
Switzerland	5.34	9.82	9.36	61.44
United Kingdom	2.50	2.91	13.82	31.65
Asia				
Australia	6.45	(0.25)	9.12	27.40
Hong Kong	n/a	21.26	8.93	141.88
Japan	5.55	14.03	27.18	(26.26)
Malaysia	n/a	n/a	n/a	220.17
New Zealand	n/a	n/a	n/a	(24.10)
Singapore	n/a	17.18	10.71	75.33
Other				
Canada	4.97	6.59	7.78	10.46
United States	3.99	1.60	12.03	71.25
EAFE Index	2.63	5.80		
World Index	3.87	2.74	15.78	

Figure 5.1   Compound annual returns: in dollars

Sources: Capital International & Morgan Stanley Capital International

have had a return of (only) 77.7 per cent. The difference in each case was the strength of the dollar against the local currencies. The story in the Far East was the reverse: a strengthening yen, in particular, turned a reasonable Japanese year in local terms (+12.2 per cent) into an excellent year in dollar terms (+25.5 per cent).

Emerging markets

Just as emerging markets are beginning to present an interesting investment destination from the standpoint of market capitalization, they also present a potentially exciting destination for investors seeking performance.

	Local price change	US dollar price change
Europe		
Austria	37.5	28.1
Belgium	34.4	23.5
Denmark	44.1	32.2
Finland	96.8	77.7
France	32.6	24.0
Germany	45.5	35.6
Ireland	64.1	42.4
Italy	48.9	28.5
Netherlands	44.4	35.3
Norway	49.2	37.6
Spain	61.9	29.8
Sweden	61.7	37.0
Switzerland	47.6	45.8
United Kingdom	27.4	24.4
Asia		
Australia	37.3	35.2
Hong Kong	116.3	116.7
Japan	12.2	25.5
Malaysia	116.3	110.0
New Zealand	54.1	67.7
Singapore	70.1	73.4
Other		
Canada	22.6	17.6
United States	9.1	9.1
MSCI World Index	20.9	22.5
EAFE Index	29.2	32.6

Figure 5.2 1993 MSCI performance - a snapshot of local-currency and dollar-adjusted market returns

Source: Morgan Stanley Capital International

Performance records do not exist in an organized, homogenous fashion for emerging markets as a group before the mid-1980s. It was a team of dedicated professionals at the IFC and their advisory panel, who constructed the various IFC indices.

Performance shown in Figure 5.3 is for two periods—1988 to 1993, and 1993. These observations may seem too short to constitute a trend, and some purists may wish to hold back until another five years of performance 'confirms' the validity of investing in emerging markets.

This recalls the early 1980s, however, when many American pension plan sponsors were analysing the 'case for international equity investing' for the investment of their pension assets. MBAs were detailed to crunch numbers and assess the portfolio risk of putting a slice of pension money overseas. There were political problems, there were custodial problems, there were risk problems, there were trustee problems. Consultants were hired, investment managers were interviewed. Managers were short-listed, they were visited in their offices in London, Zurich, Paris, Hong Kong, Edinburgh or Glasgow. Gate-keepers did the 'Grand Tour', then returned to their offices in suburban New Jersey, to recommend that a closely-monitored 3 per cent of pension assets should be dedicated to international investing. The mountains shook, and a mouse was born.

While this process was going on, the EAFE Index beat the S&P 500 every year in the 1980s. Due diligence in the investment process is highly important, but equally one should strive to avoid analysis paralysis in the face of an inexorable trend.

There are many parallels between emerging markets today and the smaller components of EAFE in the early 1980s such as size, performance, liquidity, and a recent commitment to market economies. As their economies grow, these emerging markets will provide excellent investment returns.

Retrospectively, the continent to have invested in for the five years to December 1993 was Latin America (see Figure 5.3), where the investable part of the Colombian index rose 1187 per cent in dollar terms, Argentina rose 557 per cent, Mexico 450.1 per cent and Chile rose 407.5 per cent. The enhanced performance of the Investable Index over the Global Index can be attributed to the influence of foreign money, pushing up the price of investable stocks.

A more recent investor would have benefited by being better diversified, however. Latin America had excellent returns in 1993, and Brazil rose 75.1 per cent, but there were spectacular returns elsewhere, from 272.3 per cent in Turkey to 145.3 per cent in the Philippines and 123.9 per cent in Indonesia. Other markets not represented in these indices were also strong, such as Hungary, Poland and Shenzen in China. These were not particularly accessible to foreigners, so they were excluded from the IFC Investable Index in 1993.

In 1993, there were 26 companies listed on the Budapest Stock Exchange, and Mr Jozsef Rotyis, its chief executive, estimated that there were at least 50 more companies eligible for listing. The market is small, with many favourite stocks having a strong foreign connection. For example, German retailer Tengelmann owns a majority of Skala-Coop, the Hungarian retailing group. This gives confidence to local investors, and it is often the partially foreign-owned companies that perform best in the stock market.

It is likely that more Eastern European stock markets will be included in the IFC Index. In 1993, the Budapest Stock Exchange received US$2.2m

	IFC Global Indices		IFC Investable Indices	
Market	Dec 1988 - Dec 1993	1993	Dec 1988 - Dec 1993	1993
Latin America				
Argentina	+531.6	+70.6	+557.0	+71.8
Brazil	+109.3	+79.0	+124.8	+75.1
Chile	+353.2	+32.4	+407.5	+35.8
Colombia	+618.6	+36.1	+1187.0	+49.7
Mexico	+441.7	+58.0	+450.1	+58.5
Venezuela	+272.9	-8.3	+332.5	+20.9
East Asia				
Korea	-5.3	+23.1	-5.2	+23.2
Philippines	+317.1	+124.5	+487.2	+145.3
Taiwan, China	+42.4	+91.2	+42.6	+91.3
South Asia				
India	+212.3	+37.6	+229.0	+38.3
Indonesia	n/a	+122.3	n/a	+123.9
Malaysia	+337.9	+102.7	+337.9	+102.7
Pakistan	+258.8	+56.6	-387.6	+101.4
Thailand	+526.2	+111.6	+526.2	+113.9
Europe/Mid-East/Africa				
Greece	+139.7	+37.6	+143.1	+21.5
Jordan	+60.3	+26.2	+88.6	+38.4
Portugal	-37.2	+45.2	-26.1	+45.1
Turkey	+559.9	+272.3	+559.9	+272.3

Figure 5.3 Performance of IFC indices Dec 88-Dec 93 and 1993 (US dollars)
Source: IFC

from the EC's Phare Programme and Britain's Know-How Fund (aid programmes for Eastern Europe) to install a computerized trading system. Once settlement procedures are fully reliable, the way will be open for foreign portfolio investment. The market exhibits all the volatility expected of an emerging market, with a low point of 683 in April 1993, and high in October of 1114; it rose 55 per cent in the third quarter alone.

It is desirable to have a well-diversified portfolio. Any market which can have the spectacular annual returns of Brazil or Turkey, can also fall by a similar amount. These markets act like fashionable OTC stocks in the US market, energy stocks in the late 1970s or biotechnology stocks in 1983, which can have a powerful run and then rapidly fall out of favour. In the last ten years, Latin America was on a tidal wave of deregulation, repatriation of capital, political reform and foreign investment. If there was a global slump and economic and domestic economic conditions were poor, there is the possibility of the return of undemocratic leadership and the military banana republicanism from which much of Latin America has recently emerged.

Chapter 6

Risk diversification

A third reason to invest overseas is to diversify portfolio risk. Shopkeepers earning their living from selling groceries need to offer a broad variety of produce. If they only has a pile of potatoes in the corner, and if nobody wants them on a particular day, their earnings would be slim. They must have a range of goods to satisfy customer demand and ensure a minimum daily flow of sales.

The principle of diversifying business risk is so obvious that a science has been made out of the subject. There is a branch of that science dedicated to risk diversification in investment portfolios.

Equity investors tend to want a good spread of risk. In a domestic country context, this means having exposure to many industrial sectors, and within sectors, having exposure to several companies. Portfolio analysis will determine whether to underweight or overweight a particular sector or company within a sector. Institutional investors aim to achieve adequate diversification by employing managers to handle their portfolios. These are often divided between 'core' and 'speciality' managers. Private investors usually manage to accomplish portfolio diversification by buying mutual funds. These generally offer access to a large number of individual securities, whereby an investment of US$1000 can provide an investment in tiny fractions of scores of companies.

Just as diversifying between sectors within a market provides a spread of risk, so does investing internationally provide a counterbalance to a purely domestic portfolio. In spite of the increasing links between the world's major economies through the creation of formal or informal trade zones (EC, Asean, Nafta etc.[1]) and a convergence of business cycles in the G7[2] nations, many factors which determine stock market performance are still domestic in nature. Domestic monetary and fiscal policies are subject to different operating constraints. Taxes, social structure, the political cycle, will differ be-

---

[1] EC = European Community; Asean = Association of South East Asian Nations; Nafta = North American Free Trade Area.
[2] G7 = USA, UK, France, Germany, Canada, Italy and Japan.

tween countries. Apparently monolithic 'world' events, like the Iraqi invasion of Kuwait, can affect one country more than another. Even though the immediate impact of the event on all stock markets may be the same—panic—it is interesting how quickly the information is digested and that the event can ultimately be quite beneficial for some countries (for example, petro-currencies, such as sterling, may rise and currencies from countries with no fossil fuel resources, such as the yen, may fall).

The lower the correlations between stock markets, the greater the potential for risk reduction through international diversification. Even mediocre returns from a particular foreign market can result in superior risk—adjusted returns compared to a purely domestic portfolio if the performance correlations between the markets are low.

The traditional measure of risk used by investors to evaluate portfolio diversification is beta. The risk contribution of a foreign investment to a domestic portfolio would be its beta coefficient. This is the covariance of the foreign security with the domestic portfolio divided by the variance of the domestic portfolio.

Developed markets

In the period 1975-1979, the Japanese stock market index had a total return correlation of 0.31 with the S&P 500 index, and a monthly standard deviation of 4.97 per cent compared to 4.22 per cent for the S&P 500's standard deviation. The correlation between the Tokyo and New York markets of 0.31 translated into a beta of 0.37 relative to the S&P 500 Index. If the criterion for success were strictly risk reduction, Japanese equities would have been a good investment for US investors over this period: the overall Beta of a US portfolio would have been lowered with an injection of Japanese equities.

Low correlations between markets and the S&P 500 are not a recent phenomenon. Figure 6.1 looks at correlations between markets and the S&P 500 over various periods.

The columns provide correlation data between the four largest markets in the EAFE Index and the S&P 500 for 6 timeframes over 23 years. The EAFE Index itself had a long period of low correlations with the US index, but they began to converge in the mid-1980s. This was principally because the US economy was being fuelled by the Reagan fiscal boom, falling interest rates and the western arms build-up. Japan, which derived a significant part of its export earnings from the United States, was a warrant on the propensity of US consumers to purchase high quality imported Japanese goods such as cars and consumer electronics. The Japanese stock market boomed in tandem with the US market, eventually overtaking it in performance and capitalization. The US economic boom began to taper off af-

	1970-74	1975-79	1972-82	1977-82	Jun 83-Jun 93	Jun 88- Jun 93
S&P 500	1.00	1.00	1.00	1.00	1.00	1.00
EAFE	0.53	0.48	0.51	0.36	0.80	(0.38)
Japan	0.34	0.31	0.28	0.15	0.61	(0.62)
UK	0.50	0.44	0.46	0.33	0.95	0.78
France	0.38	0.44	0.41	0.34	0.96	0.80
Germany	0.32	0.27	0.31	0.21	0.89	0.49

Note: The range for the coefficient is -1.0 to +1.0. A value of 1.0 indicates a perfect positive correlation; a value of -1.0 indicates perfect inverse correlation.

Figure 6.1 Correlation coefficients between four EAFE markets and the S&P 500 Composite Index for six timeframes over 20 years

Sources: 1970 to 1982 Bache Halsey; Stuart Shields Quantitative Research Group; Capital International 1983 to 1993 Morgan Stanley Research

ter 1988, but the Japanese capital spending boom carried on until early 1990. It was then realized in Japan that the market was wildly over-priced and its historic slide began. The Japanese economy was like a cartoon character running off a cliff who keeps running until he looks down, then plummets. Since the Japanese stock market was such a large component of the MSCI World Index, and in particular the EAFE Index, it is therefore not surprising that a correlation convergence between the EAFE and the S&P 500 Indices was seen. As has been written above, Japan hit its zenith at 39.9 per cent of the World Index. In 1990, the US market fell by 3.2 per cent, while Japan fell by 36 per cent.

Thus we see a relatively high correlation of 0.80 between the S&P 500 and EAFE Indices for the ten years ending mid-1993, but a low correlation (-0.38) for the five years ending mid-1993. This last period encompassed the Japanese crash. The influence of the Japanese index in EAFE masked other changes over the ten years. For instance, the United Kingdom, France and Germany all had higher correlations with the S&P 500 than they had in the previous ten years.

The purpose of this chapter on risk diversification is not so much to make a commentary on a particular slice of financial history, as to point out that, over time, international investing provides good diversification for investors. Harry Markowitz published a paper in a 1952 edition of the *Journal of Finance*, entitled 'Portfolio Selection', in which he observed that investors do not necessarily try to maximize return. If they were only interested in maximizing returns they would tend to hold only the single asset that they believed would yield the highest future return. Investors tend to hold portfolios of securities because they want an acceptable trade-off between return and risk.

The theory of risk and return that evolved from this observation is known as the Capital Asset Pricing Theory. The foundation of the theory is that the price of an asset is based on expectations of future cashflows from the asset.

The original theory developed with reference to the risk and return characteristics of American common stocks, but it can be adjusted to apply to any risky asset class, such as international investing. Markowitz assumed that investors act as if wealth had diminishing marginal utility. In other words, each incremental dollar of wealth provides less satisfaction than the previous dollar.

Expected utility will be maximized if the investor holds an 'efficient portfolio', which provides the maximum possible return for a given level of risk, where risk is defined as the variance of returns. Rational investors should hold portfolios along their 'efficient frontier', which is their optimal weighting in an asset class relative to their risk tolerance. The original concept of an 'efficient frontier' was developed to assess an investor's optimal weighting of American stocks. The same idea can be applied to assess the optimal weighting of international stocks for American investors. Figure 6.2 shows how, in five years during the 1980s, incremental slices of international equities would have added to the returns of a US investor and reduced the standard deviation of portfolios.[1]

For the 15 years ending 31 December 1988, there was an annualized standard deviation for a pure US portfolio of 18.3 and an annualized rate of return of 12 per cent. Each dot along the 1988 curve shows what the impact would have been over 15 years to 1988 with increments of 10 per cent tranches of international investing (The EAFE Index is the proxy for this). With 90 per cent US and 10 per cent international, the standard deviation of the portfolio fell to 17.5 and the return 13.6 per cent. With 70 per cent in the United States and 30 per cent international, the standard deviation was 17.3 and return 14.4 per cent.

Reduction of standard deviation is more pronounced in some years than in others, but is always present to some degree.

---

[1] *Harry Markowitz, 'Portfolio Selection', Journal of Finance March 1952, pp77-91. James Tobin, 'Liquidity Preference as Behaviour Towards Risk', Review of Economic Studies, 26, No. 1 February 1958. William F. Sharpe, 'A Simplified Model for Portfolio Analysis Management Science, January 1963. Jan Mossin, 'Equilibrium in a Capital asset Market', Econometrica, October 1966.*

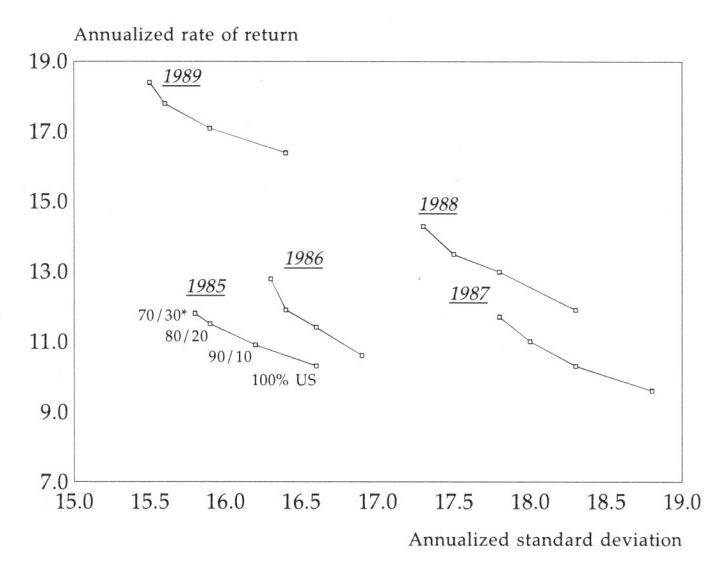

*) 7/30 represents a 70% weight in US equities and 30% in non-US equities

Figure 6.2   Long term: Increased return and reduced risk
Source: Blairlogie Capital Management

A word on crashes and high correlations

'It was the kind of market in which not even a skunk could make a scent'

Billy Henriquez

There are two types of crash: local and world-wide. A local crash happens in response to local events. This can be due to an over-inflated stock market puffed up by local speculation and the over-generous provision of margin debt. When the house of cards falls, it can fall flat indeed, such as the Kuwait Crash in the early 1980s, the Panic of 1873, the South Sea Bubble in 1720 and the Japanese Crash of 1990. These tend to be purgatives that are a reaction to excess speculation in a particular market, and will not affect other markets. An early example of such a crash is to be found in the collapse of the Darien Scheme in the 1690s. This was a plantation scheme in Panama that went wrong and ruined many Scottish families for a generation. The English barely noticed.

A world-wide crash can be caused in response to a variety of stimuli, usually happening after a period of world-wide market froth, causing over-optimistic conditions in many countries.

To take an example, in the summer of 1987, there was widespread speculation, take-over activity, increasingly tenuous leverage applied to increasingly thin deals on both sides of the Atlantic, in Hong Kong, Australia and Japan. US interest rates were creeping up in the summer. The proximate cause was the collapse of a major US leveraged buy-out deal, when some of the syndicate banks pulled out. This was the spark that lit the powder keg and the US market blew up, collapsing under the weight of accelerating margin calls. While in retrospect it could be defined as a 'financial accident', exaggerated by the failure of fail-safe systems in the Chicago pits, it seemed very real at the time.

That is what foreign markets sensed too. It was as if a huge neon sign flashed above everyone's desks, and it read, '1929'. Sell-orders came flooding in from London, Norway, Singapore, Australia, to sell equities wherever they were domiciled. Figure 6.3 is a snapshot of what occurred in a world-wide crash.

	October 1987	Nov 01 - Dec 31 1987
United States	(21.2)	(2.1)
Canada	(22.0)	4.9
United Kingdom	(21.5)	7.2
Germany	(17.6)	(7.8)
France	(18.4)	(1.9)
Switzerland	(17.6)	(3.5)
Belgium	(18.9)	2.0
Italy	(12.1)	(2.1)
Sweden	(17.5)	(6.1)
Norway	(27.9)	(15.5)
Denmark	(7.5)	8.0
Spain	(20.6)	13.4
Austria	(9.4)	8.4
Netherlands	(17.4)	0.1
Japan	(7.5)	5.4
Hong Kong	(43.4)	5.6
Singapore	(41.3)	7.5
Australia	(44.5)	14.1
Ranking of the US market	12/18	13/18

Figure 6.3   Total returns in US dollars for the month of October, and November 1st - December 31st 1987

Source: MSCI

During the 1987 Crash, there were high correlations between the US market and practically every other market. As in a crashing aeroplane, where there is a high correlation between all passengers and gravity was claiming all markets. At that time, I had many calls from clients who had been educated in the thesis of 'low-correlation diversification'. The ultimate test had failed. I counselled them to stay in the barrel as they went over Niagara Falls: they had a better chance of survival.

The true test of the Crash of 1987 was not one month's high correlations but the rapid sorting out of perceptions immediately thereafter. Investors in Toronto, London, Brussels, Madrid, Tokyo, Hong Kong and Sydney asked themselves in late October 1987, 'Is this a Japanese problem? Is this a British problem?—No, it is an American problem'. The 1987 Crash was an American crash that took the world with it at the time, but the differences between it and the Crash of 1929 were legion.

First, the US share of global GNP was over 60 per cent in 1929, but less than half that in 1987. Second, the underlying economies of much of the EC and Japan were in good shape in 1987, but not robust in 1929. Third, the Federal Reserve bank—and other central banks—made ample liquidity available to meet emergencies in 1987. The Crash of 1929 was accompanied by some errors of judgement by central bankers: money spigots dried up when they should have been in full flood.

So the key column in Figure 6.3 is not the one depicting the financial accident but the one depicting its immediate aftermath. In the two months afterwards, there was again a wide dispersion of correlations between markets. Low correlations between markets exist over time and work well for longer-term investors. If you invest internationally for a short-term speculation and Saddam Hussein invades Kuwait the next day, you will be disappointed by the high correlation characteristics of your international portfolio.

Emerging markets and diversification

Emerging markets add a new twist to the diversification-of-risk argument. It has been described how correlations between major markets have been converging in recent years. Just when investors have been potentially put off EAFE investing because of a lack of 'proper' diversification away from their domestic index, the emerging markets have provided a new pool of investments that have a low correlation with the S&P 500, the EAFE Index, and each other.

Figure 6.4 shows the correlation coefficients between some leading established markets and emerging markets indices, while Figure 6.5 shows the correlation coefficients among selected countries in the IFC Investable Index.

	EAFE	USA	UK	Japan
EAFE	1.00	0.40	0.50	0.49
USA	0.44	1.00	0.82	0.24
UK	0.05	0.82	1.00	0.20
Japan	0.49	0.24	0.20	1.00
IFCC	0.26	0.36	0.41	0.32
IFCA	0.20	0.35	0.40	0.37
IFCL	0.26	0.30	0.25	0.17

IFCC = Composite; IFCA = Asia; IFCL = Latin America

Figure 6.4 The correlation coefficients between some leading established markets and emerging markets indices.

Argentina:	Chile:	-0.09
Argentina:	Greece:	0.10
Argentina:	Korea:	-0.17
Zimbabwe:	Mexico:	-0.11
Zimbabwe:	Jordan:	0.12
Zimbabwe:	Nigeria:	-0.02
Malaysia:	Brazil:	0.07
Malaysia:	Colombia:	0.01
Malaysia:	India:	-0.03

Figure 6.5 Correlated coefficients among selected countries in the IFC index (Total returns from December 1984 to December 1990)

Source: IFC

The very act of calculating correlation coefficients between such disparate countries may seem absurd, because there is no apparent economic, political or market reason for the stock markets of these countries to have any correlation at all. It can be virtually guaranteed that the Zimbabwean market would not notice if the Argentinian market were to crash. This should not be confused with a global crash, such as the Crash of 1987, or when the Iraqis invaded Kuwait in 1990. At such times, all equity markets tend to go off a cliff together in response to an overwhelming extraneous event. It does not necessarily mean that markets are correlated to each other if they crash at the same time: it can be co-incidence rather than co-relation.

Correlation coefficients tend to be higher between countries in one region. For example, the correlation between Thailand and Malaysia is 0.52, between Colombia and Chile is 0.42, between Philippines and Indonesia is 0.63.

The key, therefore, when investing in emerging markets is to have a wide spread of countries in the portfolio, a good mix from Latin American, Asian, and Eurasian markets, that march to a different tune from each other. Investors should pay heed to the capital asset pricing theory. Evans and Archer wrote in 1968 that as the number of securities in a portfolio increases, the standard deviation of portfolio return decreases until only systematic (market-related) risk is left. As the number of emerging markets represented in a portfolio increases, the standard deviation of returns will decrease until only systematic, or IFC Index risk is left.

Chapter 7

Particular opportunities in international investing

Irrespective of the sophisticated arguments for investing overseas, such as diversification, performance, the low correlations between markets and efficient frontiers, there are many outstanding individual investment opportunities overseas, examples of which are given below.

It should be noted that mention of specific companies described should be not construed as an investment recommendation. They are being cited solely as examples of specific investment opportunities that may be available in international markets. Anyone interested in them should do their own research and satisfy themselves as to their suitability. The concepts illustrated here are historical, and may have no validity in the future.

Just as our Scottish ancestors were putting cash into Costa Rican Railroad bonds at 7 per cent in 1889 against 3 per cent at home, so it is particularly satisfying to invest in a company overseas that is in the first flush of its growth in an emerging economy. The adage that 'when everyone else is digging for gold, get into the pick and shovel business' can be applied around the world.

Cement may be a dull concept in a mature industrial economy, where growth is likely to be from gaining market share, rationalizing facilities or an occasional brilliant invention, but it can be a leading-edge investment in a country during economic take-off. Construction projects, from private enterprise office buildings and condominiums, to public sector port facilities, airports, railroads and highways, all consume concrete in large quantities.

Similarly, banks which are financing the growth of emerging countries can be an outstanding investment. They have the pulse of a country. Often, a foreign bank is a good proxy for a country's stock market because of its involvement in that country's growth. One of the best examples of a world-class bank is the HSBC Group, which includes The Hong Kong and Shanghai Banking Corporation Limited. It is one of the largest and strongest banking groups in the world, with about 3000 offices in 66 countries, of which over 600 are in Asia. Because of its long-term management style and geographical positioning, HSBC Group has had spectacular growth in recent years.

The banking group owns Hong Kong Bank, Hang Seng Bank, The British Bank of the Middle East, Marine Midland Bank and Midland Bank of the UK.

Because of its historical association with China, this banking group might be regarded as one of the best vehicles for gaining access to its rapidly emerging economy. A pick and shovel stock: when everyone is scrambling to invest in China, invest in a bank that facilitates the growth.

Figure 7.1 demonstrates HSBC's growth in a comparison between 1988 and 1992.

	1988 £ million	1992 £ million	Growth multiple
Share capital	937	2054	2.2x
Shareholders funds	3081	8011	2.6x
Assets	62,213	170,450	2.7x
Pre-tax profit	763	1710	2.2x
Dividends	150	472	3.1x
Dividends per share	9.44	19.00	2.0x

Figure 7.1   A comparison between 1988 and 1982, demonstrating HSBC's growth
Source: HSBC Holdings plc, Annual Report & Accounts, 1992

Sir William Purves, the chairman of the Group, commented in the Chairman's Statement in the 1992 *Annual Report*, 'HSBC Group's performance continued to improve in 1992. Profit attributable to shareholders was, in Hong Kong dollar terms, an increase of 68 per cent. These results are considered satisfactory.'

Not all interesting investments relate to emerging markets. The world abounds in investment opportunities. In the developed world there are three categories of stock investment that are potentially interesting to foreign investors. These are large capitalization, liquid market leaders which can be readily purchased and sold; cyclical turnaround situations; and unique corporate situations not available elsewhere.

Large capitalization stocks

While large is by no means necessarily beautiful, many of the world's largest companies are 'foreign', from whatever your perspective. Their size is important for several reasons. First, these companies can absorb the equity investment demand from around the world. Liquidity and marketability is important for many large institutional foreign investors. Second, being in-

Sector	Country	Market capitalization (billions)
Automobiles		
Toyota Motor	Japan	59
General Motors	USA	33
Ford Motor	USA	29
Daimler Benz	Germany	21
Nissan Motor	Japan	17
Banks		
Mitsubishi	Japan	171
Sumitomo Bank	Japan	64
Industrial Bank of Japan	Japan	73
Daiichi Kangyo Bank	Japan	65
Fugi Bank	Japan	60
Chemicals		
Du Pont	USA	32
Dow Chemicals	USA	16
CIBA GEIGY	Switzerland	14
Bayer	Germany	12
Asahi Chemical	Japan	6
Electrical & electronics		
General Electric	USA	81
Hitachi	Japan	26
Siemens	Germany	22
Toshiba	Japan	20
Alcatel Alsthom	France	18
Insurance		
American International Group	USA	31
Allianz Holdings	Germany	30
Tokio Marine & Fire	Japan	18
Generali	Italy	18
Allstate Corporation	USA	16

Figure 7.2 Top five capitalized companies in their fields in five representative industries
Source: MSCI 1993

dex stocks, they will always attract demand from passive investors or from investors who work to beat a benchmark. Third, many of the world's largest companies are listed on the main exchanges of the world, which are New York, London and Tokyo, and have cosmopolitan underpinnings. For example, there are over 1000 foreign companies listed in the form of American Depository Receipts on various US exchanges.

Figure 7.2 shows the top five capitalized companies in the world in five representative industries.

Size, of course, has no bearing on whether a company is an interesting investment. It is often the case that very large companies are inefficient, bureaucratic and political hierarchies, with a streak of hubris at the top. For substantial international investors, however, there is usually no choice but to own a cross-section of large market capitalization stocks.

Cyclical turnaround stocks

Given that not all countries experience synchronized business cycles, it is often possible to invest in companies at the bottom of one country's cycle when those same industries elsewhere are in full swing. Some of the largest profits and opportunities in international investing can be derived from early investment in 'bombed-out cyclicals'. A company like Barratt Developments, the British house construction group, after nurturing its way painfully through the UK housing slump in the early 1990s, saw its share price rise from a low of 94 pence in early 1993, to a high of 195 pence by late summer. This was in response to falling mortgage rates and a forecast UK economic recovery of 1.6 per cent, which is pretty sluggish by Asian standards. During the same period, British building societies were exaggerating the importance of every move in house prices and leading the public to believe the United Kingdom was on the brink of a sustained housing recovery. This may or may not occur, but it had an electrifying effect on the share price of a leading house-builder. The art is to identify such out-of-favour cyclicals and buy them when nobody else wants them. The science is to apply a fool-proof methodology to security selection so that what appears speculative on the surface is actually a well-balanced business decision where the odds are high in your favour. As Jesse Livermore found in 1923, 'Everything happened as I had foreseen. I was dead right and—I lost every cent I had. I was wiped out by something that was unusual'.

An investor does not need to go overseas to be a successful cycle-spotter. Every market has depressed cyclical opportunities for the patient investor. An investor in US oil service stocks in 1986 would have experienced spectacular returns over a 2-3 year waiting period. Companies like Baker-Hughes and Schlumberger were discounting ever-lower oil prices, so that when there was evidence of a bottom in oil, the share price of oil service stocks soared upwards.

There are usually three responses to a serious business downturn by cyclical companies, namely, go out of business, merge, or manage your way out. In a downturn, the share price tends to get hit in line with falling earnings. It is important to watch how the management reacts to business conditions. During the depths of recession, well-managed companies tend to shed surplus labour, close marginal facilities and invest in equipment to add to their productivity—to the point where they are down to a hard nut of profitable business. When business conditions improve, these companies have good operational leverage: a 1 per cent rise in GNP can translate into a 60 per cent rise in profits. Investors should always be careful with cyclical stocks, because every robust capitalist economy must subscribe to the maxim, 'Capitalism without bankruptcy is like Christianity without Hell'.

Unique investments

There are so many individual companies around the world that have unique features unavailable elsewhere, that it would be impossible to list them in one book let alone one chapter. Each market has indigenous and unusual opportunities. In Japan, there are electronics, semiconductors, computer games, automobiles, 'new materials' and robotics. In Germany, there are precision engineering, chemicals, metallurgy, and specific plays on Eastern Europe (pick and shovel stocks). In France, there are food companies, telecommunications, wine, luggage and world-class water treatment companies. Britain, because of its historical relationships, has unusual plays on Africa, pharmaceuticals on the leading edge of the fight against Aids and companies with a substantial stake in the United States. Also, because of early privatization, many of Britain's cyclicals are more profitable than their counterparts elsewhere (like British Steel, British Airways, British Telecom).

In the United States, there are scores of companies that are unique in their field, which would have to be considered for inclusion in global sector portfolios: cellular radio (Motorola), oil service (Baker Hughes, Schlumberger), microprocessors (Intel), irrigation equipment (Lindsay Manufacturing).

What follows is merely a scattering of interesting stories in some representative markets.

Kyocera

Kyocera Corporation is a Japanese corporation, formerly Kyoto Ceramic, founded in 1959. It has been the world leader in advanced ceramic technology for thirty years, with 1992 sales of US$3.8bn, net annual income of US$208m and total assets of US$5.4bn. About 23 per cent of Kyocera's earnings are in ceramic packaging for the semiconductor industry, in which it has 62 per cent of the world market. Ceramics have three major qualities over competing materials: heat dissipation, protection against moisture and durability under harsh conditions. Plastic is cheaper, but there will continue to be a niche for ceramics: Pin grid arrays with up to 512/1024 pins are housed only in ceramic and are used in telecommunications equipment. Since the telecommunications industry is growing explosively world-wide, there should continue to be handsome sales for this application of ceramic technology for the foreseeable future. Analysts estimate that Intel's Pentium chip, housed in ceramic, will see sales rise twenty-fold in the three years to 1996.

In its electronic equipment division, Kyocera brought out two new products in 1992. The first is its light-emitting diode (LED) printer that needs no cartridge replacement. It is known as Ecosys, because users do not have to throw out cartridges for recycling. While other manufacturers have cartridges with a typical life expectancy of 7000 pages of text, Ecosys can produce 300,000 pages. For an average user printing 1300 pages a month, the savings on cartridges alone can recoup the cost of the printer. The printer also doubles as a copier at a cost per copy lower than that of an office copier.

Output of the printers is rising sharply—7000 a month were produced in early 1993 and the company projects sales 20,000 in mid-1994.

The second new product is a portable phone that functions on one charge for 160 minutes, as opposed to the current best time of 60 minutes by competing products. Kyocera is raising production to meet demand in all markets.

Kyocera owns 25 per cent of Daini Denden Inc. (DDI), the Japanese provider of long-distance telecommunications services, which owns a majority of eight regional mobile telephone companies in Japan. In mid-1993, it had 360,000 subscribers and was adding 5000 a month. This will be a valuable channel for the sale of equipment throughout the 1990s.

One project which makes Kyocera a company to watch for the twenty-first century is its stake in Nihon Iridium. This is the multinational satellite communications system based on 66 satellites in low orbit that form a global telecommunications network, allowing portable phone users to call other users anywhere in the world. The system will be in service in 1998 and expects 1.5m subscribers by the year 2000. The US$3.4bn Iridium project was conceived and initially financed by Motorola, of the US, and the development of the project is now being shared by a multinational consortium which includes Kyocera.

Consumer-related products account for a small part of the company's sales (8 per cent), but there are exciting developments here. Its Bioceram unit has developed ceramic bone-substitutes for artificial hips and dental transplants. Ceramics have the flexibility of bone, but greater strength. They do not deteriorate or corrode like metal bone replacements, nor do they set off the hi-jack alarms at airport security checks.

Kyocera is a world leader in photovoltaic cells. They have produced them so far with a 17 per cent conversion efficiency, which is one of the best in the world—but still a long way below the 45 per cent conversion efficiency of fossil fuels.

Products like Ecosys, photovoltaic cells and Bioceram point the way forward. They are part of Kyocera's over-reaching philosophy of applying 'green' policies world-wide. Wherever possible they apply green principles to the manufacturing and service function, also in the design and function of their products. A key philosophy of the company's founder, Kazuo Inamori, is 'to promote human well-being'.

The fact that Kyocera did well in the first thirty years of its life as part of one of the great economic phenomena of history, Japan's post war growth, is not necessarily a prescription for future success. It is important to look hard at the management to get a sense of future direction—indeed, to detect for hubris and analyse whether they can handle a new world in which Japan can not expect to be treated as indulgently by its trading partners as in the past.

Kyocera is realistic. As stated its 1993 *Annual Report*, the company faces the challenge squarely. Its priority is 'to build a strong company structure capable of withstanding external pressures such as intensified competition and the continuing appreciation of the yen. Our first priority is to bring our ratio of operating profit to net sales back up to 10 per cent in the shortest possible time'.

For illustration, Kyocera's profit margins for the five years to March 1993 were:

1989	13.6 per cent
1990	12.6 per cent
1991	11.7 per cent
1992	7.9 per cent
1993	7.7 per cent

This decline is broadly in line with the world-wide decline in demand for ceramic packaging for microprocessor chips over the period.

The company has devised three strategies to achieve its 10 per cent margin target:

■ **1. Expand sales by cultivating new markets and introducing new products.**
The company will focus on developing new technology and create new markets. For instance, the amorphous silicon drum used in the

Ecosys printer is based on a non-cartridge concept, and produced only by Kyocera. Applications for ceramics are expanding to automotive and fibre optic communication equipment. The integration of technology around the company can lead to interesting synergies, such as the production of telephone hardware for Daini Denden.

■ **2. Promoting globalization of the production system.**
This is in response to the rapid growth of smaller Asian and other developing countries. Kyocera is setting up facilities from Batam in Indonesia to Shilong Town in China. The company believes that the key to survival is to compete locally in local markets with no labour disadvantage. By setting up production facilities in the EC and North America, Kyocera employs local people and avoids the accusation of unfair competition in each area.

■ **3. Pursuing management efficiency based on efficient investment and productivity.**
Kyocera will be seeking a higher return on capital and R&D investments, as well as working to monitor continually the environmental impact of its operations. In 1992, the company eliminated the use of chlorofluoro-carbons (CFCs) in its processes. The company seeks to achieve greater productivity per employee and to upgrade product lines to achieve optimal product yield.

As an investment, Kyocera has exhibited many cyclical characteristics. When rumours of slower microprocessor growth circulate, or when the debate between plastic and ceramic packaging tilts towards plastic, Kyocera's share price can fall sharply. But such volatility does not detract from the long-term technologies being developed by the company, such as satellites for cellular phones, solar power and ceramic bone replacement. Kyocera is a company with a 100-year vision, and is powerfully placed for the technology and consumer trends of the early 21st century.

The Body Shop

The Body Shop may or may not survive for the long-term as an independent company, but its place in commercial history is assured. It is a classic example of a concept which has influenced the way business is done, and has attracted a wide following of international shareholders. It is still a small company, with a market capitalization of about £375m ($570m), which tends to exclude many large investors, but this is balanced by a large following of devotee shareholders to whom The Body Shop concept is the way forward.

The Body Shop opened its first store in England in 1976. By 1993, it had over 900 stores in 41 countries. The management of the company is driven by 'green' concepts, from the sourcing of raw materials, to an employee share option scheme. It was the first company to publish a statement in line with the EC's ECO Management and Audit Regulation. The company has no environmental liabilities.

The Body Shop differs from many cosmetic enterprises, because it does not claim that its products are the elixir of youth. They produce hair and skin care cosmetics that have not been tested on animals in the research phase, and which are made from renewable resources. For example, a pineapple facial wash with exfoliating properties, jojoba moisture cream, banana shampoo and Brazil nut conditioner. The company has pioneered the use of unusual crops in its preparations. In the case of its Brazil nut conditioner, the Brazil nut oil is harvested by Kayapo Indians in the Amazon rain forest though a 'Trade Not Aid' programme. The company claims to be the first UK cosmetics company to use jojoba oil, pointing out that one acre of jojoba bushes yields the same amount of oil as 30 sperm whales.

Cosmetic companies are notoriously wasteful with their packaging, and The Body Shop has tackled the problem imaginatively. There is a refill bar at its stores, where customers can return used containers for refilling, rather than simply throwing away the plastic containers. The management recognizes the obscenity of manufacturing an item at great expense to the environment and the consumer, having it used once and then discarded, to lie in a landfill for generations before it decomposes. Archaeologists are still finding garbage discarded by Roman troops at sites near Hadrian's Wall 1800 years ago. The company states in its *Annual Report* that customers refill a bottle every 13 seconds in the United Kingdom—or 2.4m times a year—which translates into a lot of prevented waste.

Their manufacturing facilities were designed as a model production site. There is a 4000 square foot crèche—day care centre—for an average of 48 children of the 626 employees. Tours are encouraged, and 2300 visitors a week are taken on a tour-buggy powered by electricity generated by the company's wind turbine. The offices use as much natural light and ventilation as possible and can recycle 6000 cubic metres of waste water in an ultra-filtration plant.

The company demonstrates that it is possible to have a technologically-advanced production system that is frugal in energy and raw material use. This is an important trend which other manufacturers would do well to emulate.

Good corporate citizenship also extends to the communities in which the company operates. In November 1992, the 118th branch of The Body Shop opened in Harlem in New York City. Fifty per cent of the shop's profits are earmarked for donation to community organizations within Harlem. The company makes a special effort to support the homeless and it sponsors over 600 community projects world-wide. These include helping Aids patients in the United Kingdom, Eastern European Relief in Romania and youth projects in Canada.

The company makes money, too. Earnings retreated in 1992 owing to recession in the United Kingdom, but its turnover (revenues) rose from £73m in 1989 to £168m in 1992, and operating profit from £15m in 1989 to £24m in 1993. This represented profit margin slippage, however, from 20.6 per cent to 14.4 per cent, but the management is committed to improving the ratio. Short-term debt has been reduced, and inventories have fallen. Given a target to open its 1000th outlet in 1993, it is likely that the overseas sales ratio will rise relative to the United Kingdom, so that a local recession in the United Kingdom becomes less negative to the company, as the novelty of Body Shops in new markets stimulates new sales. Growth in Japan, Singapore, the United States, Spain, Holland and elsewhere testifies to the success of the 'exportability' of the concept. Whereas much of what The Body Shop does is often dismissed by financial analysts as gimmicky, the company is setting important trends in corporate governance that will be emulated by other companies around the world.

Global sector themes

A fourth area of opportunity is to invest in themes that can be found simultaneously around the world.

In the third quarter of 1982, interest rates in the United States fell sharply. The Federal Reserve Bank under Paul Volcker perceived a serious risk of a major bank collapse as a result of defaults of loans to the developing world.

In particular, some major US money centre banks were having difficulty with their Mexican loans. The Mexicans offered a stark choice: reschedule our debt on more favourable terms, or we default. The Federal Reserve Bank reduced interest rates, which enabled the banks to reschedule more easily. It did not prevent the inexorable decline of some banks, but at least the financial system withstood the strain. There were jokes flying around, such as 'How do you buy a small New York bank? Buy a big one and wait!'.

There was an electrifying effect in the bond market and, in leading blue-chip stocks, the bull market of the eighties was born, in August 1982.

As the effect of lower interest rates rippled around the world, so interest-rate sensitive stocks moved sharply over the next two years. Bank stocks, insurance companies, over-borrowed cyclicals and bond markets had dra-

	December 1984 capitalization ($bn)	% move 1984	P/E 12/83	P/E 12/84	Yield %
Sumitomo Bank	16,234	237.4	18.9	50.7	0.4
Dai ichi Kangyo	13,379	160.9	27.2	57.6	0.5
Fuji Bank	12,231	148.9	17.5	47.6	0.5
Mitsubishi Bank	11,967	143.4	27.3	48.8	0.5
Sanwa Bank	11,176	132.3	25.3	47.6	0.6

Figure 7.3   The top five Japanese banks' performance in 1984
Source: Capital International

matic upward moves. Japanese bank stocks rocketed upwards in 1984. Figure 7.3 shows the performance of the top five banks.

These were the top five banks in the Capital International World Index, and as such they strongly influenced the EAFE Index, much to the frustration of international investment managers. Firstly, they thought that buying a Japanese bank at over 20x earnings was crazy, given that they could buy Deutsche Bank at 8.5x or Hang Seng Bank at 14.9x earnings. Secondly, it was an insiders' market, as the average free float of shares in the top Japanese banks was only 13 per cent. It was as if the Big Four broking houses (Nomura, Daiwa, Yamaichi, Nikko) decided in January 1984 that banks were the place to be, so up they went, leaving EAFE-related managers stranded with lots of underperforming 'good value' stocks.

Energy stocks flew upwards in the late 1970s, culminating their bull market in 1980. Stocks of pharmaceutical companies associated with cures for fashionable diseases had a strong move in the late 1980s, and stocks with any relationship to biotechnology were popular in 1983. Stockbroker analyst reports were grouping odd bedfellows into the biotechnology sector. For example, BSN, the French food company, was included because of its yoghurt manufacturing (Dannon) and brewing activities—it was therefore a biotech company. Danish United Breweries (Carlsberg and Tuborg) formed a subsidiary, Carlsberg Biotechnology, to exploit their knowledge of enzymes. Gist-Brocades, in the Netherlands, built on its experience in yeast fermentation to make antibiotics and enzymes. Toyo Jozo, the Japanese producer of sake, developed enzyme-based drugs from yeast and fermentation by-products. Even Grand Metropolitan was in this group, because it derived 40 per cent of revenues from brewing and distilling (J&B and Bailey's Irish Cream are two of its brand names), and therefore was deemed to be a biotechnology play.

A late-1990s sector theme: telecommunications

If energy was the global sector theme of the 1970s, it can be confidently argued that telecommunications is the global sector theme of the 1990s. This is not predicting there will be no crises of shortages, panics and booms in other sectors of the world's stock markets. For instance, meteorological ravages in America's Midwest on the scale of the 1988 drought or 1993 floods could lead to food shortages and fashion-buying of food stocks. Political anxieties in Saudi Arabia could lead to a rush into energy stocks. But telecommunications as a concept looks set on a rapid growth track for the next ten to fifteen years irrespective of short-term interruptions that may favour other sectors. The background is as follows:

- World-wide, there are 46 telecommunications companies with separate stock market listings. By 2000, that number will probably have doubled. There are 20 privatizations of national public telecommunication operators slated to take place by 1994. The estimated market capitalization of those operators once they have been privatized is over US$140bn. The privatization of British Telecom in 1984 was a major event in financial history. It led governments world-wide to assess the revenue impact of privatization, and also to ask what business central governments had in running phone companies. They came up with the answer—'none at all'.

- The privatization revolution triggered by Mrs Thatcher will continue for years. Even though the concept may be running its course in the Anglo-Saxon countries, it has taken hold in many other countries, from Argentina to Poland, the Czech Republic and Japan. Figure 7.4 shows relative P/E ratios of some key telecommunication operators in the world.

- International telecommunications traffic is growing at 15 per cent a year. It dipped in 1993 to 13 per cent, but that was ten times the growth of global GDP.

- Telecommunications growth goes hand in hand with GDP growth. This suggests great potential in the emerging markets. Baring Securities estimate that phone-line installation in the Far East will surpass North America's by 1997.

- Mobile communications—cellular telephones—are soaring in popularity, and in many parts of the world they actually precede the installation of lines. Whole urban populations are going straight to 1990s

Opportunities in international investing 61

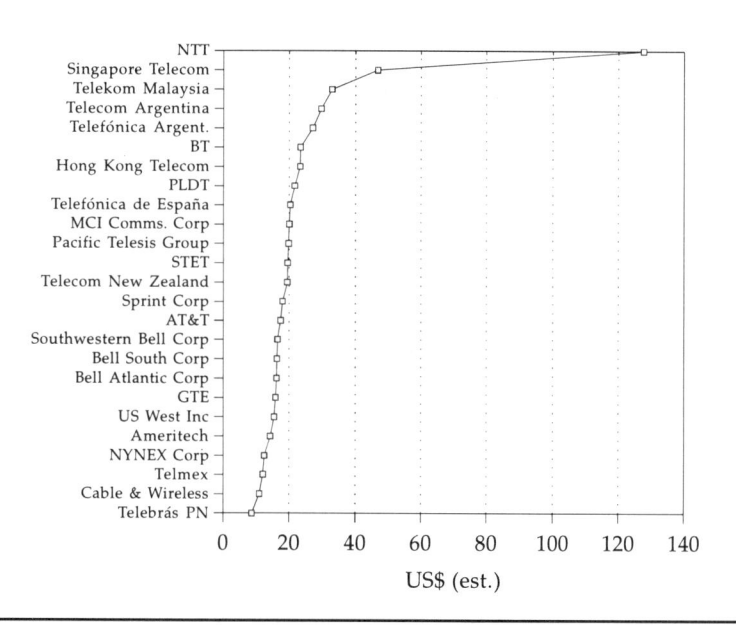

Figure 7.4   Global telecommunications P/E ratios for year 1993
Source: ITU data, Baring Securities estimates

technology without having graduated through a conventional telephone system. First-time owners of telephones in Mexico City and Shanghai are more likely to be users of cellular phones than fixed lines.

Capital commitments of billions of dollars have been made to develop a global cellular network. In the description of Kyocera above, reference was made to its stake in Nihon Iridium, the multinational satellite communication system based on 66 satellites in low orbit. By the year 2000, it conservatively expects to have 1.5m subscribers.

- The emergence of new carriers. In 1993, for the first time, the volume of international traffic added by new carriers was greater than that carried by more established carriers. MCI added more traffic than AT&T in the United States, Mercury added more than BT in the United Kingdom, IDC and ITK together outperformed KDD in Japan.

- All the major EC countries, except Spain, have agreed to allow new operators to compete with their domestic public telecommunications operators (PTOs) by 1998.

- BT is now fully privatized, Telefónica of Spain and STET of Italy are partially privatized, a minority stake in Tele Denmark is being sold. PTT Turkey, Deutsche Telecom, Belgacom and KPN, the Dutch telecoms operator, are at various stages of the process.

- Population growth and industrialization is leading to vast new markets. There are expected to be 60m new lines in China by the year 2000, as part of the Beijing government's commitment to a modern network. This will necessarily mean significant foreign participation, because the capital and technology is not available on a sufficient scale to enable it to happen through domestic resources. To put this into perspective, it means installing more new lines in China than currently exist in Germany and the United Kingdom combined. In 1993, there were 17m phone lines in China, or about 1.7 telephones per hundred people. Public pay phones have a 90 per cent usage rate and low efficiency. The largest foreign market in China is for equipment manufacturers, and the Chinese authorities initially permitted three foreign companies to set up joint ventures—Shanghai Bell (Alcatel of France), Siemens of Germany and NEC of Japan. Northern Telecom, Ericsson and AT&T are heavily involved in selling equipment or expertise in China. Motorola is growing rapidly, with over 300,000 subscribers to cellular services in China.

    Figure 7.5 shows the extent of line-diffusion in 41 countries around the world in 1991, from fewer than one telephone per hundred people in three countries, to 68 per hundred in Sweden.

- Competition and technology lead to falling costs. Mercury One-2-One, the UK network owned jointly by Cable and Wireless and US West, launched its network in September 1993 with a special residential tariff, offering free local calls in the London area in the evenings and at weekends. Rival operators have slashed their London prices.

- Mega-relationships are forcing the pace. AT&T spent US$12bn in August 1993, buying McCaw Cellular; BT of the UK spent US$5.3bn purchasing 20 per cent of MCI of the US; and Spain's Telefónica owns 44 per cent of CTC, Chile's national operator, where line growth is 23 per cent a year and long-distance traffic has grown 25 per cent a year since 1988.

- Long-term potential in Eastern Europe. The Communist fear of open communication meant that civilian telephone services were not an investment priority. The fewer the phones, the easier the bugging. The number of main telephone lines per 100 people—the tele-diffusion

Opportunities in international investing   63

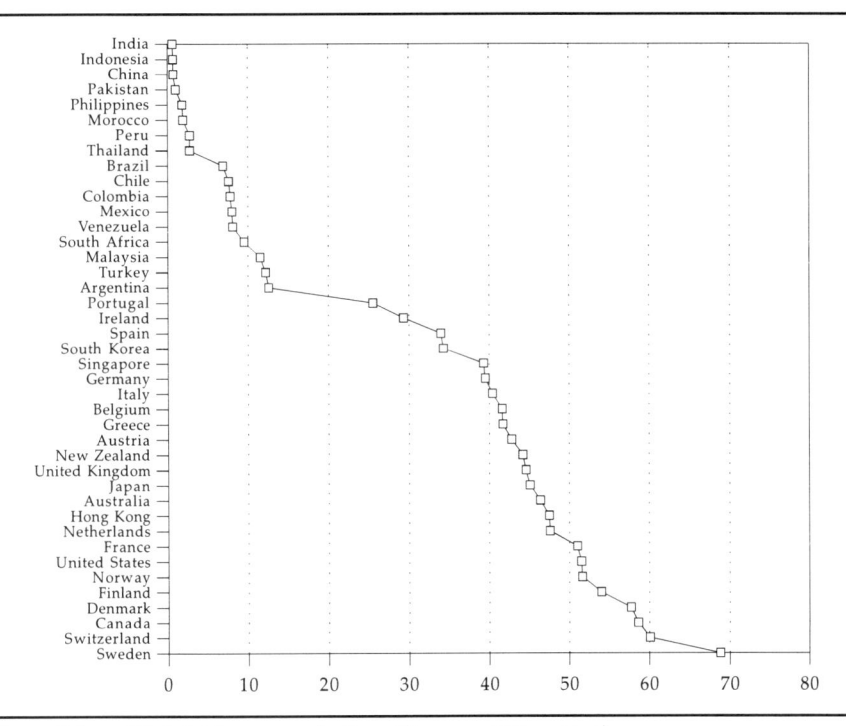

Figure 7.5   Global telecommunications (lines per 100 persons)
Source: ITU, Baring Securities, Telecommunications Valuation, Autumn 1993

ratio—is consequently low is Eastern Europe. In Russia in 1991, there were 14.7 telephone lines per 100 people, or 22m lines in a country of 150m people. Contrast this with the United Kingdom, where the ratio was 45 phones per hundred people and 26m lines for 56m people.

- Technology leapfrog is actually an advantage. Some exchanges date from the 1930s—as the Financial Times correspondent in Budapest, Nicholas Denton, observed. 'Visiting Western engineers with a yen for telephone history beg for a glimpse of the Jozsef Varos rotary switch in Budapest'. Perhaps former Communist countries could attract industrial archaeology tourists to visit their telephone exchanges and boost revenues.

Some equipment is so antiquated that it is not worth adapting for incremental use, but is being completely scrapped to enable state-of-the-art equipment to be installed. Siemens, AT&T and Alcatel have all recently made significant investments in equipment factories in Poland.

The OECD calculates that US$129bn needs to be spent in Eastern Europe to bring line density up to 35 per hundred by the year 2000. Local funding is limited by the inability of companies to raise tariffs to prohibitive levels. Although the European Investment Bank, World Bank and European Bank for Reconstruction and Development all favour the telecommunications sector for lending, the debt load of these enterprises cannot be allowed to be excessive.

Foreign equity investment is the solution being most actively discussed at present. Hungarian Telecommunications Company, the Hungarian state-owned operator, has privatized 30 per cent of the company, and placed the equity in a 50/50 joint venture between Deutsche Bundespost Telekom of Germany and Ameritech of the US, to ensure technology transfer and management expertise.

In late 1993, there were 14 telecommunication infrastructure projects in Eastern Europe approved for investment by the European Bank of Reconstruction and Development, totalling US$2728m. These ranged from a US$660m project for a digital overlay project in Romania, to a US$43m cellular development in the Slovak Republic and an international access programme with Belarus International Telecoms, for US$44m.

The point of mentioning these vast sums is not necessarily that outside investors can participate directly in the investments in Eastern Europe (nor would wish to), but that Western and Japanese equipment companies are garnering large production contracts and will benefit from the trend. They can selectively be bought as 'pick and shovel' stocks.

Despite the projected growth in Eastern Europe, analysts are confident that the Asia Pacific region offers the most growth potential in telecommunications in the next ten years. The growth of main lines in the Far East is expected to surpass that in North America by 1997. There is a link between per capita GDP growth and the installation of main telephone lines, and given the expectation of superior growth in this region, it is not surprising that telecom equipment use and installation patterns should be close on its heels. Figure 7.6 illustrates this point.

Line-diffusion is expected to expand rapidly in these markets, and it is arguable that investing in local telecom operators will offer an enhanced means of participating in many stock markets, compared to other sectors. These are also pick and shovel stocks.

The evidence is that investing in telecommunications companies are an effective proxy for stock markets in the early stages of growth. Once a country achieves economic maturity, and line-diffusion is up to 40/100, telecom operators and in particular, equipment manufacturers, tend to settle into a mature pattern where growth comes from increasing efficiency, better management, competition, deregulation and market share. They cease to be the main warrant on economic growth in a country.

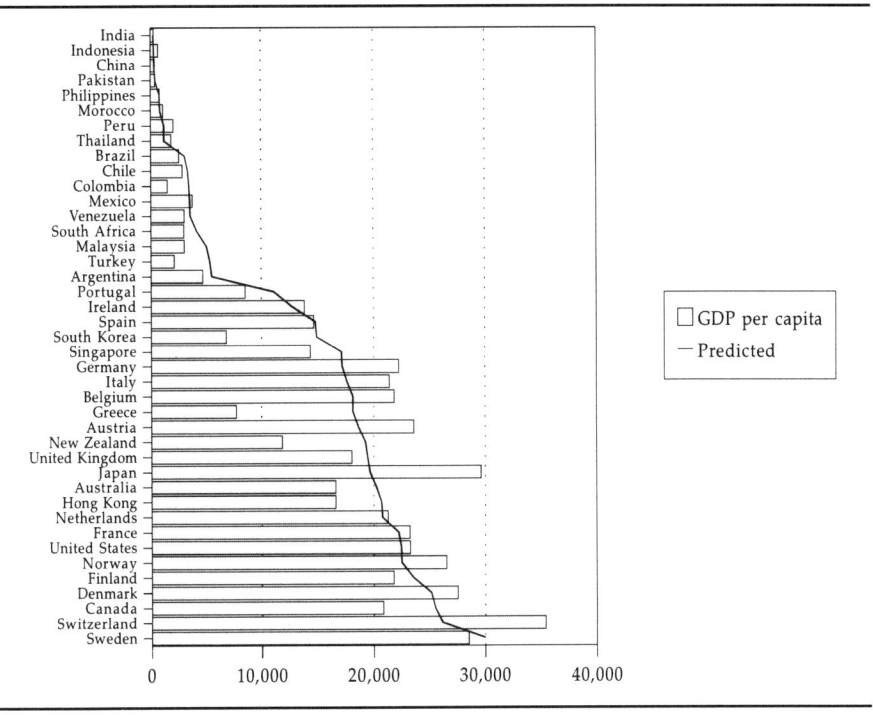

Figure 7.6 GDP per capita and that predicted by telephone line diffusion
Sources: ITU, Baring Securities estimates, Autumn 1993

Conclusion

To conclude, there are numerous particular opportunities in foreign investing for the observant analyst. There are unique situations in every market in the world that could be potentially interesting to outside investors. This chapter has outlined a fraction of such opportunities, but the point has been to illustrate a new reality for investors and increase their awareness of situations outside their own countries.

Chapter 8

The weight of money

Another compelling reason to consider international investing is the weight-of-money thesis. In many countries, there are three dynamics at work:

- 1. The strategic reallocation of institutional, mainly pension, assets;

- 2. The ageing of baby boomers; and,

- 3. A shift out of cash equivalents in search of yield or compensatory capital appreciation.

The strategic reallocation of institutional assets

Figure 8.1 shows the size of total pension assets in the 15 largest pension markets in the world. It should be noted that only funded pension plans are included. Pay-as-you go, book reserved and insured plans are excluded. 1985 and 1990 amounts are converted at contemporary prevailing exchange rates, and 1995 estimates are based on 1990 rates. All projections assume no change in current legislation affecting pension funds or foreign investment.

The total is projected to grow from US$2.4 trillion in 1985 to US$6.6 trillion in 1995, or a 2.7-fold increase. Much of this can be accounted for by reflows within each market, such as reinvested income and capital gains. In some markets, there is clearly a fundamental shift into funded pension plans which accounts for part of the increase: Canada and Australia are examples in this category.

Figure 8.2, also compiled by InterSec Research, shows the actual figures for 1985 and 1990, and estimated figures for 1995, of the size of non-domestic investment. In other words, the total amount of foreign investing from home base.

From the figures given in Figure 8.2, the US was projected to leap eightfold, from US$31bn (actual) to US$252bn (estimated) in the ten years. InterSec is often conservative in its estimates, so it is likely that the 1995 figure will prove to have been understated. Similarly, Japan is projected to rise

	1985	1990	1995 (projected)
United States	1490	2425	3184
Japan	210	583	1051
United Kingdom	228	489	607
Netherlands	105	230	323
Switzerland	65	176	267
Canada	89	171	240
Germany	41	98	134
Sweden	34	71	104
Australia	25	54	110
Denmark	15	36	58
France	10	20	29
Ireland	4	14	22
Norway	6	12	19
Hong Kong	3	12	40
Belgium	2	6	12
Rest of the World	75	182	366
Total	2402	4579	6566

Figure 8.1   Total pension assets (year-end value in US$ billion)
Source: InterSec Research Company

over eighteen-fold in the same period. In 1985, only US$7bn out of US$210bn of Japanese pension assets, or 3.5 per cent of the total, was invested overseas. By 1990, that had risen to US$48bn, or 8.2 per cent of the total. A significant percentage of this was invested in US Treasury bonds in an attempt to mitigate the trade imbalance between the two countries.

The United Kingdom is forecast to rise 4.2 fold over the period, from US$35bn to US$149bn overseas. This still represents a move from 15.3 per cent to 24.5 per cent of total pension assets invested overseas. For the historical reasons outlined in section one, British fund managers have always had a big percentage of assets overseas. Firstly, because they have often dealt with compatriots as their counterparts in distant lands (Hong Kong, Canada, United States, Australia etc.). Secondly, because the structure of the British pension fund industry was shaped by the 'contracting out' choice from state pension plans in the 1970s, there is a more entrepreneurial flavour to the management of these funds. Thirdly, because investment funds in Britain have long outgrown the ability of the British stock market to absorb the volume of cash. Fourthly, political, fiscal economic and currency

	1985	1990	1995 (projected)
United States	31	93	252
Japan	7	48	128
United Kingdom	35	125	149
Netherlands	6	26	54
Switzerland	2	11	24
Canada	6	13	36
Germany	1	4	7
Sweden			5
Australia	1	7	24
Denmark			
France		1	2
Ireland	1	4	8
Norway			
Hong Kong	2	7	24
Belgium	1	2	4
Rest of the World	2	6	17
Total	95	347	734

Figure 8.2 Total pension assets: Size of non-domestic investment (year-end value in US$ billion)

Source: InterSec Research Company

uncertainty taught British fund managers the value of international diversification long before it became a science.

Switzerland has a twelve-fold projected rise in overseas assets, from US$2bn to US$24bn—from 2.6 per cent to 8.8 per cent of pension funds over the period.

The bottom line is that there is expected to be an overall increase of nearly eight-fold in this ten year period, from US$95bn to US$734bn, of pension funds invested outside home base. This is already having a major impact on markets.

Consider that US$150bn, or approximately 20 per cent of the total, may be destined for emerging markets. The late-1993 market capitalization of the IFC Investable Index is US$272bn, and even if foreign money is allocated in a smoothed, orderly way into these markets (which it will not be), the impact will be colossal. No wonder Hong Kong stockbrokers talk of a 'wall of foreign money' entering that market.

It could be the result of no more than a strategic reallocation programme by hundreds of American, Canadian, Dutch, Australian, Swiss and British

	1985	1990	1995 (projected)
United States	2.1	3.8	7.9
Japan	3.5	8.2	12.1
United Kingdom	15.3	25.6	24.5
Netherlands	6.2	11.3	16.7
Switzerland	2.6	6.3	8.8
Canada	6.7	7.7	14.9
Germany	2.6	4.5	5.2
Sweden	-	-	5.0
Australia	5.1	14.4	21.5
Denmark	-	0.5	-
France	2.0	5.0	6.0
Ireland	20.0	25.0	35.0
Norway	-	-	-
Hong Kong	60.0	54.2	59.8
Belgium	30.0	35.0	35.0
Rest of the World	2.3	3.2	4.6
Total	4.0	7.6	11.2

Figure 8.3   Percentage of non-domestic investment (percentage of total pension assets)
Source: InterSec Research Corporation 1991

pension funds and not a speculative shift of short-term money flows.

Figure 8.3 shows the percentage of total pension assets allocated overseas by fifteen countries at three separate periods.

The high percentage of international investing from Hong Kong is for two reasons: a relatively small market for the wealth being created there, and long-term risk diversification inspired by uncertainties after 1997. There have been few credible guarantees that, after 1997, domestically-invested pension assets will be recoverable. Belgium and Ireland are two small countries that have small stock markets and also for diversification purposes, need to spread the risk elsewhere.

The ageing of baby boomers

There are approximately 60m North Americans entering middle-age, the vanguard of whom will be reaching retirement in the year 2005. These baby-boomers were born between 1945 and 1960 and after the glorious irresponsibilities of the 1960s, inflation of the 1970s and leverage of the 1980s, this generation is coming to the realization that the US social security system may not deliver the goods when they retire. Evidence is mounting that this generation's savings ratio will steadily rise. The more affluent quadrant is ceasing to define itself by consumerism and more by net worth, to the point where it is no longer chic to be sporting the more extreme symbols of affluence, à la Bonfire of the Vanities. The Clinton administration is trying to exacerbate the process by redistributing wealth via higher taxes. But mostly, it is fears about security in old age that is confronting millions of baby-boomers.

The same demographic forces are at work even more acutely in Japan and Western Europe. Already, Germany is not replacing itself organically. Immigrants are filling many employment gaps in semi-skilled and unskilled categories. A multitude of stresses sustains the high savings rate in Germany.

The standard measure of the number of people in a population who are of working age is the age dependency ratio: the population over 65 as a percentage of the population aged 15 to 64. For the OECD as a whole, the age dependency ratio is predicted to rise from 19 per cent in 1990, to 28 per cent by 2020 and 37 per cent by 2040. Germany and Japan will both have age dependency ratios of 34 per cent by 2020.

Germans are becoming particularly edgy about population decline. In a recent study published by the Institut für Wirtschaft und Gesellschaft in Bonn (Miegel and Wahl) (*Das Ende des Individualismus: die Kultur des Westens Zerstort sich selbst*), it was predicted that by the year 2000, deaths will exceed births by 300,000 a year, and by 2030, they will exceed births by 600,000 a year—equivalent to eliminating the city of Frankfurt every year. In the next 40 years, the number of Germans will decline by about 15m. If the country intends to remain an industrial power, Germany will have to let in over 15m immigrants over the same period, which would be politically intolerable. Naturally, this assumes that these extrapolations are accurate.

A similar crunch is looming in France. Since the late 1940s, the state pension system has been run by the Caisse de Retraite on a cash management basis. Pensions were paid out of contributions received from active workers. In the 1950s and 1960s demographics favoured this system, when there was a young, large working population to support pensioners. The pension system moved to an annual deficit of 20bn francs (US$ 3.4bn) by the early 1990s, with 3.3 workers supporting each retiree. It is estimated that by the year 2005, there will be 1.9 workers supporting each retiree, and that this figure will be 1.3 by 2040. Using the existing cash management system, this means that in 2040, 35 per cent of each employee's salary will have to be deducted in pension contributions, against 19 per cent in 1993. It is likely that the French government will encourage the growth of private pension plans to prevent inter-generational conflict in the early years of the 21st

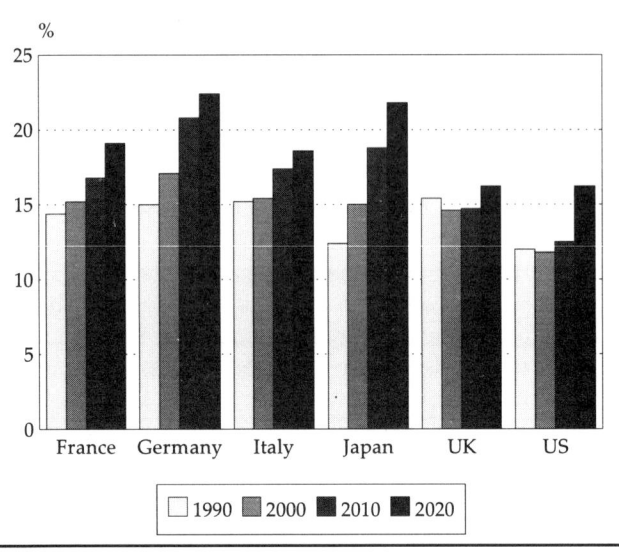

Figure 8.4 Population aged 65 and over (as percentage of total)
Source: OECD/FT 25 October 1993

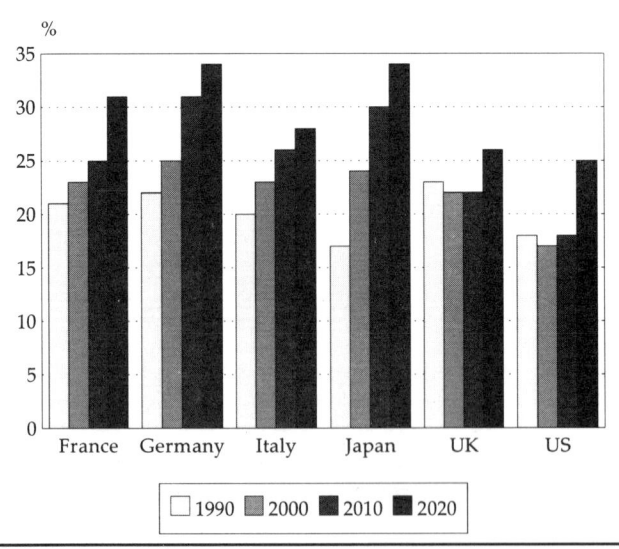

Figure 8.5 Age dependency ratio (population aged 65 and over as percentage of the population aged 15-64)
Source: OECD/FT 25 October 1993

century. The initial beneficiary will be the domestic equity market, because France being French, there is likely to be a regulation which steers private pension money into their own stock market. But there will probably also be the ability to invest a portion internationally, which will be a further tributary into the global river of transnational assets. Apart from the large institutionalized pension funds, individual savers are also a major contributor to international investment flows.

Typically, people in the 35 to 55 age group tend to invest in vehicles that give them maximum capital appreciation. This means equities, in particular, equity mutual funds. Most financial planning and stockbroking firms in the United States offer an asset-allocation advisory service, whereby a client can define the degree of risk tolerance and be pointed in the appropriate investment direction.

International mutual funds are nearly always on the investment menu of financial advisers in the United States. At least one financial planner—the Alpha Group—will recommend to suitably-qualified investors that 50 per cent of their investments should be international, of which 50 per cent should be in emerging markets. The case for international investing discussed in earlier chapters applies equally to retail and institutional investors. The result according to the Investment Company Institute[1], was a flow of over US$20bn into international mutual funds in 1993, more than in the six previous years combined. This amounts to about US$85m in each working day of 1993.

By late 1993, there was a total of approximately US$50bn of US money invested in international or regional mutual funds. Global funds, which invest a portion in the United States, accounted for a further US$30bn. Moreover, it is not unusual to find ADRs or other foreign stocks within US mutual fund portfolios. Fidelity's Magellan Fund, the Phoenix Growth Fund and many other ostensibly US equity mutual funds, have large numbers of foreign securities in their portfolios. It is probably not wide of the mark to estimate that over US$100bn of mutual fund money was invested overseas by early 1994, whether in international, regional or global funds, or whether buried within US equity funds.

As returns become more attractive overseas, and GNP growth patterns increasingly tilt in favour of the 'emerging world', it is fairly certain that an increasing percentage of the ageing OECD's pension funds will be shifted in that direction.[2]

---

[1] *Barrons 10 Jan 1994*
[2] *Population tables, ratio tables, FT 25 October 1993*

The shift out of cash equivalents in search of yield or compensatory capital appreciation

In January 1994, 3-month money market rates in the following currencies were:

Sterling	5.38 per cent
Deutschemark	5.80 per cent
US dollar	3.29 per cent
Dutch guilder	5.15 per cent
Swiss franc	4.00 per cent
French franc	6.20 per cent
Yen	2.04 per cent

Source: The Economist 8 Jan 1994

The 30-year US Treasury bond yielded under 6 per cent, and 25-year British gilts yielded around 7.2 per cent

Millions of retired people in the Anglo-Saxon world have had a real income drop in the early 1990s, as their CDs[1] and bonds matured and they had to accept significantly lower deposit rates on the rollover. With money market fund rates in the United States at thirty-year lows (2.5 per cent), many normally risk-averse, unsophisticated, investors have been forced or persuaded to put an increasing amount of their capital into investments which carry capital risk.

This is in contrast to the early 1980s when retirees benefited greatly from high interest rates. This caused a certain amount of inter-generational conflict: young people were borrowing at high rates to the benefit of older lenders (depositors) in the system. That situation was reversed by the early 1990s with mortgage rates at 25-year lows, to the benefit of borrowers but the detriment of depositors and those relying on fixed incomes.

It has been estimated that, since 1990, cash totalling the equivalent of US$120bn has shifted from money market funds and CDs into mutual funds with capital risk. Of these mutual funds, 65 per cent has been into bond funds and 35 per cent into equity funds, of which 10 per cent has been invested internationally. These figures may not seem dramatic, but few people who invested retirement capital into capital risk funds from 1990 to 1993 would have experienced a capital loss, so they are encouraged to invest more. In 1993, the EAFE Index rose 32.6 per cent, and IFC Index

---

[1] *Certificates of deposit*

rose 63.7 per cent, versus the S&P 500—which rose 9.1 per cent itself.

It is likely that such differences in performance will lead to further substantial flows into international equity funds.

Summary

To summarize the case for international investing, there are five broad reasons why investors should look outside their own markets, whether they are based in Stockholm, Brussels, Tokyo or New York.

- The size of market capitalizations now available outside home base. Twenty years ago, it could have been argued that one's local market was large enough to invest in. Today, international markets are big enough to absorb most investment flows.

- The performance of stock markets around the world is such that there will nearly always be a market, or group of markets, that outperform one's home market. If a pension fund director has to meet certain performance targets, there is a high statistical probability that diversifying the equity portfolio into other markets will help to accomplish them.

- The need to diversify risk is paramount. Many countries have guidelines for the degree of diversification that is deemed prudent for pension funds. ERISA specifically addresses the concept of the 'prudent investor' and watchdogs for pension funds are being set up in Europe.

- There are myriads of individual investment opportunities outside home base for all investors, and a few examples of interesting international concepts from HSBC, Kyocera and Body Shop to the telecommunications sector were discussed above.

- The weight-of-money phenomenon described above will undoubtedly have an impact on markets as pension funds and mutual funds grow around the world. This trend is inextricably bound up with the demographics of the mature industrial world, in the longer term, but also depends on short-term interest rate trends. If interest rates rise in the United States and Europe, the temptation to risk capital in foreign equity markets will be diminished.

PART III

The practice of international investment

Chapter 9

Background

'An investment operation is one which upon thorough analysis, promises safety of principal and a satisfactory return. Operations not meeting these requirements are speculative.'

Benjamin Graham

Given sums of money to invest internationally, how do practitioners go about their art? What are the steps they take to put that money to work?

There are many approaches. Some international managers are resolutely 'bottom-up', which is to say they focus on individual securities so that country weightings are a residual of the geographical location of their preferred equities. They have a well-defined methodology applied to stock selection, and no particular methodology applied to country weightings.

Other international managers feel that the most appropriate approach is 'top-down', that 'getting the country weighting right' is the most important determinant of good performance. Once they have ascertained their preferred country weights, they then search for the best means to invest in each country. Some managers apply elements of each methodology. They see the importance of having a well-defined top-down process, while at the same time applying a recognizable security selection system.

There are managers at each extreme who invest hundreds of millions for clients and produce excellent performance. There is no intrinsically 'right' or 'wrong' approach to international investing. What makes a person's approach 'wrong' is when it produces consistent underperformance of an agreed benchmark. Then it is time to look for another job.

As in any walk of life, a successful style evolves for individuals or groups, and works as long as the inspiration behind the style remains intact. There are millionaire lawyers and failed lawyers. There are rich oil men and busted oil men. There are great portfolio managers and lousy portfolio managers. The 'greats' are often great for different reasons and have their own unique approach to the problems that life throws at them. There are many routes to the top of the mountain. All of them involve discipline and a recognition of the practitioner's limitations, for, as was once pointed out, 'a great many smashes by brilliant men can be traced directly to the swelled head.'

When Warren Buffet was asked about technology stocks in 1985, he said he had never bought one, adding that the technology revolution had 'gone right past me... It's OK with me. I don't have to make money in every game. I mean, I don't know what cocoa-beans are going to do. You know, there are all kinds of things I don't know about, and that may be too bad; but you know, why should I know all about them?'

John Templeton's response to this view was, 'It would be a mistake for somebody to say "I am not going to buy high-tech stocks because I don't understand them". If you think that a high tech stock could really be an investment, a real bargain, you should investigate it.'[1]

Warren Buffet and John Templeton are among the most successful investment managers of the 20th century. Their methods of managing money are quite different, and each is apparently at least a centi-millionaire.

They do have a virtue in common, however: patience. Both take the long view of investing, confident that their investments will eventually pan out. Buffet talks of a sense of owning a piece of business: 'The real test of whether you're investing from a value standpoint or not is whether you're one who asks if the market will be open tomorrow.'

---

[1] 'Global Investing: The Templeton Way', Berryessa and Kirzner

Chapter 10

The top-down approach to international investing

Top-down investing is the approach which considers macroeconomic factors as a guide to making investment decisions. There is arguably no 'right' or 'wrong' way to select those factors, except they must work over time to give a manager consistent outperformance of a benchmark.

Some managers have been quite successful for a time using one or two variables to determine their country weightings, and others use multi-factor variables. I believe the key is to have a dynamic model, which is flexible in the light of new information and which is not afraid to admit that some factors are becoming obsolete.

In the 1970s, there were many managers who keyed off the oil price, and many became professional OPEC-watchers. The oil analyst would be the most important analyst in the firm, and predicting the oil price direction was among the most important decisions the firm had to make. Many other decisions would spin out of that central analysis, such as the weighting in gold stocks, the relative attractions of the 'mineral markets', such as Australia, Canada and South Africa. One factor—oil—would have a powerful influence on the disposition of the firm's investment assets.

Many people believed in 1980 that the oil price would rise to US$100 a barrel, triggering inflation that would push the gold price to US$2000 an ounce. Investors sought the most leveraged way to profit from this trend, and out of the woodwork came the promoters of shale oil schemes in Australia and marginal gas-drilling partnerships in Louisiana.

The flaw with following one or just a few factors is that the investor often does not see other variables in the ascendant which could eclipse his pet factors in importance. In retrospect, gold's fate was sealed when President Carter appointed Paul Volcker to be chairman of the Federal Reserve Bank. Volcker's mandate was to crush inflation, which he did by raising interest rates until a new US industry flourished: money market funds. Seventeen per cent money market rates were enough to persuade asset-speculators, especially the leveraged precious metal bugs, to cash out their positions as fast as they could. By 1981, the gold price had fallen back and silver crashed, taking with it some colourful players and adding a new word to the financial lexicon: 'bunkered.'

The point here is that while single factor analysis can work quite well for a time, an effective long-term strategy should include a good spread of different factors, to ensure consistent performance.

For a top-down manager to make a balanced decision on how much to invest in a country, he must analyse variables relative to two areas: the economy at large, and the stock market. The weightings he puts on each factor is the 'ingredient X' of his style. Some managers tilt weightings towards stock market factors, others towards economic factors. Still others believe in equally weighting all variables, to ensure that the model is less corrupted by subjectivity. Some of the more important factors are discussed below.

Economically-related factors

'Economics is the study of mankind in the every day business of life'

Alfred Marshall.

The following description of economic factors is not a 'how to' discussion. There are as many models as there are top-down managers, so to claim that one model, or one particular set of factors, is the Rosetta Stone of investment management, would be inaccurate. One should not forget Goodhart's Law, which wryly states that as soon as you rely on any economic indicator, it will start to mislead.

For those of you with degrees in advanced economics, please forgive the simplicity of what follows. I have found, despite the complexity of the world, that the adherence to first principles often helps us to stay on track.

It is helpful to go back to one of the most elementary concepts in economics. In order to correctly analyse a country, the manager has to be aware of the fundamental constituents of that country. There are 21 markets represented in the EAFE Index of developed countries and 20 markets in the IFC Emerging Market Index. The manager must have a framework to know those 41 countries: how else could he apply portfolio weightings with any reasonable hope of success?

The elementary concept is that of 'factors of production'. To know a country is to know its economic potential, and looking at the classic factors of production is a good place to start.

Factors of production[1]

■ Land
Land is taken to mean all the resources provided by the 'bounty of nature'. This includes the physical size of the land in a country, the breakdown between agricultural land, mineral resources and other products deriving from the land and surrounding oceans. It is a fair bet that China, which has been an economic laggard under communism, but which has a land area of 9.6m square kilometres, will eventually outperform Singapore, which has been an economic star for 20 years, but which has a land area of 618 square kilometres. Historically, Britain has been fortunate in the resources provided by its land. Coal, iron ore, fertile ground, ample ocean fishing and recently, North Sea oil, have all been 'bounties' that have spawned important industries and contributed to national wealth.

■ Labour
Labour represents the human resources of a country, including all the skills and organizational talents that make up the productive processes of a country. A country with a population of 156m has greater human resource potential than a country with a population of 7m. But there is no question that Switzerland enjoys a higher standard of living than Brazil. The key lies in the actual effectiveness, education and training of a population, not necessarily in its untapped potential.

Relative labour costs between countries are a key determinant of economic potential. One of the reasons why developing countries are so interesting to foreign manufacturers is the cheapness of their labour, which can be trained quickly to perform tasks that cost a fraction of labour costs back home. In early 1994, US labour costs were US$16.70 an hour, Japanese labour was US$19.30 an hour and German labour, US$25.50, plus substantial benefits in each case.[2] Depending on the rate of inflation used, and exchange rates, Ukrainian labour will work for US$20 *a month*. It is granted that there may be other reasons why a multinational may not want to set up in the Ukraine, but the point is there: developing countries are cheap.

Japan's fabled labour force may be on a decline. There are indications that Japanese corporate under-employment—for example in the case of the smart elevator ladies in Tokyo stores—may soon become unemployment. The custom of employment for life is being questioned as companies are

---

[1] *Geoffrey Whitehead, 'Economics Made Simple'.*
[2] *Wall Street Journal Europe, 10 January 1994.*

forced to rationalize, and battalions of *madogiwazoku* (people sitting by a window with little work to do) are likely to be laid off. There is another angle, which is that during their economic ascendancy, millions of Japanese travelled overseas, to find that foreigners often work less hard and live better. There is a disillusionment in Japan and it is not uncommon to find young Japanese reflecting views that John Stuart Mill espoused in the 19th century: 'I confess I am not charmed with the ideal of life held out by those who think that the normal state of human beings is that of struggling to get on; and that the trampling, crushing, elbowing and treading on each others' heels, which form the existing type of social life, are the most desirable lot of human kind, or anything but the disagreeable symptoms of one of the phases of industrial progress.'[1] Could it just be happening that the Japanese, scared of *karoshi* (death by overwork), are turning their priorities to more 'civilized' pursuits?

■ Capital

Capital is the stock of physical assets created in the past and available for present use. This includes social capital, such as transport infrastructure, schools and hospitals, and so-called producer goods, or capital equipment. The total sum of factories, machine tools and the productive capacity of a country is its productive capital. This may not tell the whole story, because this capital may be obsolete. Eastern Germany had a vast amount of factory capacity, machine tools and other capital equipment. The problem, as Truehand[2] discovered, is that it was largely obsolete and of little interest to potential purchasers. On the other hand, there may be little capital in a country, but that very fact defines its potential. Today, countries can industrialize quickly by importing foreign capital and know-how. A country with few capital resources which can offer the other two factors of production—labour and land—could have the prescription for an economic boom on its hands. Mexico, Thailand, the Philippines and China are examples of this: foreign industrialists are attracted to them because of their undeveloped local markets, as well as offering a labour arbitrage over goods produced at home.

Today, economies do not need to go through the gradual evolution of industrialization that was necessary two hundred years ago. Great Britain

---

[1] J.S. Mill, 'Principles of Political Economy'.

[2] Truehand is the abbreviated name given to Truehandanstalt, the agency created in March 1990 by the former East German government charged with the privatization of former state-run East German companies ('Kombinate'). The new federal government is committed to ensuring that Truehand transfers most of the companies into private hands.

took 150 years, from 1700 to 1850, to accomplish industrialization. Using and building on British know-how, it took Germany, France and the United States 50 years, from 1860 to 1910, to industrialize to the same degree. Today the process could take as long as it takes to build a cellular phone factory in a jungle. There are more subtle requirements to successful take-off, however, such as a compliant government, tax breaks, a reasonably well-educated work-force and the general business climate in a country.

■ The entrepreneur as a factor of production
Entrepreneurs should be regarded as the fourth factor of production, because they are the catalyst that makes the other factors coalesce into a capitalist economy. People prepared to risk their capital, time, experience and livelihoods to start a business should be regarded as a national treasure. It is the immense energy and risk-taking characteristics of the overseas Chinese that have been the catalyst for economic take-off in so many smaller countries in Asia, just as a handful of nonconformists were the backbone of the British Industrial Revolution.

Once investment managers have built a base of knowledge about each country along these lines, they have a good foundation to analyse the investability of countries. Managers are measured on their performance, both against an index and also against their peers. It is no good investing only in countries with long-term potential if there is no short or intermediate-term reward for doing so. We all know what Lord Keynes said about the long-term.

So a methodology must be developed to take the long-term into consideration at the same time as allowing managers to beat agreed benchmarks and their peer group in the shorter term. To make a balanced decision on top-down country allocation, the two areas that have to be analysed are (a) each country's economy and (b) each country's stock market.

Other economic factors

There are many cogs in the machinery of a modern economy. Different managers put different weight on the various cogs in their assessment of a country, but the following economic factors should generally be included in country analysis.

■ Real GNP/GDP growth
The total productive capacity of a country and the trend of its growth should be measured. It is not necessary for each manager to do original research on the subject, because there are many services available that pro-

vide data and country statistics. Major stockbroking firms have country research departments, most countries have central statistical data banks which provide economic information and leading newspapers and periodicals such as the *Financial Times* and *Economist* can be relied on to provide up-to-date estimates of growth for the world's economies.

A good place to start is a publication that provides consensus data, so that the manager has a digest of what leading economists and forecasters around the world are thinking. The information in Figure 10.1 is from Consensus Forecasts from its survey of Italy of 4 October 1993.

Information up to the end of 1992 was historical, and the subsequent

	Year	Gross domestic product %
Historic:	1989	2.9
	1990	2.1
	1991	1.3
	1992	0.9
Forecast:	1993	-0.1
	1994	1.4
	1995	2.3
	1996	2.6
	1997	2.3
	1998	2.3
	1999-2003	2.2

Figure 10.1 Consensus forecast for Italy
Source: *Consensus Forecasts, 49 Berkeley Square, London*

figures were long-term forecasts compiled by Consensus Forecasts in London. Their methodology is to survey leading financial and economic forecasters around the world each month, and provide consensus figures. Some might argue that the resultant figures are a consensus sludge that is meaningless, but it is a useful place to start if the manager is not in the business of original data-gathering from the central statistical office of each country.

'Real' GNP growth analysis is important, particularly in countries with high inflation rates. There is a lot of slippage in countries like Brazil, with an estimated inflation rate over 2000 per cent and there are no prizes for sensational returns on that stock market if they do not translate into real returns for investors. Nonetheless, Brazil was offering 'real' economic growth—after inflation—of about 3 per cent in early 1994.

■ Inflation

The top-down manager must consider the inflation rate of each country. This includes consumer price and wholesale, or producer price trends, wage rates and the extent to which an economy is subject to outside inflationary pressures which it cannot control. In the early 1990s, oil prices have been trending downwards and providing a boost to the major economies in recession. In the 1970s, the shock of sharply rising oil prices had a destructive effect on inflation rates everywhere, particularly in countries like Japan which were not oil producers.

Politicians tend to congratulate themselves on their countries' low inflation rates at the bottom of business cycles, when international demand is slack. They attribute low inflation to successful government policies. It is worth looking at a country's marginal propensity to inflate, historically. The United Kingdom, Italy, Australia and Canada have poor records. Germany, Japan and Switzerland tend to be tougher inflation managers. The promiscuous ease of credit in Anglo-Saxon countries tends to fuel economic booms unsustainably.

The manager must therefore not just look at today's inflation rate, but at future inflation trends, because these will have an impact on the investment climate. British politicians made a lot of noise about having inflation at 25-year lows in early 1994—the consumer price index (CPI) was recorded at 1.4 per cent—but the seeds of future inflation were being laid by the government itself through heavy tax increases which will lead to wage demands in years ahead. Figure 10.2 sets the UK inflation record against Japan's.

	Year	Japan	UK
Historic:	1989	2.3	7.8
	1990	3.1	9.4
	1991	3.3	5.9
	1992	1.6	3.7
Forecast:	1993	1.2	1.7
	1994	0.7	3.6
	1995	1.2	4.5
	1996	1.5	4.3
	1997	1.8	4.1
	1998	1.8	4.2
	1999-2003	1.7	3.8

Figure 10.2   Japan vs. UK inflation record (per cent)
Source: Consensus Forecasts, October 1993

■ Budgetary condition

The absolute level of a country's budget deficit is not as relevant as the ability of its economy to sustain it. Someone with a US$100,000 mortgage can theoretically service it more easily on an income of US$150,000 a year than can someone earning US$50,000 a year. What often happens, though, is that the big earner tends to be more profligate and has a higher marginal propensity to squander, and get into just as much financial trouble as his 'poorer' neighbour.

A top-down manager will look at the budget deficit to GDP ratio and at trends of deficit—or surplus—growth. Deficits tend to rise in recessions, as a country's tax base shrinks through unemployment combined with a reduced consumer tax take and lower corporation taxes. Social security payments rise and the government is squeezed. A rising deficit under these circumstances is not necessarily a 'bad' thing. It should just be contained within sustainable boundaries. Figure 10.3 shows estimates for budget deficits or surpluses as a percentage of GDP for a number of countries in early 1994.

	1994 estimates	Historic average
Australia	-3.8	-1.1
Belgium	-7.2	-10.7
Finland	-14.6	-2.6
France	-4.5	-2.5
Germany	-4.4	-3.0
Italy	-9.5	-12.2
Japan	1.0	-3.0
Singapore	6.5	4.3
Turkey	11.5	n/a
UK	-6.9	-1.4
USA	-4.0	-4.3

Figure 10.3 Budget deficits or surpluses as a percentage of GDP
Sources: 1994 estimates by Blairlogie Capital Management; Historic figures (average 1981-1992) by BZW

What has made the US budget deficit so frightening to Americans over the last ten years is its absolute size, rising from US$152bn in 1989, to US$290bn in 1992. When seen in the context of the ability of the US economy to sustain that debt, it is not so serious. There is a generation of Americans, however, which remembers when the United States was a capital exporter and when there was a balanced budget. The outrage occurs when it is realized that a huge percentage of the deficit is spent on debt service. Approximately forty-two per cent of today's government spending goes towards servicing debt-paying interest in the United States. The outrage is further compounded when it is estimated that the federal bail-out of the savings and loans will cost the US taxpayers more than World War II.

The British record has been mixed. There was a time in the mid-1980s when the proceeds of government privatizations, oil revenues and a booming economy conspired to push the government into surplus. There were rumours of gilt-traders threatening to vote Labour at the next election, because they saw the supply of government bonds drying up—if there was no government deficit, there would be no need for a government bond market. That was a fanciful notion. The government now has a debt/GDP ratio of 6.9 per cent, which should keep gilt-traders voting Conservative for a long time to come. As in all factors in a model, however, one should watch for trends. The British budget deficit may have hit its nadir, just as economic indicators are pointing upwards and tax revenues start to pick up.

■ Balance of trade

The analysis of trade flows provides a useful guide to the vitality of an economy. A country in chronic deficit in its visible trade may not be in as poor shape as appears. The rapid importation of capital goods characterizes newly industrializing countries, and is often the prelude to sustained economic growth which eventually redresses the deficit.

A trade deficit may not convey the whole story. Many economies have a thriving 'invisible' export sector, making up in services what they do not achieve in goods. Tourism, banking, transport and, indeed, portfolio management, are 'invisible' services that contribute to a country's trade balance.

In assessing a country for investment purposes, this is one of the variables that contributes to the full picture. Figure 10.4 shows the current account balance for merchandise in some leading economies.

Monetary factors

■ Interest rates

The level and trend of interest rates in a country has a profound effect on its financial markets.

Figure 10.5 sets out short rates (90 days where possible) and long bond yields (10 years where possible) in the developed and some emerging markets. The 'now' column refers to real figures available in January 1994 and the estimated 12-month column is from figures generated by Blairlogie Capital Management.

The value of a table such as this is to focus on expected trends. It is easy to ascertain where current interest rates stand in two key areas: 90-day Treasury paper and 10-year bonds. Based on what we know about eco-

	1992	1993	1994 (estimated)
Australia	-10.7	-11.8	-12.8
Belgium	6.5	5.1	5.1
Canada	-22.9	-21.0	-18.8
France	3.7	5.0	3.6
Germany	-25.8	-24.5	-17.9
Italy	26.5	-10.6	-5.8
Japan	117.6	141.4	135.7
Netherlands	6.7	6.3	6.8
Spain	-18.5	-13.8	-11.9
Sweden	-4.9	-1.3	2.0
Switzerland	12.6	16.1	15.9
United Kingdom	-15.2	-21.7	-25.4
United States	-66.4	-92.0	101.0

Figure 10.4   Current account balance for merchandise (per cent)
Source: Consensus Forecasts

	Short rates		Long bond rates	
Developed countries	Now	12 months	Now	12 months
Australia	5.2	4.5	7.3	6.6
Austria	5.8	4.5	6.4	6.0
Belgium	7.3	4.5	6.8	6.5
Denmark	8.0	5.0	7.6	7.0
Finland	8.6	5.0	9.5	7.0
France	6.3	4.0	6.2	5.8
Germany	6.2	4.5	5.9	6.0
Hong Kong	3.1	3.5	4.1	4.6
Italy	8.4	6.8	8.7	8.5
Japan	2.0	1.4	3.1	3.0
Malaysia	6.4	6.4	6.8	6.4
Netherlands	5.8	4.5	5.8	6.0
New Zealand	4.8	4.8	5.9	6.0
Norway	6.8	4.5	7.2	6.5
Singapore	3.5	3.6	3.5	3.6
Spain	9.1	7.3	8.6	8.5
Sweden	7.2	4.0	9.3	7.0
Switzerland	4.1	3.5	4.3	4.0
United Kingdom	5.5	5.0	6.4	6.4

Note: All figures are rounded up to one decimal place

Figure 10.5   Short rates vs. long bond rates - developed countries
Source: Blairlogie Capital Management, January 1994

nomic growth trends, money supply and consensus estimates, one can estimate rate levels in one year's time. This can either reveal bullish expectations (as in Australia, for example, where short rates are predicted to fall from 5.2 per cent to 4.5 per cent, and long rates from 7.3 per cent to 6.6 per cent) or relatively bearish expectations (as in Singapore, where short rates are expected to rise—from 3.5 per cent to 3.6 per cent and long rates also from 3.5 per cent to 3.6 per cent).

In a model like this, constant changes must be made in the light of new facts. It is not aiming at 100 per cent correct figures, or pinpoint forecasting, so much as to identify a trend that will help in the country weighting of an overall portfolio.

Figure 10.6 sets out the same data for emerging markets. There are some dramatic interest rates here, but again the focus should be on trend. We would expect Brazilian short rates to fall in response to an easing in the inflation rate of 2500 per cent. That country is hostage to fortune, because a lot will depend on government policies working to bring down the inflation rate. Other countries have high rates by developed country standards, but

Emerging markets	Short rates *Now*	Short rates *12 months*	Long bond rates *Now*	Long bond rates *12 months*
Argentina	10.8	7.0	n/a	-
Brazil	2530.0	2230.0	n/a	-
Chile	18.0	14.0	n/a	-
Colombia	24.0	24.0	n/a	-
Greece	20.0	15.0	n/a	-
India	15.0	14.0	16.5	15.0
Indonesia	8.8	9.0	n/a	-
Jordan	2.5	2.5	n/a	-
Korea	12.2	11.4	n/a	-
Mexico	12.5	10.5	n/a	-
Pakistan	12.4	10.9	n/a	-
Philippines	16.4	16.6	n/a	-
Portugal	11.6	7.5	n/a	-
Taiwan	8.1	8.0	7.4	7.5
Thailand	6.8	6.8	n/a	-
Turkey	82.0	80.0	n/a	-
Venezuela	60.0	40.0	n/a	-

Note: All figures are rounded up to one decimal place

Figure 10.6 Short rates vs. long bond rates - emerging markets
Source: Blairlogie Capital Management, January 1994

that is mainly because of the price rises caused by a flood of foreign capital, increased demand for factors of production (for example, land and buildings for factories in Guangdong Province in China, capital in Mexico and labour in Hong Kong).

Stock market related factors

The other key area that top-down managers must analyze is the current valuation of the stock market. Once they have assessed the market for its investability, and married it with their economic view of that country, they have the beginnings of a country allocation model.

At this stage, analysts are looking at the market as a whole, and not yet making any judgement on individual stocks. What should they look for?

Below is a step-by-step analysis of the Spanish stock market in the summer of 1993. Each of the main relevant factors in assessing a stock market will be covered with examples from Spain.

The dividend yield to 90-day interest rate ratio

This is one ratio that measures the value of a stock market.

	Current	Historic average
Dividend yield:	4.72%	6.10%
3-month rate:	10.70%	14.92%
Yield ratio:	2.27	2.76

What this measure is trying to determine is whether the market as a whole is cheap or expensive relative to the absolute risk-free proxy of holding 3-month Treasury bills. On this criterion, the yield ratio is favourable. Although the current dividend yield of 4.72 per cent is lower than its historic average of 6.1 per cent, 3 month bills are lower, at 10.7 per cent against an average of 14.92 per cent, so the ratio is favourable. Figure 10.7 shows the progress of this ratio back to 1982. In simple terms, if the graph is below the line, the market is cheap (by this criterion), and if it is above the line, it is expensive. It is worth looking at the build-up of over-valuation in 1987, and the dramatic correction that brought the market back to the invisible line of fair valuation after the Crash.

Price/earnings ratios (P/E)

Benjamin Graham pointed out that the term price/earnings ratio can be a misleading concept. Do the earnings refer to the past year, the current year

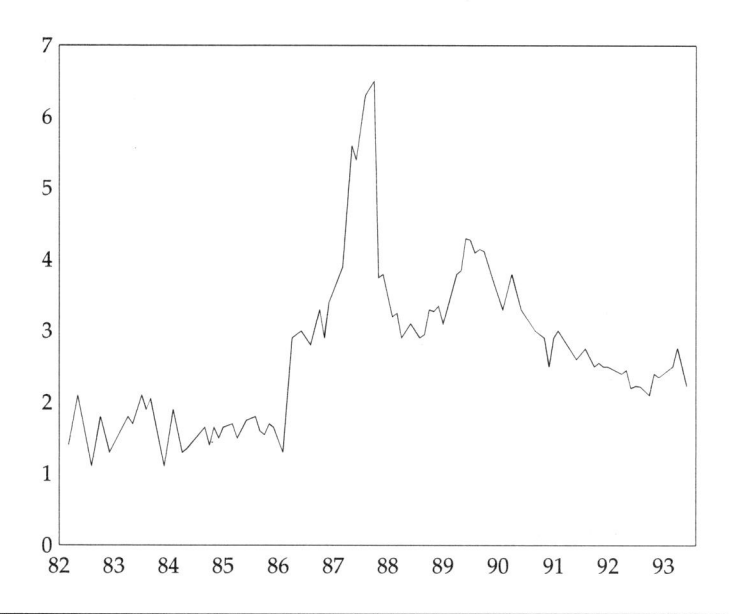

Figure 10.7 Spain: Yield ratio (short rate/dividend yield)
Source: Blairlogie Capital Management

or the future? While it is desirable to qualify the term by saying '*x* times average earnings' for a stated period in the past, or '*x* times anticipated earnings' for a stated period in the future, this qualification is rarely made.

Unless stated to the contrary, the term price/earnings ratio should be taken to apply to the current full year's earnings figure.

In Spain in mid 1993, the market multiple was at 11.90x earnings, compared to a historic average of 11.84x earnings. By this criterion it was expensive, but there was a cyclical factor at play here: the market's earnings were hit by recession in Spain, so on this criterion it might have been a mistake to sell the market in an economic trough. In other words, it is important to consider the context of each set of figures.

Price/cashflow (P/CF)

This measure relates to the ability of a market to support its price level by the cashflows it generates, expressed as a ratio. Again, it can be misleading, particularly when a stock market begins to discount recovery while the economy is still in recession.

Spain had a price/cashflow ratio of 5.8x at the end of 1993, compared to a five-year average of 4.63x. By this criterion it was expensive, but not so bad when compared with other countries. Sweden's P/CF was 21.3x, compared to a five-year average of 9.6x. Japan was 10.5x (five-year average 12.36x), the US 10.1x (average 8.63x), UK 11.6x (average 8.45x). One of the only markets that seemed cheap on this measure was Singapore, at 5.8x cashflow compared to its five year average of 12x.[1]

Price/book value (P/BV)

The book value per share of a common stock is found by adding up all the assets (excluding intangibles), subtracting all liabilities and stock issues ahead of the common stock, then dividing by the number of shares.[2] The book value of a stock market is, effectively the replacement value of all the assets represented by the companies listed in it. The price to book is therefore the value attributed to the stock market by investors relative to its replacement value.

Spain has a five-year average P/BV of 1.17x. It was valued at 1.49x at the end of 1993.

Singapore's five-year average P/BV was 1.87x, and it was trading at 1.84x at the same time. It was the only major market trading below its book value.

Debt/equity ratios

What is the ability of a stock market to sustain the level of debt it has collectively incurred? Where possible an analysis of the capital structure of the components of a stock market should be measured. This involves delving into the leading index stocks and taking a view of the average. The traditional acceptable working capital ratio was a minimum of 2 units of current assets for each unit of current liabilities. The second measure, the 'acid test' of corporate financial strength, requires that current assets exclusive of inventories should be at least equal to current liabilities. Such measures can be applied to the leading stocks of a market to obtain a market ratio.

Consensus estimates for markets

While the consensus is often exactly where you should not be, it is useful to see what leading economists, financiers and investors predict for markets. They provide a useful resource that presumably reflects the future investing

---

[1] Source: Goldman Sachs

[2] Benjamin Graham, 'Security Analysis', 4th Edition

plans of some of the most influential institutional investors in each market. The data in Figure 10.8 were compiled by Consensus Forecasts for Japanese 10-year bond yields in late 1993.

A useful way of generating one's own consensus is to take the average of the forecasts of three leading stockbroking firms in each market.

	Year	%
Historic:	1989	5.7
	1990	7.0
	1991	5.4
	1992	4.5
Forecast:	1993	3.8
	1994	4.3
	1995	4.6
	1996	5.2
	1997	5.7
	1998	5.3
	1999-2003	5.1

Figure 10.8 Ten-year government bond yields for Japan
Source: Consensus Forecasts, 49 Berkeley Square, London

Other ratios

It is worth the analyst's effort to dig out information whenever possible on other key ratios relating to markets. In effect, the more factors put into the model, the more likely it will end up as a representative means of comparing the investability of one country versus another. Some other ratios would be:

Profitability ratio

The best gauge of the success of an enterprise is the percentage earned on invested capital. In other words, on the long-term debt and preferred stock, plus the book value of the common stock. The rate of return is the ratio to total capital of the final net profit available for capital funds. It is helpful to find an overall market average for the profitability of the companies in the leading indices.

Measures of stability

Just as it is possible to develop arithmetical indices on the stability of earnings of a company over a period of years, so it is possible to do the same for the market as a whole. It is useful to understand this characteristic within markets, as it helps in the diversification decision between countries.

Technical analysis

'Don't sell stocks when the sap is running up the trees.'

Addison Cammack

The use of charts is sometimes regarded as a superficial timing device by value managers. But they can be a useful snapshot to see where a market has been recently, what its ranges have been historically, and they are an excellent aid to timing. If all the fundamental analysis points in one direction, namely that one should invest heavily in a market or in a region, it is worth casting an eye on recent price action, to satisfy oneself that the timing is appropriate. It could well be worth waiting before becoming fully invested, because a correction appears imminent. Figure 10.9 shows the price action of the three Nordic markets in 1993. The components of the Index are the Finnish HEX Index, which rose 91 per cent in 1993, the Norwegian Oslo Stock Exchange Index, which rose 65 per cent, the Swedish Affärsvärlden Index, which rose 54 per cent, and Denmark's Copenhagen Stock Exchange which rose 40 per cent.

There were some good fundamental reasons for the markets to rise: the collapse of interest rates owing to protracted recession, the first buds of recovery, the fruits of corporate restructuring, a surge of exports caused by weak domestic currencies, and economic regulations getting into line with the EC. It is not suggested that these markets will necessarily collapse in 1994, but the chart suggests caution and that perhaps the best action has already taken place.

As a final check on the top-down process, technical analysis is a useful discipline to prevent over-enthusiasm towards a market that someone else discovered before you reached the conclusion that it was the place to be.

Country ranking

Top-down managers normally go through an exhaustive list of variables in their analysis of countries. The next question is how to rank countries to enable a systematic and credible weighting between one country and another.

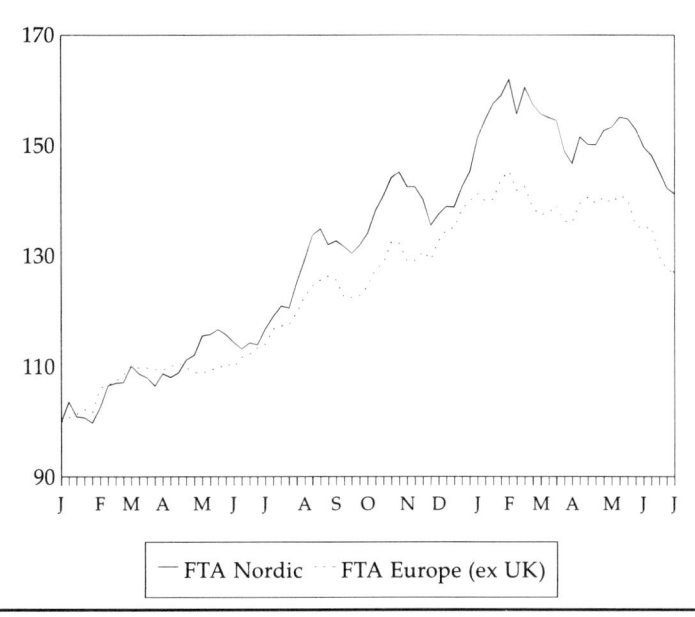

```
                                              170 ┐
                                              150
                                              130
                                              110
                                               90
                                                  J F M A M J J A S O N D J F M A M J J

                                                   ── FTA Nordic    ⋯ FTA Europe (ex UK)
```

Figure 10.9 FTA World Nordic Price Index vs. FTA World Europe Price Index (ex UK), January 1993-July 1994

Source: Financial Times/Datastream

There are managers who focus on fewer variables. Some will swear by a dividend discount model as the leading determinant of market positioning and not waste their time on multi-factor analysis. It all depends on the individual uses of models, and how successfully they are made to work.

The ranking of countries will depend on the weighting given to each factor. Long-term fundamental 'value' investors may put more stress on the secular opportunities available in markets, and really not be concerned about the price that today's investors attach to those values. So their top-down weighting will be more influenced by macroeconomics than market factors. Other managers may have to demonstrate quarterly outperformance when they advise, for example, a mutual fund or more aggressive growth-orientated clients, and pay more attention to current market factors.

The James Capel Strategy Group construct a matrix at the beginning of each year, breaking down countries into what they regard as five key variables: Three are 'directional drives' and two are 'support variables'. They get a total score for each country, which will influence the subsequent country weighting against the relevant world index. Figure 10.10 is their first quarter matrix for 1994.

Having a high or a low score for a country is one step towards defining favourability, but deciding on the actual amount to invest in each country is a major decision in itself.

Managers differ radically on how they approach this problem. When American institutions give money to an international manager, the benchmark against which they will be measured is generally defined in the management agreement at the outset. In other words, US Inc. gives US$50m to a manager to be invested against the EAFE Index. The job of that manager, whether active or passive, is to play in the 'EAFE sandbox' to quote Chris Nowakowski. The job of the active manager is presumably to beat the index over a number of years, and his or her compensation may well depend on outperforming it by x per cent each year over a market cycle. The manager may outperform the index by taking carefully-nurtured weighting risks in markets within the index, and scalping 'lots of little alphas' which amount, over time, to clearly defined superior risk-adjusted returns. Alpha is the return a manager accomplishes above the market return.

Other managers sign on to manage money against an EAFE mandate, then opportunistically inject stocks from markets that are not even on that index. It can significantly enhance the returns of those managers, but at a huge risk against the EAFE Index. It is evident that many pension fund clients in the United States—and presumably the United Kingdom and elsewhere too—do not have a clear idea of the risks taken on their behalf by their managers.

There is no substantive difference between this style of international investing and giving money to a real estate manager who invests in pork bellies 'to enhance returns against the real estate index'.

If managers seek to invest internationally in all markets, crossing betwixt and between the IFC Global and EAFE Indices, they should define an appropriate benchmark with their clients at the outset.

Many clients of international managers are not concerned about benchmarking, but are seeking 'absolute returns' and leave their money to be managed with that in view. They may have a sense of well-being after a good year of 'absolute returns', but they may equally have no idea as to how well their manager has done against a measurable benchmark.

The weighting decision

Most managers working against an EAFE, MSCI World or IFC Investable Index tend to develop an acceptable range of weighting to reflect the importance of markets within the indices. For example, Japan, the United Kingdom, Germany and France between them represent 78 per cent of the EAFE Index capitalization. Japan alone represents 48 per cent (a long way

	USA	Canada	Mexico	Germany	France	Italy	Netherlands	Spain	Sweden	Switzerland	UK
Monetary conditions	1	1	2	4	4	2	4	3	1	0	2
Earnings	2	3	-1	1	2	2	2	1	3	1	3
Uncertainty	0	-1	2	-2	0	0	0	0	0	1	0
Directional drives	**-3**	**3**	**3**	**3**	**6**	**4**	**6**	**4**	**4**	**2**	**5**
Liquidity	1	1	0	2	3	3	1	2	2	2	3
Valuation	-1	-1	2	0	1	0	1	2	-2	2	2
Support variables	**0**	**0**	**5**	**2**	**4**	**3**	**2**	**4**	**0**	**4**	**2**
Total score	**3**	**3**	**3**	**3**	**6**	**4**	**6**	**4**	**4**	**2**	**5**
Forecast return %	14.9	18.4	21.7	14.1	27.1	18.0	21.6	27.8	16.8	16.1	15.8
Forecast return in $ %	14.9	17.6	17.8	5.4	16.3	9.3	12.3	16.0	2.8	9.3	9.7

	Hong Kong	Singapore	Malaysia	Thailand	Korea	Taiwan	Australia	Japan	Average World	Previous
Monetary conditions	1	1	1	4	1	1	0	2	1.8	1.7
Earnings	3	2	1	-3	0	-1	4	-2	1.2	1.3
Uncertainty	-1	0	1	-1	0	-1	0	0	-0.1	0.2
Directional drives	**3**	**3**	**3**	**0**	**1**	**-1**	**4**	**0**	**2.9**	**3.2**
Liquidity	2	2	2	4	2	3	3	2	2.1	2.2
Valuation	1	0	-2	-3	2	-2	1	2	0.3	0.3
Support variables	**3**	**2**	**0**	**1**	**4**	**1**	**4**	**4**	**2.4**	**2.4**
Total score	**6**	**5**	**3**	**1**	**5**	**0**	**8**	**4**	**5.3**	**5.6**
Forecast return	29.8	11.8	-2.2	-4.9	31.9	7.2	20.7	15.3	16.9	12.5
Forecast return in $ %	29.4	11.1	-3.2	-5.2	31.9	7.7	21.4	4.6	12.1	12.3

Figure 10.10 Country weighting against the relevant world index
Source: James Capel Global Investment Strategy, Q1 1994

down from the 64 per cent position it once held in 1989), the United Kingdom is 18 per cent, Germany and France each 6 per cent.

Clearly, the most important decision that top-down EAFE managers can make in a given year is the weighting accorded to Japan. If they significantly underweigh the market—even if it is for all the right analytical reasons—and the Nikkei Index moves up by 20 per cent, the ground lost against the index will be exceedingly difficult to regain without taking inordinate risks elsewhere. Similarly, if they overweight the market and it collapses, as it did between 1990 and 1993, there will be a lot of running to do to catch up with the index. Given that Japan is such a key part of the index, and that the index will fluctuate significantly as Japan fluctuates, why take excessive bets away from Japan, when to be wrong can blow a huge hole in performance relative to the index?

It is therefore advisable to set ranges of potential overweights and underweights for the key markets within each index, so as to control the portfolio risk. There are quantitative programs that can be either bought (BARRA is one such service) or developed internally, so that managers can manage and, at all times define, the risk which they are taking against a stated benchmark. Conversely, there are many small markets, such as Finland or New Zealand in the EAFE Index, representing respectively 0.2 per cent and 0.21 per cent of total index capitalization. With all due respect, it is virtually irrelevant how managers do in those markets if they get the Big One—Japan—wrong.

Managers should set themselves maximum/minimum investment guidelines for each market to control risk against the index. The figures in Figure 10.11 are typical of the bands which managers have set since 1985.

The IFC Investable Index for emerging markets has a similar problem. There are two giant markets, Mexico and Malaysia, which between them represent over 50 per cent of the index. As with Japan in the EAFE Index,

	EAFE weight (%)	Suggested investment bands relative to index (%)
Japan	48	-30 to +12
United Kingdom	18	-10 to +7
Germany	6	-6 to +6
France	6	-6 to +6
Other	23	+0 to +4

Please note: These figures illustrate a methodology and are not recommendations

Figure 10.11 Risk guidelines for key markets in the EAFE Index

the key decision in emerging markets is 'getting Mexico right'. There is an additional anomaly in Mexico, which is that one company, Telefonos de Mexico (Telmex), represents 28 per cent of the Mexican stock market capitalization, and 8 per cent of the entire IFC Investable Index. It is almost as if that one company, whose market capitalization exceeds that of India, Pakistan, Sri Lanka, Jordan, Portugal, Greece and Venezuela combined, should be treated as a country in its own right. There is, of course, significant portfolio risk in deviating too far away from Telmex's weighting in the Index.

The figures in Figure 10.12 are typical of the bands in the IFC Index that managers might have set themselves since 1990.

You will note an asymmetry in the weighting of the largest markets in

	IFC weight (%)	Suggested investment bands relative to index (%)		
Mexico	28.8	-10	to	+8
Malaysia	22.9	-10	to	+5
Brazil	11.8	-4	to	+4
Argentina	7.0	-3	to	+3
Other	30.0	+0	to	+2

Please note: These figures illustrate a methodology and are not recommendations

Figure 10.12 Risk guidelines for key markets in the IFC Index

both indices. This is to prevent continually increasing weights in the largest markets as they rise. There were many passive investors who were not tilted against Japan in the late 1980s who took serious losses when the market began to slide from early 1990.

Figure 10.13 shows the recommended weightings of James Capel's Strategy Group in the first quarter of 1994. It is for global equity management, and includes the United States as a component. Note Mexico and South Korea.

Conclusion on the top-down process

It should have become evident that there are many ways to slice the cake. There are managers who do fundamental research on economics and markets, who come to country allocation decisions through multi-factor and multi-variable analysis. There are managers who employ one factor or just a handful of variables. There are managers who use proprietary technology to create their own 'black box' whose components are obscure and whose results are sometimes highly lucrative, sometimes shaky.

	MSCI Index	JC
USA	38.2	30.0
Canada	2.3	0.0
Mexico	-	2.5
North America	40.5	32.5
Australia	1.6	5.0
Hong Kong	2.6	5.0
Japan	24.4	20.0
Malaysia	1.3	-
Singapore	0.6	2.5
South Korea	-	1.0
Thailand	-	-
Taiwan	-	-
Asia	30.5	33.5
France	3.8	7.0
Germany	4.0	3.0
Italy	1.2	2.0
Netherlands	2.0	3.7
Spain	1.1	2.3
Sweden	0.9	-
Switzerland	2.9	1.0
United Kingdom	10.8	15.0
Other	2.3	-
Europe	29.0	34.0
Cash	0.0	0.0
Total	100.00	100.0

Figure 10.13 Global equity portfolio
Source: James Capel Investment Strategy, Q1 1994

My experience is that whatever the manager's style, it must be clearly definable, repeatable and, of course, successful.

What is the next step, once a top-down methodology is in place?

The next step depends on the manager's philosophy. There are various choices at this point, namely:

    1) Buy derivatives, where available, to get the desired country weightings synthetically;

2) Buy the leading index stocks in each market, on the assumption that if the country weightings are correct, the leading stocks will catch the flow of money and provide the required performance;

3) Invest by sector;

4) Actively manage the stock selection in each country.

The next chapter will deal with these alternatives.

Chapter 11

Portfolio construction

Once the top-down process has been performed, and a country preference is in place, the next step is to implement the country weightings.

It is usually desirable to act quickly, in this turbulent world, because country rankings get stale quickly. Market action can be swift, and one month's cheap market can be next month's bubble. This is particularly true in the case of emerging markets. In December 1993, the Malaysian market rose by 25.6 per cent, followed by profit-taking in the first two weeks of January 1994 that pushed the market down 21.7 per cent.

It is important to draw a distinction between performance-driven funds (about 98 per cent of all equity assets in the world) and patient, long-term investing. Long-term investors are content to be in the long-term accumulation business, whereby a market collapse is welcomed as an opportunity to buy cheaply. Most investment managers do not have the luxury of patient clients so they must take steps to keep up with, and preferably exceed, benchmarks on a quarterly basis.

Rapid implementation by the use of futures

> *'A man may know what to do and lose money—if he doesn't do it quickly enough'*
>
> Jesse Livermore

Managers of EAFE portfolios should have the ability to shift market weightings quickly, efficiently and cheaply by using stock index futures. For American investors, the appropriate contracts must be approved by the CFTC (Commodity Futures Trading Commission, in Washington DC), which limits the markets that can be traded by this method. But at least the major markets, which represent about 70 per cent of the EAFE market capitalization have contracts that are CFTC-approved. At the time of writing, Figure 11.1 represents the CFTC-approved futures contracts and exchanges.

For investors not bound by CFTC approval, other markets are available, so they can get futures coverage for about 80 per cent of the EAFE Index. If the portfolio is of hundreds of millions of dollars, it can become a cumber-

Country	Contract	Exchange	Location
UK	FT-SE 100	LIFFE	London
Australia	All Ordinaries	SFE	Sydney
Japan	Nikkei 225	OSE	Osaka
Japan	Nikkei 225	SIMEX	Singapore
Japan	Topix	TSE	Tokyo
France	CAC 40	MATIF	Paris
Canada	TSE 35	TFE	Toronto
Pending approval:			
Netherlands	EOE 25	EOE	Amsterdam
Hong Kong	MSCI HK	SIMEX	Singapore
Switzerland	SMI 25	SOFFEX	Zurich

Figure 11.1 **CFTC-approved futures contracts and exchanges**
Source: CFTC

some process involving the sale of millions of shares in market *a*, *b* and *c*, confirming settlement, then reinvesting the proceeds in markets *d*, *e* and *f*. While this process is going on, the events that triggered the shift in the portfolio in the first place may have moved on. It is costly to buy and sell stock on this scale.

Futures provide a way to get immediate implementation. Managers can buy futures to get the required country coverage as soon as the weighting decision is made. Once the futures position is in place, managers can do several things; (1) trade it as their sole investment bet on a market, thus becoming the chosen representative instrument, or (2) keep it in place until the weighting/percentage gap has been filled by common stocks.

Conversely, managers may sell futures to cover their retreat from a market. If the portfolio shift is from 30 per cent to 20 per cent in a market, they may decide to get immediate implementation of the shift without waiting to sell stocks.

Futures can be useful in facilitating the timing of a shift. Instant positioning is obtained without the need to buy or sell stocks disadvantageously. They are usually seen as an insurance premium which allows portfolio shifts to occur in good time rather than as an investment destination in their own right.

The example below is of a futures contract commonly used in the circumstances described:

A manager wishing to create a 'synthetic' portfolio representing the Tokyo Stock market might buy the Topix index. Each futures contract is for

10,000 yen, multiplied by the index level. If the Topix index level is at 1507, the cover would be for 15,070,000 yen's worth of index, or US$125,583 at an exchange rate of 120 yen to the dollar. The contract cycle is quarterly, and contracts expire in March, June, September and December. Liquidity is low for far-out contracts, and tends only to build up towards the end of each contract for the following quarter's contract.

The last trade date for each contract, and trading hours are clearly defined by the Tokyo Stock Exchange, settlement is by cash and margin is 30 per cent of the contract value. In the 1980s it used to be 9 per cent, but margin requirements were raised to deter excessive speculation.

Stock index futures are thus a useful way to obtain rapid implementation of a top-down investment process. Some managers are content to leave their implementation at a futures level alone. They have faith that their biggest contribution to adding value is their top-down process and therefore do not waste energy, time and expense in finding individual securities to own. They might further argue that the index of a market captures the biggest flow of capital, the biggest part of a market move, and that to be 'cute' in stock picking within a market is a waste of time. Other managers see futures as an excellent way of getting synthetic positions in place immediately, to be followed at leisure by backing and filling with real equities. They are also cheap. Figure 11.2 refers to the cost of trading futures on the Tokyo Stock Exchange. Contrast this with the figures for the cost of trading options on the same exchanges, in Figure 11.3.

Stock options may be used in the same way as futures. Most markets that have futures contracts on their indices tend to have options. They have advantages over futures, such as risk limitation, but they also have disadvantages, such as a higher cost and, often, less liquidity.

Since there are in excess of 150 equity and stock index contracts worldwide, it would be impractical to list them here. Any readers who wish to explore the vast array of contracts currently available should consult *The World's Futures & Options Markets*[1].

---

[1] *The World's Futures & Options Markets*, Nick Battley (Ed.) Probus Publishing ISBN 1 55738 513 0.

Trade amount	Commission
Less than ¥100m	0.080%
> ¥100m to ¥300m	0.060% + ¥20,000
> ¥300m to ¥500	0.040% + ¥80,000
> ¥500m to ¥1bn	0.020% + ¥180,000
> ¥1bn	0.010% + ¥280,000

Tax = 0.001%

Figure 11.2 The cost of trading futures on the Tokyo Stock Exchange
Source: TSE, August 1992

Trade amount	Commission
Less than ¥1m	4.00%
> ¥1m to ¥3m	3.00% + ¥10,000
> ¥3m to ¥5m	2.00% + ¥40,000
> ¥5m to ¥10m	1.50% + ¥65,000
> ¥10m to ¥30m	1.20% + ¥90,000
> ¥30m to ¥50m	0.90% + ¥185,000
> ¥50m	0.60% + ¥335,000

Tax = 0.001%

Figure 11.3 The cost of trading options on the Tokyo Stock Exchange
Source: TSE, August 1992

Chapter 12

Stock selection

'Whenever I have lost money in the stock market I have always considered that I have learned something. The money really went for a tuition fee.'

Jesse Livermore

Managers do not have to take big risks to beat an index. If they have the specific brief to beat a particular index—say, the S&P 500, or the 50 leading Australian stocks, they would be advised to stay close to the stock universe which they are playing to beat.

Once country weightings have been set, managers who do not just stay at the derivatives level, must pick stocks. Ideally, managers should be adding value over the local indices (alpha) in which they invest. If this is not possible, they would be better to stay at the futures level.

Some managers are not too concerned about beating each country's local index, but aim to match its performance. They believe that their value-added comes from being in the market, and that having once set a country weight, simply matching its index will suffice. In this case they would be advised to buy a weighted portfolio of the leading stocks in the index and re-weight occasionally to take account of market movements. This would be known as an active/passive strategy. *Active* on country selection and *passive* on stock selection.

Stock options

Managers need not always invest in stocks themselves, because in many cases, options are available for leading index stocks. If for some reason managers do not want futures or options on a particular index, they may test their prowess by buying options on particular issues. Figure 12.1 shows some leading European companies with equity options available. The largest part of the market capitalization in each developed country is covered by individual stock options, so it would be relatively easy to match the index this way.

It can be useful to buy options to obtain synthetic positions in a stock prior to buying the underlying equities. It can also be expensive if the

Austria	Ca-Bv Vorzug, EVN, ÖMV, Verbund, Weinerberger
Denmark	Den Danske Bank, Unidanmark, Sophus Berendsen, ISS, East Asiatic Company, Carlsburg, Danisco, Novo-Nordisk
Finland	Amer Group Limited, Enso-Guzeit Oy, Huhtamäki Oy, Kansallis Banking Group, Kesko Oy, Kone Corporation, Kymmene, Nokia, Okaobank, Partek, Repola, Unitas Bank, Pohjola Insurance, Kop, Ubf, Partek,
France	Accor, Alcatel Alsthom, Axa, Bouygues, BSN, Carrefour, Cerus, CMB Packaging, Elf Aquitaine, Euro Disney, Eurotunnel, Havas, LaFarge Coppée, Lyonnaise Des Eaux, L'Oréal, Michelin, Paribas, Pechiney, Pernod Ricard, Perrier, Peugeot, Rhône Poulenc, Saint Gobai, Société Générale, Suez, Thomson CSF, Total
Germany	Allianz, BASF, Bayer, BMW, Commerzbank, Daimler Benz, Deutsche Bank, Dresdner Bank, Hoechst, Mannesmann, Siemens, Thyssen, Veba, VW, RWE
Netherlands	ABN-AMRO Bank, ACF Holding, Aegon, Ahold, Akzo, Amev, Begemann Groep, Bols Wessanen, Borsumij Wehry, CSM, DSM, Elsevier, Fokker, Gist-brocados, Getronics, Hunter Douglas, Heineken, Hagemeyer, IHC-Caland, Internatio-Müller, Internationale Nederland, Ned. Hoogevens Bijenkorf Beheer, Koninklijke, Luchtvaarte Mij., Royal Dutch Petroleum, Nedlloyd, Nijverdal-Ten Cate, Verenigde Bedrijven Nutricia, Océ-van de Grinten, Pakhoed, Philips, PolyGram, Stad Rotterdam, Stork, Unilever, VNU, Van Ommeren, Volmac Software, Wolters Kluwer
Norway	Bergesen, Hafslund, Kværner Norsk Hydro, Saga Petroleum
Sweden	Electrolux, Ericsson, Procordia, S-E-Banken, Skanska, Trelleborg, Asea, Astra, Atlas Copco, Kinnevik, Nobel, SCA, Skandia, Volvo, Avesta, Celsius, Investor, Nordström & Thulin, Sandvik, SKF, Stora, Svenska Handelsbanken
Switzerland	Alusuisse, BBC Brown Boveri, Ciba-Geigy, Credit Suisse, Nestlé, Roche, Sandoz, SMH, Swiss Bank Corporation, Swiss Re-Insurance, Union Bank of Switzerland, Zurich Insurance
United Kingdom	Abbey National, Allied Lyons, Amstrad, Argyll, ASDA, BAA, Barclays Bank, Bass, BAT, Blue Circle, Boots, BP, British Aerospace, British Airways, British Gas, British Steel, British Telecom, BTR, Cable & Wireless, Cadbury Schweppes, Commerical Union, Courtaulds, Dixons, Eastern Electricity, Eurotunnel, Fisons, Forte, GEC, GKN, Glaxo, Grand Metropolitan, Guinness, Hanson, Hillsdown, HSBC, ICI, Kingfisher, Ladbroke, Land Securities, Lasmo, Lonrho, Lucas, Marks & Spencer, National Power, P&O, Pilkington, Prudential, Redland, Reuters, Rolls Poyce, Royal Insurance, RTZ, Sainsbury, Scottish & Newcastle, Scottish Power, Sears, Shell, Smithkline Beecham, Storehouse, Tarmac, Tesco, Thames Water, Thorn Emi, Trafalgar House, TSB, Unilever, United Biscuits, Vodaphone, Wellcome, Williams, Zeneca

Note: Check with a broker as to which particular securities of each companies are optionable. There are many restrictions as to A shares or B shares, ordinary and preferred, in different countries.

Figure 12.1 European stocks with equity options
*Sources: The World's Futures & Options Markets, Probus Publishing
Baring Securities*

decision proves wrong.

Similarly stock options exist in Brazil, Canada (Montreal and Vancouver), Australia, Hong Kong, Japan, the United States and other leading markets. Owing to the fluidity of world markets, investors should check with their broker to find out if options exist on a particular stock.

Investing to replicate or approximate the index

There is a school of thinking that if managers are going to invest in a market, they should own the leading capitalized stocks in it, which will (a) capture the lion's share of investment money entering the market; (b) approximate the local index performance; (c) ensure liquidity and marketability; (d) be cheaper; (e) be safe, free of surprises and visible for risk-averse clients.

This approach if often best in smaller markets where stock prices move closely with the index (high systematic risk), or if investors have such large funds under management that they are not able to be nimble in smaller stocks, so effectively have to own the index constituents.

In the US context, this is equivalent to owning a mutual fund investing in S&P 500 stocks, or blue chips, as opposed to owning a micro-cap, or OTC-style mutual fund. It depends entirely on the manager's style and clients' requirements.

Sector analysis within stock markets

If you decide to invest in a stock market, it is worth considering the systematic risk (beta) of each stock.

The Capital Asset Pricing Model (CAPM) states that the risk inherent in each stock consists in (1) unsystematic, or company-specific risk, and (2) systematic, or market risk. Company-specific risk can be mitigated by good diversification, but market risk cannot be. If the top-down model dictates that you should invest x per cent in New Zealand, then owing to the relatively small size of the stock market, companies tend to have a high systematic risk relative to the market. It is not worth spending too much time analysing individual issues in the New Zealand market, when to buy eight of the top ten capitalized index stocks would capture the market move you are hoping for. There is an argument for restricting analysis to these ten stocks, and not looking for smaller, spectacular high fliers in the market.

Larger markets are different, because of the number and capitalization of issues available. It is important to select the right sectors in these markets to beat the index. Some market sectors, however large, can remain moribund for most of a cycle, and the best chance of beating the market is to be under-weight, or out of such sectors altogether. Similarly, being over-weight in an important sector when it rises can go a long way to help a manager beat the Index. Reference is made earlier in the book to Japanese bank stocks in 1984 (page 57). An investor in those stocks at the beginning of 1984 (few international investors were) would have had a good chance of beating the index. If an investor did not hold those shares, there would have been a remote chance of beating the index. Sumitomo Bank's share price rose 237.4 per cent in 1984, to make it the largest bank in the world at the time, in terms of market capitalization, at US$16.2bn. In the same year Daiichi Kangyo Bank rose 161 per cent to a capitalization of US$13.4bn, Fuji Bank rose 149 per cent, to US$12.2bn, Mitsubishi Bank rose 143 per cent to US$12bn, and so forth.

Japanese banks represented 25 per cent of the Japanese Index, and 11 per cent of the EAFE Index. It was a year in which lucky sector analysis would have been very valuable. Lucky, because the ratings and value of those banks at the beginning of 1984 made them unattractive according to conventional Western bank analysis.

The term 'sector analysis' sounds straightforward, but the first thing a manager must do is define what is meant by a 'sector'. There are conventional guidelines available from Capital International and leading broking firms, who tend to break their analytical functions down into industry groupings.

The Financial Times London Share Service breaks the UK market into the following sectors:[1]

Banks	Life assurance
Breweries	Media
Buildings & construction	Merchant banks
Chemicals	Oil exploration & production
Distributors	Oil integrated
Diversified industrials	Other services businesses
Electricity	Pharmaceuticals
Electronic & electrical equipment	Printing, paper & packaging
Engineering	Property
Engineering vehicles	Retailers, food
Extractive industries	Retailers, general
Food manufacturers	Spirits, wines & ciders
Gas distribution	Support services
Health care	Telecommunications

[1] *Financial Times, 12 January 1994*

Household goods   Textiles & apparel
Insurance   Tobacco
Investment trusts   Transport
Investment companies   Water
Leisure & hotels

The listings provide amusing juxtapositions, such as food manufacturers followed by gas distribution, and spirits, wines & cider followed by support services. The Financial Times sector breakdown is highly comprehensive, and even the wealthiest stockbroking firm is unlikely to have analysts specific to each sector.

Security Pacific Investment Managers, Inc. developed a system in the 1970s for the US stock market that characterized industries by financial and market characteristics with identifiable relationships to economic variables. First, they classified all stocks in the S&P 500 into 43 industry groups. Second, they aggregated all individual company financial characteristics in each group. Third, they applied a statistical technique called cluster analysis to sort the industries on the basis of their common key characteristics. Fourth, they divided companies into sectors that related to their economic characteristics.

They found that price characteristics of each sector were different in trend, volatility and economic sensitivity, while within each group, price movements were similar. The resulting economic sectors in the US market were:[1]

   Consumer discretionary durables
   Consumer discretionary non-durables and services
   Consumer non-discretionary
   Energy
   Retail
   Capital spending
   Technology
   Utilities
   Finance
   Industrial commodities

Knowing which sector reacts to different economic forces is a valuable tool. It enables the most effective implementation of a top-down strategy, as

---

[1] *Edmund A. Mennis, 'Techniques of Portfolio Adjustment', an article in 'Investment Manager's Handbook', edited by Sumner Levine (Dow Jones Ind.).*

well as theoretically providing out-performance in a market.

A similar methodology can be applied to sectors in international stock markets.

If it was the manager's view that the US dollar was going to rise sharply in the next year, and he or she was managing a non-US equity portfolio for an American pension fund, then damage-limitation is the challenge which must be faced. Currency hedging can be used to protect the value of the portfolio. For example, if the portfolio has 10 per cent in German equities, and the Deutschemark (DM) is expected to fall against the US dollar, the DM risk can be hedged out by buying DM put options, or dollar calls, or currency forwards or futures to cover the 10 per cent DM exposure in the portfolio. Simple. But what if that manager is not permitted by his clients' trustees to use currency hedges?

Nothing is more painful to investment managers than to succumb to a trend they saw coming, but were unable to act upon.

There are other ways available to international managers of mitigating a rising dollar in international portfolios:

- First, hold all cash in the portfolio in US dollars;

- Second, there are many markets, particularly in Asia, whose currencies are linked to the US dollar. Weightings in these markets (e.g. Hong Kong and Singapore) are thus relatively dollar-neutral;

- Third, a manager may analyse foreign stock markets and individual issues for their dollar sensitivity. By buying—or avoiding—such stocks, there can be a significant 'implicit hedge' built into a portfolio.

Dollar-sensitive stock markets

For historical reasons, some stock markets have a tight linkage with the US economy. The British, Dutch and Japanese are the largest investors in the United States. The British own many American companies, such as Smith & Wesson (Tomkins), Stewart Warner (BTR) and Sohio (BP). The Japanese have tended to be direct investors in the US economy, such as constructing car factories in green-field sites from Kentucky to Tennessee, as well as owning trophy properties like 80 per cent of the Rockefeller Center (Mitsubishi Estate) and Pebble Beach Resort. The Dutch, through ownership of Royal Dutch, Philips and Unilever have a huge stake in the primary US economy. More recent acquisitions, such as the LaSalle National Bank in Chicago by ABN AMRO Bank, have deepened their stake in the service economy. Goldman Sachs prepared data on the dollar-sensitivity of European markets. They took a sample of leading stocks and analysed them for

Country	%
Netherlands	35
Switzerland	25
UK	20
Sweden	15
Germany	15
Italy	10
France	7
Spain	3

Note: Proportion of earnings from US subsidiaries and exports to the 'US dollar' area.

Figure 12.2   Earnings that are US dollar sensitive (% of total earnings)
Source: Goldman Sachs June/July 1993 Portfolio Strategy

	Effects of a 10% dollar appreciation		
Country	First year	Second year	Total effect
Netherlands	4.9	2.6	7.5
Norway	2.7	4.2	6.9
Germany	0.1	5.4	5.5
Sweden	2.8	2.3	5.1
Finland	2.1	2.3	4.4
Switzerland	1.3	1.1	2.4
UK	1.2	1.1	2.3
France	0.6	1.5	2.1
Italy	0.1	1.9	2.0
Spain	0.3	0.5	0.8
Japan	0.3	0.4	0.7
USA	3.0	-3.9	-0.9

Note: Based on a regression of stock returns on % change in exchange rate, with relevant controls (valuation indicators, change in interest rates) also included. In most cases, sample period is 1973-93 (monthly data). The exceptions are Finland (1979-1993) and France (1979-93). In the German case, coefficients reported are for the first 6 months, and the period between 6 and 18 months.

Figure 12.3   The dollar and stock markets
Source: Goldman Sachs

their sensitivity to a dollar move (see Figure 12.2).

If the dollar rises, the European countries to consider for investment would be the Netherlands, Switzerland and the United Kingdom, for the size of their dollar-sensitivity.

Further work by Goldman Sachs showed that the effects on stock markets of dollar exchange rate changes are gradual, and that a 10 per cent dollar appreciation would have an effect for at least two years on stock markets with high dollar-sensitivity.

Figure 12.3 shows their estimates—in mid-1993—of the effect of a 10 per cent dollar appreciation on the local currency returns in each country. The two-year benefit demonstrates the multiplier effect of a currency working its way through the economy into higher earnings and into the stock market. If 35 per cent of the earnings of leading Dutch companies are in the US dollar, and the dollar rises, there is a healthy jolt into the Dutch income stream.

This analysis is useful for those wanting to cut the cake into dollar-sensitive slices. Some country allocation models may particularly seek to mitigate negative currency risk.

If it was considered that the dollar would rise, the manager can also seek out particular stocks that benefit from dollar appreciation, which at the same time provide an adequate proxy for the market index. Examples are given in each of six countries below:

Japan:	Sony, Toshiba, Mori Seiki, Honda, Nintendo
UK:	British Petroleum, Glaxo, Cable & Wireless, ICI, Shell
Germany:	BMW, Bayer, Lufthansa, Schering, Siemens
France:	Air Liquide, Club Med, LVMH, Michelin, Total
Netherlands:	ABN-AMRO, Hunter-Douglas, KLM, Royal Dutch, Akzo
Switzerland:	Ciba-Geigy, Nestle, Sandoz, Swissair, Roche

However, dollar-sensitive stocks can be anathema to a portfolio if the dollar is declining. In such a case, the manager should reverse out of these sectors and focus on proxies for the domestic economy in local markets. American investors would want the undiluted effect of a declining dollar to flow into their equity portfolios.

Interest-rate sensitive stocks

Another example of where sector analysis is required is in the area of interest-rate sensitive stocks. As the recession gathered pace in Europe in the early 1990s, it was clear that tensions would build among the weaker members in the exchange rate mechanism (ERM). In late 1992, the pressures on the ERM caused by the German Bundesbank's high interest rate policy forced Italy and the United Kingdom out of the mechanism 'temporarily'.

The problem was that the integration of East and West Germany was more inflationary than originally anticipated. East German workers wanted living conditions and wages as high as their counterparts in the West, even though their productivity was lower. Costs of cleaning up pollution in the East, dismantling old factories and providing social benefits to the unemployed, all conspired to increase the demand for public borrowing which led to higher German interest rates. Unfortunately, because of the design of the ERM banding, the signatories to the ERM agreement were forced to raise their interest rates along with the Bundesbank. Domestic economic conditions outside Germany, which may not have warranted high interest rates, were ignored in this process.

European unemployment, exacerbated by these interest rate levels, rose to higher levels than would have been expected in a normal economic downturn. Politically, the situation became untenable in the United Kingdom and Italy, which burst out of the ERM in a undignified fashion. This enabled the United Kingdom to reduce its interest rates without constraint. The pound fell sharply on the foreign exchange market (from US$2/£1 to US$1.49/£1 in a few months), which had the effect of re-liquefying corporate balance sheets with US earnings. Mortgage rates fell sharply, and the British economy slowly came to life again. A year later, unemployment had fallen from nearly 12 per cent to under 10 per cent, there were signs of revival in the property market, consumers were regaining confidence and industrial production began to rise. In the meantime, countries which remained bound to the ERM were suffering high unemployment (such as Spain with 25 per cent unemployment), and falling production. It was becoming politically untenable in Europe for this scenario to continue. Social tensions were erupting, from neo-Nazi attacks on Turkish immigrants in Germany to scuffles between Algerians and French nationalists in Paris.

Given this background, there was a strong case for investing in interest-rate sensitive securities across Europe. Figures 12.4, 12.5 and 12.6 show dividend yields and long interest rates for the United Kingdom, Germany and France from 1973 to December 1993.

With a falling interest rate scenario, Richard Davidson at Morgan Stanley screened the MSCI Europe data base for four criteria:

- 1. Stocks with a current dividend yield greater than 4 per cent. This reflected the desire to keep income close to existing levels, but also had the hope of capital appreciation.

- 2. Stocks with a current pay-out ratio under 75 per cent. This was conservative, but reflected Davidson's caution on Europe and the need for safety in his model.

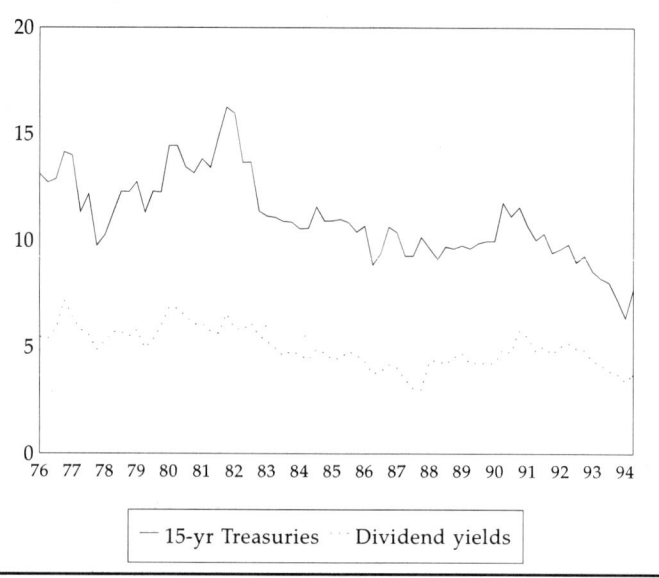

Figure 12.4 UK: Dividend yield and long interest rates
Source: Smith New Court

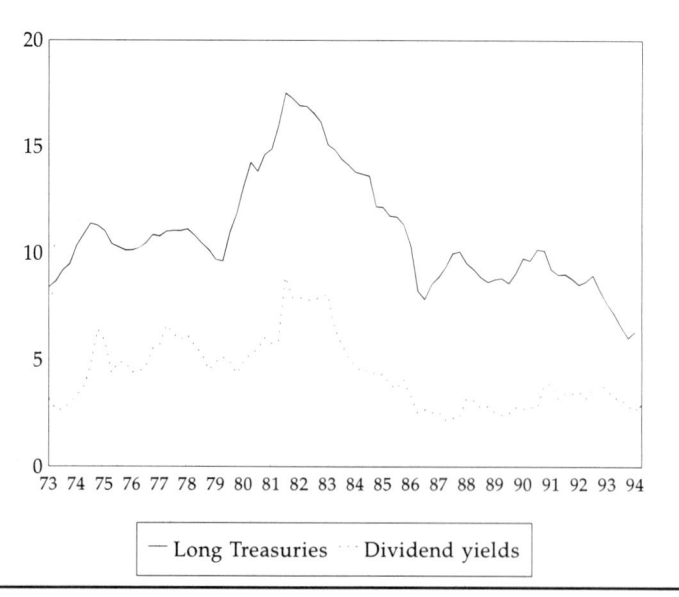

Figure 12.5 France: Dividend yield and long interest rates
Source: Smith New Court

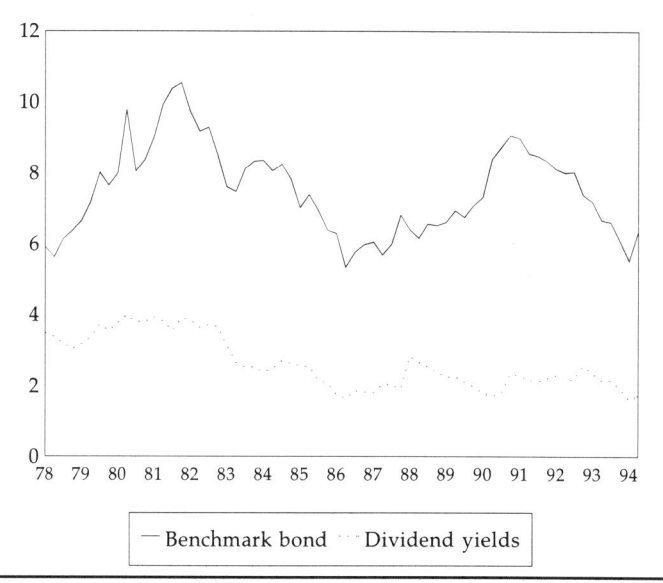

[Chart showing benchmark bond yields and dividend yields in Germany from 1978 to 1994]

Figure 12.6 Germany: Dividend yield and long interest rates
Source: Smith New Court

- 3. Stocks with a current dividend yield greater than the average for a company's global competitors.

- 4. Stocks with annualized dividend growth greater than 3 per cent over two consecutive years. In other words, real dividend growth that would at least match expected inflation.

It is interesting to note how much these criteria are influenced by safety. Given the declining interest-rate scenarios illustrated above for Germany, the United Kingdom, and France, an investor might be tempted to be more reckless and invest in poorer quality interest plays in those markets. This strategy would probably be fairly successful if the portfolio was well-diversified, but in an uncertain financial environment, investors are advised to stick to quality.

Figure 12.7 shows some of the companies that came out of Davidson's screen in four European sectors: financial, food retail, UK utilities and 'other'. The list is purely illustrative, not exhaustive and its inclusion here should not be construed as a recommendation for purchase.

The sector analysis described above gives examples of top-down influenced analysis. One example shows the consequences of an expected rise in the US dollar, and the markets likely to benefit from this scenario. The

	Latest payout ratio	5-yr payout ratio	Latest dividend yield	5-yr dividend yield	Yield relative to country	Yield relative to industry	Dividend growth 1992-94
Financials							
ABN-AMRO	50.0	53.4	4.1	6.7	1.3	2.3	4.3
BAT	60.2	97.9	4.3	5.6	1.2	1.5	7.9
Dresdner Bank	18.6	n/a	4.1	4.9	1.7	2.3	4.2
Generale de Banque	54.6	91.3	4.7	6.2	1.2	2.6	7.0
Food & food retail							
Argyll	49.7	56.2	5.0	4.0	1.4	2.8	8.5
Bodegas y Bebidas	49.5	57.1	4.0	3.8	1.2	1.5	8.3
Tate & Lyle	42.8	43.0	4.1	4.3	1.2	1.8	6.5
UK utilities							
Anglian Water	47.5	44.5	4.6	5.3	1.3	2.5	8.7
South West Water	43.9	41.8	4.8	6.6	1.4	2.6	8.2
Welsh Water	29.0	30.7	4.3	5.4	1.2	2.4	9.4
London Electricity	47.6	45.0	3.9	4.5	1.1	1.1	14.1
Northern Electricity	38.2	38.2	4.0	4.6	1.2	1.1	14.3
Other areas							
RWE Vorzug	71.1	68.0	4.2	5.0	1.8	1.1	8.3
Zeneca Group	66.5	67.9	4.1	4.8	1.2	1.6	n/a
United Newspapers	64.5	82.8	4.1	6.8	1.2	2.6	5.0

Figure 12.7 Safe high-yield stocks with dividend growth
Source: 'European Markets: Invest in Disappointment and Safe Income', Richard Davidson, Morgan Stanley Global Strategy, 12 January 1994

other shows the steps that can be taken on the expectation of falling interest rates in Europe.

Top-down sector analysis can be played using many scenarios. What if the oil price were to rise by 20 per cent? What if militancy were to increase in Russia? Given any expectation, an investment response can be constructed.

Risk optimization in the stock selection process

Managers must always be aware of the benchmark they were hired to invest against. In the same way as the country allocation process should constantly be aware of the implicit risk of investing away from benchmark country weightings, so a stock-picker should always be able to quantify the risk of weighting particular sectors, or stocks within sectors.

This should not be construed as recommending a passive, or near index-weighting within countries. On the contrary, it is recommending that managers should at all times be able to quantify and understand the implicit and explicit risks inherent in their investment behaviour. It is a useful guide to managers' risk-taking profiles to compare their portfolio holdings within a market with the sector weight of those stocks in that market.

For example, as mentioned above, Telefonos de Mexico (TelMex) represents approximately 28 per cent of the capitalization of the Mexican Index. If a manager has 10 per cent of his Mexican weighting in TelMex, he is taking a big risk against the index, even though it may seem like an intrinsically large position in one stock. It is unusual for managers of internationally-diversified portfolios to invest more than 4 per cent of a portfolio in one stock. Indeed, many mutual fund prospectuses specifically prohibit portfolio concentration above 5 per cent in one stock. For investors in the IFC Investable Index, they are taking an immediate risk against the index, because TelMex represents approximately 8 per cent of that index. The risk inherent in any portfolio should always be quantifiable and understood by investment managers.

International stock selection

Analysing stocks for their interest-rate or dollar-sensitivity is a useful approach for specific scenarios. Companies should, however, generally be analysed for a wider range of criteria. This chapter will deal with a range of possible tools with which to analyse companies around the world, suggest some common ratios that enable the rapid ranking of stocks, discuss information sources and cite one case-study by Goldman Sachs on major accounting differences between the United States and Germany.

Analytical tools in security analysis

> *'The objective of financial statements is to provide information about the financial position, performance and financial adaptability of an enterprise that is useful to a wide range of users in making economic decisions.'*
>
> Accounting Standards Board Draft Statement of Principles.

When filing a business plan with its lawyers, a recently incorporated Scottish investment firm referred to its need for investment professionals. The lawyer indignantly crossed out the word 'Professional' because he did not regard anyone outside his conventional definition to be a professional. The firm tried to explain about the Institute of Chartered Financial Analysts in the US and the Institute of Investment Management & Research in the UK, whereby security analysts are given a professional standing similar to that of certified public accountants, but this fell on deaf ears.

Admittedly, there is a difference in professionalism between an Edinburgh lawyer drafting the lease on a fish and chip shop and an investment manager merely doing asset allocation for a Fortune 500 pension fund.

In the previous section on top-down allocation, reference was made to ways of analysing the overall value of stock markets. These included various ratios, such as price/earnings (P/E), price/cashflow (P/CF), price/book value (P/BV), debt/equity (D/E), profitability and stability ratios. This section deals with those same ratios, but applied to individual companies.

Significant reference will be made to Benjamin Graham, whose work in the 1940s and 1950s on the subject of security analysis laid the groundwork for much of our methodology today. He would have argued that the analysis of foreign stocks should be subject to the same disciplines as the analysis of US stocks. The analysis of stocks everywhere must start from the premise that it is the application of scientific method, albeit in an inexact field.

Graham described security analysis as comprising the following:

- **1. Description function**
  This sets out the facts on a company for a quick appreciation of its standing. It should show how the company has evolved over the years, compare it with its rivals and project earnings forecasts.

- **2. Selective function**
  This provides the analyst with an essential view on whether to buy, hold or sell a stock. Graham refers to three approaches: a stock's anticipated market performance, its absolute value and its relative value.

- **Anticipation approach**
  Analysts who adopt this approach anticipate the market in the future and structure their portfolio accordingly. They attempt to project future results that may be different from what is implicit in today's share price.

- **Value approach**
  With this approach, analysts attempt to value a stock independently of its current market price. This is the 'intrinsic value' approach (alias 'indicated value', 'central value', 'normal value', 'investment value', 'reasonable value', 'fair value', 'appraised value', etc.).

  This approach was in vogue in Japan from 1985 to 1990, when analysts bought stocks—rather, justified holding stocks—at P/E multiples of 100 times, 200 times or higher, on the basis of 'hidden values'. Real estate and railroad stocks were favourite candidates for these investors. The argument ran that a railroad company which was chartered in 1895 still held its real estate assets at book price in its accounts and that if those assets could be unlocked, the 'value' of the security was 'worth' a great multiple of the current share price. This was against a background of soaring Japanese real estate prices and railroad companies which bought empty land in 1895 were now sitting on extremely valuable property as Japanese cities swelled into the countryside during the intervening years. Seasoned investors in Japanese equities pointed out that the 'hidden asset' theme rolls around periodically in the stock market, but that the 'values' are seldom realized as expected.

  Figure 12.8 shows the share price from 1971 and P/E ratio from 1982 of Kinki Nippon Railway, the regional railroad company. The share price rose from 280 yen in 1984 to 1670 yen in early 1990. Much of that move came from punters betting that the hidden assets of the company would be realized during the staggering rise in real estate prices in the second half of the 1980s. The P/E ratio rose to 250 times earnings, attributing a fantasy to the stock that could never possibly be realized.

  During this period, it was calculated that the land on which the Imperial Palace in Tokyo stands was worth more than the entire State of California. Prices have since corrected.

  Figure 12.9 for Mitsubishi Estate shows a similar price explosion from 1984, when the price was below 500 yen, to its peak in 1987 (pre-Crash) of 3520 yen. The P/E ratio was up to 160x earnings, but has since fallen back to below 40x earnings. It is easy to imagine the hubris of this company when it bought 80 per cent of the Rockefeller Center in New York. Presumably it looked cheap compared to Tokyo real estate at the time.

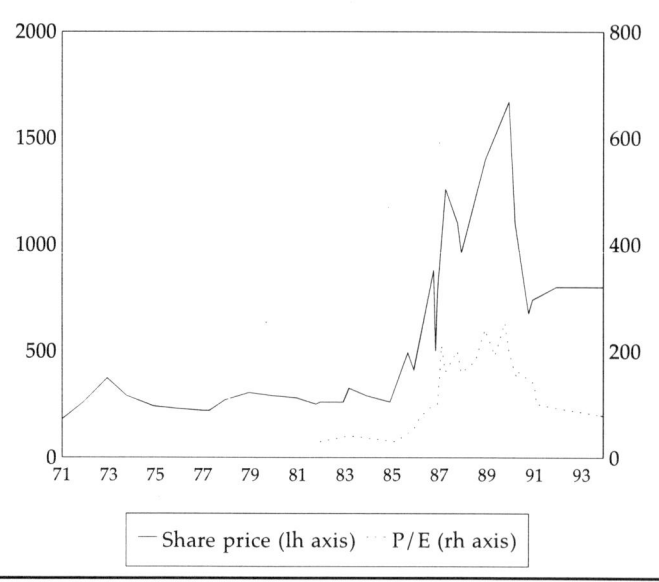

Figure 12.8 Kinki Nippon Railway: Share price and P/E ratio
Source: Datastream

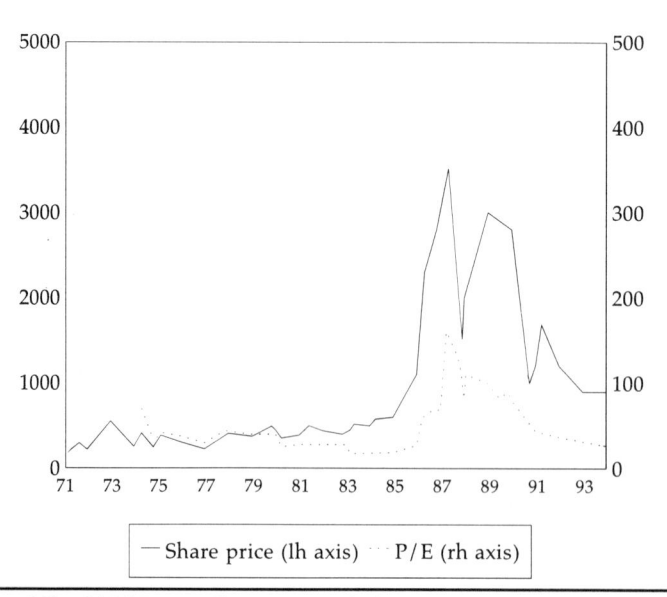

Figure 12.9 Mitsubishi Estate: Share price and P/E ratio
Source: Datastream

- **Relative approach**
   With this approach the analyst seeks to determine the value of a stock relative to the market, or to that relevant cross-section of the market, which is the stock's peer group.

Intrinsic value

It is important at this point to consider what exactly is meant by 'intrinsic value', because 'value' is an ephemeral concept. The value of a company could be computed in terms of net assets, earnings, dividends, work in hand, management and goodwill. Graham distilled it down to one overriding factor: indicated average future earnings power, that is, estimated future earnings for a period of years. 'Intrinsic value' was found by forecasting this earnings stream, then multiplying it by an appropriate 'capitalization factor'.

Graham undertook an exercise in 1948 with General Motors. He assumed average future earnings of US$4.50 to US$5.50 a share, and a multiple of 14 to 16, giving an indicated range of between US$63 and US$88 a share: this would be its 'intrinsic value' band. So by analysing the 'level of earnings trend' and choosing an appropriate multiplier, a 'theoretical value' for a stock can be reached. The difference between the current price and the theoretical value will determine whether the stock is worth buying at current levels. This approach deals with concepts that have nothing to do with current market prices, and there is some satisfaction in being able to detach oneself from the noise of the market. But there are plenty of potential pitfalls—estimates of future earnings may not be fulfilled, and the multiplier may be incorrectly chosen.

Key ratios

There are six categories of key ratios in security analysis identified by Graham 45 years ago which are still useful today. These, which are described below, are:

- 1) Profitability ratios;
- 2) Growth (progress) ratios;
- 3) Stability ratios;
- 4) Pay-out ratio (dividend policy);
- 5) Credit ratios;
- 6) Price ratios.

■ 1. Profitability ratio

One gauge of the success of an enterprise is the percentage earned on invested capital—i.e. long-term debt and preferred stock, plus book value of the common stock. This percentage is the ratio of total capital to the final net profit available for capital funds. There are various qualifications here—for instance, the treatment of depreciation varies between companies depending on accounting conventions and these must be taken into account. It is important to ensure the comparison of like with like, so the ratios can be expressed as follows:

- a) Earnings before depreciation per dollar of capital funds;
- b) Earnings per dollar of capital funds;
- c) Sales per dollar of capital funds;
- d) Earnings per dollar of sales.

■ 2. Growth ratio

The figures usually compared for company growth rates are:

- a) Dollar sales;
- b) Net profit for total capital in dollars;
- c) Earnings per share.

Growth rates differ between industries; for instance, there may be a 30 per cent growth rate in one industry (e.g. software) and negative growth in another (e.g. meat packing), but an average growth of 8 per cent across all industries might be expected.

■ 3. Measure of stability

The stability of earnings over a period of years can be calculated arithmetically. There are different ways of doing this, but a suggested route is to select the lowest net income over a period of 10 years and calculate the ratio of such earnings to the average of the preceding three years. This will give the ratio of the maximum decline in the earnings rate on total capital.

■ 4. Pay-out ratio

This is calculated by dividing the earnings into the dividend. This is not so relevant for international investors in high growth economies, whose objective is aggressive capital appreciation. Few foreigners investing in the equity markets of Brazil, Jordan or Thailand are after dividend yield.

■ 5. Credit ratios
These relate to working capital and to the capital structure of the company.

- a) The ratio of working capital to current liabilities should generally be in excess of 2 to 1, but this depends on the industry in which the company operates;

- b) The common stock ratio is obtained by dividing the total capital fund, at book-value, into the common stock component;

- c) Coverage of senior charges is calculated by dividing the balance available for senior charges by (i) the fixed charges, or (ii) fixed and contingent charges, or (iii) total prior charges plus preferred dividends. The quality of common stock is influenced strongly by the margin of safety shown above senior charges.

■ 6. Price ratios
No investment decision relating to equities can be made except with reference to a specific price. There are four ratios that a security analyst should ascertain for each security:

- a) Sales per dollar of common stock;
- b) Earnings per dollar of common stock (earnings yield);
- c) Dividend per dollar of common stock (dividend yield);
- d) Net assets (equity) per dollar of common stock (asset ratio).

These ratios should be calculated on the basis of the last full year's figures, and in relation to average earnings for five years.

Ratios commonly used for a quick assessment

Investment managers covering eight European markets have thousands of companies in their universe, of which hundreds merit further scrutiny. It would be one thing if the body of knowledge relating to these companies was static, and if every aspect of these companies could be known, with enough studying and analysis. It is not realistic to expect managers to have the depth of knowledge that full-blown traditional analysts might once have had in a handful of leading companies in several industrial sectors in one country. However, the use of computers and the ability to tap into pools of research can enable a manager to screen companies rapidly for specific financial criteria. Companies are organic, and while all sorts of predictions can be made with varying degrees of success, they depend crucially on the foibles of management and the work force, as well as extraneous dynamics. It is useful to have a few 'quick and dirty' analytical tools by which to obtain a financial snapshot of a company.

The data shown in Figure 12.10 is for Sandoz, the Swiss pharmaceutical company. It comes from a report in January 1994 by Morgan Stanley, and focuses on the following headline data: net income, earnings per share (EPS), price to earnings ratio (P/E), cash earnings per share (cash EPS), price/cash earnings (P/CE), net dividends and net yield. Other ratios are included, which will be discussed below.

Year to Dec.	Net income SFr mill.	EPS SFr	P/E	Cash EPS SFr	P/CE	Net div. SFr	Net yield %
1992	1495	197.4	20.9	306.8	13.4	47.0	1.1
1993[e]	1708	225.5	18.3	341.0	12.1	55.0	1.3
1994[e]	1981	261.5	15.8	386.7	10.7	62.0	1.5
1995[e]	2311	305.1	13.5	442.9	9.3	70.0	1.7

[e] = Morgan Stanley Research estimates

Figure 12.10 Sandoz: A financial snapshot
Source: Morgan Stanley Research, January 1994

The first column lists fours years under scrutiny—one actual (1992) and three estimated (1993-1995). The second column lists the actual and expected net income for the company in Swiss francs (SFr). The third shows earnings per share growth estimated over the period. The fourth shows a falling P/E ratio, which is the January 1994 share price divided by projected earnings per share at various dates. The share price on January 14, 1994 is the 'key-off' price for this data. It was SFr 4120 on that date. The P/E for 1992 is shown at 20.9x, which was calculated by dividing the SFr 4120 price by the actual earnings of SFr 197.4 for the year to December 1992. The P/E for 1993 is shown at 18.3x, while for 1994 it is 15.8x and for 1995, 13.5x.

The 1992 P/E ratio was calculated here by taking 1992's earnings and a January 1994 share price. As Ben Graham pointed out, 'The statement that a common stock 'is selling at *n* times earnings' is not without some ambiguity.'

The next column shows cash earnings per share. This is a higher figure than the first EPS figure, because it is stated before tax and depreciation. It is arguably a more accurate picture of a company's cash-generating abilities than the earnings-per-share figure, because it is not tainted by tax and depreciation distortions.

Price to cash earnings is the ratio between the current price and the

Share data

Price at 14 January 1994	SFr 4120
52-week range	SFr 4200 - 2820
1-, 3-, 12-month relative performance (%)	-2, 4, -11
Shares outstanding	7.57m
Market capitalization	SFr 31,166m
Reuters symbol	SANZn.Z

Ratios

NAV/share at 31 December 1992	SFr 1337
Price/NAV	3.1
Net debt/equity	Nil
EPS growth (next five years - estimated)	15.0%
Dividend cover	4.2
Return on equity at 31 December 1992	15.7%

Figure 12.11 Sandoz: Share data and ratios
Source: Morgan Stanley Research, January 1994

stated cash earnings. Then there is the net dividend expressed in Swiss francs, and the yield on the stock.

Figure 12.11 gives share data on the company and other ratios: the net asset value (NAV) per share in December 1992 was SFr 1337. If that figure prevailed in January 1994, the NAV to share price ratio would have been 3.1x. The company appeared to have no debt, had an estimated earnings-per-share growth rate for the next five years of 15 per cent. Dividend cover (the ratio between dividends paid and earnings per share) was 4.2 and return on equity based on 1992 data was 15.7 per cent.

The information in Figure 12.12 also relates to Sandoz, but it refers to the American Depository Receipts (ADRs) of the company. An ADR is a certificate issued by a US depository, usually a bank which evidences the ownership of a foreign security held by the bank on behalf of the ADR holder. In this case, the certificate would evidence the ownership of Sandoz. ADRs will be discussed more fully in Chapter 17.

Many Swiss companies have 'heavy' shares. In this case, Sandoz shares trade at SFr 4120, or approximately US$2800 (assuming an exchange rate of 0.68 SFr/US$1). There would be relatively little interest in the United States in a share this heavy, particularly among smaller investors, so the ADR was created at 1/50 of the underlying common stock to make it at least optically cheap. This data is expressed in US generally accepted accounting principles (GAAP) form, for the benefit of US investors following the stock.

These data and ratios given for Sandoz are typical of what can be pro-

ADR per ordinary shares		50			
ADR symbol		None			
Price at 14 January 1994		$55.68			
52-week range		$56.75 - 38.11			
Market capitalization		$21,058m			

Year to Dec.	US GAAP EPS $	P/E	Net div. $	Yield %	Exchange rate SFr/$
1992	2.67	20.9	0.64	1.1	1.48
1993[e]	3.05	18.3	0.74	1.3	1.48
1994[e]	3.54	15.7	0.84	1.5	1.48
1995[e]	4.13	13.5	0.95	1.7	1.48

e = Morgan Stanley Research estimates

Figure 12.12 Sandoz: American Depository Receipt data
Source: Morgan Stanley Research

duced on a large number of companies by the research departments of stockbroking firms. The information provided by one researcher can be corroborated with other firms by the investment manager, or compared with data provided by a consensus service, such as Institutional Brokers Estimate System (IBES). But the headings for data tend to be common to all stockbrokers' research departments.

The reason why both cash-earnings-per-share and earnings-per-share are present is to attempt to identify some distortions caused by local country depreciation rules. Cash earnings are after-tax income plus depreciation, whereas earnings are simply after-tax income. It should be noted that when comparing companies in the same industry between countries, the EPS figure will tend to obscure massive local accounting differences.

The German Investment Analysts Association (DVFA) devised a formula to obtain profit figures used in calculating EPS. The analysis of Daimler Benz that follows later in this chapter will help to explain the EPS adjustments recommended by the DVFA. It will be evident that Daimler Benz has been applying conservative depreciation and other provisions over the years, and by US GAAP standards, has significantly understated the worth of its earnings and assets.

Accounting differences

Questions are often asked about the difficulties involved in analysing companies overseas. How can an analyst in one country really understand the accounting conventions, and trust the honest practice of the profession in other countries around the world? There are no guarantees that the accounts in some countries are a fair representation of what they purport to be but, in recent years, strides have been made in this area which help the analyst significantly.

There is confusion on many domestic matters, even within the US accounting profession. In a recent study of the annual reports of 600 US corporations, the terminology for shareholders' funds differed widely and included the following terms: stockholders' equity, shareholders' equity, common shareholders' equity, shareowners' equity, shareholders' investment, common stockholders' equity and stockholders' investment.[1]

There is a perception in the United States that company managements 'over there' may be less than honest, and await the unwary foreign investor like a Venus fly trap awaits insects. To put this into perspective, some of the greatest financial frauds in history have been perpetrated in the United States and the United Kingdom, who pride themselves on the sophistication of their accounting professions. The collective corruption surrounding the US savings and loans in the 1980s was a fraud of epic proportions that the Third World would have been hard-pressed to match. The shenanigans surrounding Robert Maxwell, Ferranti and Polly Peck in the United Kingdom are worthy of note too.

There are various accounting traditions in the developed world, which can be split into four broad categories, as shown in Figure 12.13.

Other accounting traditions operate in Eastern Europe, Africa, Scandinavia and many 'emerging' markets. It is important to realize that differences exist, and to allow for them in approaching the world's equity markets.

Some of the areas in which accounting differences tend to occur from one country to the next are flagged below:

- 1. The valuation of currency and receivables in non-local currency;

- 2. Taxation differences;

- 3. The philosophy towards valuation of assets, such as buildings, equipment, inventory, etc. For example, German tax regulations have a scale of depreciation rates for particular assets. By contrast, in the United Kingdom, Statement of Standard Accounting Practices (SSAP) 12 states, 'Management should select the method regarded as most

---

[1] *'Comparative International Accounts'*, by Christopher Nobes and Robert Parker, Third Edition, Prentice Hall.

US model	Latin American model	Continental European model	British Commonwealth model
Canada	Argentina	Belgium	Austria
Japan	Bolivia	France	Kenya
Mexico	Brazil	Germany	Netherlands
Panama	Chile	Italy	New Zealand
Philippines	Colombia	Spain	Pakistan
USA	Ethiopia	Sweden	Singapore
	India	Switzerland	South Africa
	Paraguay	Venezuela	UK
	Peru		
	Uruguay		

Figure 12.13 Categories of accounting traditions
Source: Nais and Frank, Accounting Review, July 1980

appropriate to the type of asset and its use in the business so as to allocate depreciation as fairly as possible.';

- 4. Consolidation practices;

- 5. The ability to smooth income through manipulation of provisions from one year to the next;

- 6. The extent to which accounting rules are applied uniformly within a country, and by companies in a similar industry;

- 7. How strict the law is on details, and to what extent judgement is given free rein;

- 8. Degree of required disclosure.

There are many other potential pitfalls and differing treatments of accounting around the world, but at least if the analyst is aware of these issues, it will be a start towards understanding the analysis of non-local companies.

Daimler Benz — A case study in international accounting differences

An event recently occurred which provides a graphic illustration of the differences between two accounting conventions, as well as new insights into an established company's accounting practices. In October 1993, Daimler Benz listed its shares on the New York Stock Exchange (NYSE). One of the requirements of foreign companies listing on the NYSE is to report net income and shareholders' equity under US Generally Accepted Accounting Principles (US GAAP).

Daimler Benz filed its 20-F document (the Stock Market Listing Application) with the NYSE, which showed its accounts restated under US GAAP. There are a number of areas in which German and US GAAP differed, mostly demonstrating the greater conservatism of German accounting, which tends to understate assets and income.

The impact of adjusting for US GAAP was evident in many areas and for illustration, an 'adjustment effect' is shown in five categories. These are, differences in the treatment of depreciation and other provisions, pensions, currency, deferred taxes and goodwill. The differences are shown for the profit & loss account (P&L) and net assets. The range is significant. For example, German provisions understated profits in 1992 by 55 per cent and assets by 54 per cent, when compared with figures obtained if calculated under GAAP.

Each of these items is shown for its impact on the adjusted US GAAP accounts. A summary of the figures, including items not discussed here, is at the end of this section.

■ 1. Depreciation

German companies tend to take higher depreciation charges and make more generous provisions for potential liabilities, contingencies and asset risks, than their US or UK counterparts. This is illustrated in Figure 12.14, in terms of Daimler Benz's provisions in its profit & loss account, and its statement of net assets.

Under German GAAP in 1992, the profit and loss account (P&L) is understated by 55 per cent when expressed in US GAAP terms, as are net assets by 54 per cent in the same year. 1992 was a difficult year for the company and this conservatism reflects potential losses to a degree not acceptable under US or UK GAAP.

■ 2. Pension provisions

The calculation of pension provisions is quite different under each accounting convention. Daimler Benz had accounted for pension obligations under stockholders' equity, and it had also accounted for post-retirement benefits supplementary to pensions. The adjustment effect is shown in Figure 12.15 as being somewhat overstated relative to US GAAP.

US GAAP: Provisions and P&L

	German GAAP*	US GAAP	Adjustment effect
1990	DM 1.684bn	DM 1.684bn	+44%
1991	DM 1.872bn	DM 1.936bn	+3%
1992	DM 1.418bn	DM 2.192bn	+55%

* Net income minus net minority interests

US GAAP: Provisions and net assets

	German GAAP*	US GAAP	Adjustment effect
1991	DM 18.2bn	DM 25.2bn	+38%
1992	DM 18.5bn	DM 28.4bn	+54%

* Stockholders' equity net of minority interest

Figure 12.14 Daimler Benz: Provisions and P&L/net assets
Source: Goldman Sachs

US GAAP: Pensions and P&L

	German GAAP*	US GAAP	Adjustment effect
1990	DM 1.684bn	DM 1.531bn	-9%
1991	DM 1.872bn	DM 1.806bn	-4%
1992	DM 1.418bn	DM 1.514bn	+7%

* Net income minus net minority interests

US GAAP: Pensions and net assets

	German GAAP*	US GAAP	Adjustment effect
1991	DM 18.2bn	DM 17.2bn	-6%
1992	DM 18.5bn	DM 17.3bn	-7%

* Stockholders' equity net of minority interest

Figure 12.15 Daimler Benz: Pensions and P&L/net assets
Source: Goldman Sachs

US GAAP: Exchange rate and P&L

	German GAAP*	US GAAP	Adjustment effect
1990	DM 1.684bn	DM 1.730bn	+3%
1991	DM 1.872bn	DM 2.027bn	+8%
1992	DM 1.418bn	DM 1.324bn	-7%

Net income minus net minority interests

US GAAP: Exchange rate and net assets

	German GAAP*	US GAAP	Adjustment effect
1991	DM 18.2bn	DM 17.6bn	-3%
1992	DM 18.5bn	DM 18.1bn	-2%

Stockholders' equity net of minority interest

Figure 12.16 Daimler Benz: Exchange rate and P&L/net assets
Source: Goldman Sachs

US GAAP: Deferred taxes and P&L

	German GAAP*	US GAAP	Adjustment effect
1990	DM 1.684bn	DM 0.926bn	+45.0%
1991	DM 1.872bn	DM 1.746bn	+7.5%
1992	DM 1.418bn	DM 0.772bn	-45.6%

Net income minus net minority interests

US GAAP: Deferred taxes and net assets

	German GAAP*	US GAAP	Adjustment effect
1991	DM 18.2bn	DM 19.5bn	+7.1%
1992	DM 18.5bn	DM 18.4bn	-0.7%

Stockholders' equity net of minority interest

Figure 12.17 Daimler Benz: Deferred taxes and P&L/net assets
Source: Goldman Sachs

US GAAP: Goodwill and P&L			
	German GAAP*	**US GAAP**	**Adjustment effect**
1990	DM 1.684bn	DM 1.433bn	-15%
1991	DM 1.872bn	DM 1.602bn	-14%
1992	DM 1.418bn	DM 1.342bn	+5%

* Net income minus net minority interests

US GAAP: Goodwill and net assets			
	German GAAP*	**US GAAP**	**Adjustment effect**
1991	DM 18.2bn	DM 21.0bn	+15%
1992	DM 18.5bn	DM 20.4bn	+10%

* Stockholders' equity net of minority interest

Figure 12.18 Daimler Benz: Goodwill and P&L/net assets
Source: Goldman Sachs

■ 3. Currency

The treatment of currency translation is different under each system. Under US GAAP, assets and liabilities denominated in foreign currencies are translated at rates prevailing at the end of the accounting period. Gains and losses are charged to the income statement. Income statements are translated using average rates. Daimler Benz used historic rates for receivables and payables, unless period-end rates show a lower result. Unrealized currency losses are recognized currently while unrealized gains are deferred.

Figure 12.16 shows there is a slight over-statement of currency appreciation *vis-à-vis* US GAAP in 1992 in the P&L account and balance sheet.

■ 4. Deferred taxes

In line with the general conservatism of German accounting, Daimler had a much larger figure for deferred taxes than would have been allowable under US GAAP (see Figure 12.17).

■ 5. Goodwill

Goodwill can be charged either to shareholders' equity or capitalized and depreciated from 5 to 15 years in Germany. Daimler capitalized all its goodwill for US GAAP, and depreciated from 15 to 40 years.

	1991	**1992**
Stated net income		
German GAAP	19,448	19,719
Minorities	(1214)	(1228)
Adjusted net income		
German GAAP	18,234	18,491
Changes in:		
Provisions	6984	9931
Long-term contracts	188	131
Goodwill	2737	1871
Pensions et al	(1082)	(1212)
Foreign currencies	(624)	(342)
Financial instruments	134	580
Disposals	(490)	0
Deutsch Aerospace	1124	
Other	(1746)	(1708)
Deferred taxes	1286	(138)
Total changes	(8511)	9113
as of stated net income	47%	49%
US GAAP	26,745	27604

Figure 12.19 Daimler Benz: Stated shareholders equity
Source: Goldman Sachs

The results are shown in Figure 12.18.

When all the differences are summarized in one table (see Figure 12.19) they add up to a massive difference in the valuation of the company. Under German GAAP, in 1992, stated shareholders' equity was DM 18,491 and under US GAAP was DM 27,604, which is a 49 per cent difference amounting to DM 9.1bn.

There were reverberations after the Daimler Benz listing. The first and most obvious was a sudden interest by international investors in Daimler's stock, particularly by Americans. Before the listing, the company reckoned that between 5 per cent and 10 per cent of its equity was either US- or UK-owned. One of the objectives of the listing was to push foreign ownership, particularly American, to 10 per cent.

Secondly, it helped to explain why so few German companies are listed on the NYSE. If a corporation the size of Daimler Benz understates itself to this degree by American standards, it could be uncomfortable for it to reveal its hand to its German shareholders. Thirdly, it implied that the German market is a lot cheaper by international standards than was realized at the time. Fourthly, it begged the question as to why Daimler wanted to list its shares at all in the United States. It seemed to make itself unnecessarily naked to the world. The answer is probably (a) to increase the marketability of its shares and (b) in recognition of setting up a plant in the US with annual capacity of 60,000 cars.

As the world's economy 'globalizes', we are likely to see an increasing number of companies which had previously kept accounting details close to their chest, opening up to the scrutiny of outside financial analysis.

Chapter 13

Currency

In the early days of international investing in the United States, currency was often cited by pension plan sponsors as their single largest objection to investing internationally. It was common to be told by the sponsor that 'I really like the concept of international investing, but the Board do not like currency risk in the pension fund.'

A brief perusal of the portfolio of US equities held by the fund in question would reveal stocks like Boeing, Coca Cola, General Motors, Archer-Daniels-Midland, McDonalds and Ford; good American companies with no currency risk, because they were listed on the New York Stock Exchange. This was not quite accurate. There is more exposure to non-dollar currency fluctuations in many American multinationals than there is in many 'foreign' companies. Coca Cola, for instance, derives over 60 per cent of its revenues outside the US, whereas Hanson Trust of the UK derives approximately 50 per cent of its revenues in the United States. Arguably, Hanson Trust has less currency 'risk' to an American investor than Coca Cola has. It is all a matter of perception.

Analysts can make a career out of exploring the implicit and explicit currency risks of investing, and devising strategies to lower risk, or at least minimize the perception of risk in this area.

The common perception among many US investors is that it is an uncontrollable wild-card which can eliminate hard-earned equity profits. They see it as an instrument of speculation with high volatility. These observations need to be addressed. Currency is merely the unit in which a country's assets are denominated. The objective of international investing is to own equity assets that provide a real return above a stated benchmark. Such equity assets are generally part of that benchmark, and the currency in which they are denominated is also part of the benchmark. The currency may fluctuate, but the benchmark will fluctuate with it, thus providing no extra 'risk' against the benchmark. There is 'risk' against the home currency of the international investor, which will be addressed later.

Controlling currency risk

When Americans invest overseas against an EAFE benchmark, and the Japanese yen collapses against the dollar, it is not their concern that EAFE falls proportionally too. What they generally understand by 'risk' is an absolute loss against the dollar, and they are not mollified when they are told that their portfolio was currency-neutral against EAFE, therefore had no risk, even though it fell.

If an American investor has a diversified portfolio invested throughout the markets represented in the EAFE Index, there are various mechanisms for mitigating currency volatility. These were discussed from page 109, in the section on sector analysis and are summarized below.

- 1. If the dollar is expected to rise, portfolio cash should be kept in US dollars. If the dollar is expected to fall, cash should be kept in those currencies which are expected to rise.

- 2. If managers like US dollar-linked markets, such as Hong Kong, Malaysia, Singapore, or Australia, and the dollar is expected to rise, they would be advised to keep a full weighting in these markets because the portfolio would not be dented as the dollar rises.

- 3. A rising dollar can be beneficial for earnings in some markets, (see Chapter 12) and the rise in earnings could outpace the decline in local currency. US investors may be net better off in such markets than they perceive when the currency falls.

- 4. Manager should invest in dollar-sensitive stocks (see Chapter 12), if the dollar is expected to rise.

- 5. Managers may hedge currency risk by using forward currency contracts. If the dollar is expected to rise against the Deutschemark (DM), a contract can be executed to sell DM and buy it back in 60 or 90 days. If the decision proves correct, then the DM can be bought back more cheaply at the end of the contract, thus mitigating the dollar loss on DM-denominated assets in the portfolio.

    The expected event—a rising dollar—may not take place and the forward contract can go the opposite way. Managers may find themselves in the irritating position of buying back the DM at a higher rate than they sold it for. The problem with forward currency contracts is that their open-ended nature can prove costly.

    An alternative choice is to buy currency options. These are more expensive for the currency insurance obtained, but they have an overwhelming advantage over currency forwards, namely loss limitation. If options costing DM 200,000 are bought to cover a certain risk, and the currency does the opposite of what was expected, when the option expires, the manager will only lose DM 200,000. Options are exactly like insurance premiums, if the house burns down, you get your money back. If it doesn't burn down, some people may regard last year's fire insurance premium as a waste of money, but they will generally by grateful that the fire did not occur.

Currency options are liquid, tradeable and easily available on a number of exchanges. As noted earlier with regard to equity contracts, readers wishing to know what contracts are available should consult *The World's Futures & Options Markets*[1].

An equity investor should probably regard currency hedging as a defensive mechanism, not an operation to generate profits in its own right. Opinions differ widely on the subject, but the analysis in this section will be restricted to defensive hedging. The hedging strategies below are typical of those used by international equity managers:

- 1. Only execute covered hedges. In other words, if you have DM 10m worth of equities, hedge up to DM 10m and no further, into the US dollar (or appropriate base currency).

- 2. Avoid speculative cross-hedging. It is not unusual for managers to decide that a particular currency is under-valued and to boost holdings of that currency above the level of equities denominated in it. For instance, if the equity position in Japan is 40 per cent of an EAFE portfolio and managers are bullish on the yen, they can hold 40 per cent in the yen and also hedge other currencies into the yen in order to play on their hunch. There are cross-currency options and future strategies available to play this game (see footnote). It is theoretically possible to have 40 per cent in Japanese equities, 15 per cent in UK equities, 7 per cent in Germany, 7 per cent in France and 31 per cent in eight other countries, and for the entire portfolio to be denominated in yen. Such strategies are not recommended for equity managers because there is a significant risk against the benchmark—EAFE—which is unwarranted.

---

[1] *The World's Futures & Options Markets*, Nick Battley (Ed.) Probus Publishing ISBN 1 55738 513 0.

- 3. Hedging up to the benchmark. To continue the yen example: in January 1994, the Japanese stock market represented approximately 44 per cent of the EAFE Index. Whether or not managers held stocks in Japan, 44 per cent of the EAFE Index was denominated in yen. There is a case, to neutralize the risk of betting against the EAFE benchmark, for hedging the difference between what managers hold in Japan—say, 30 per cent—and the weighting of Japan in the EAFE Index. In other words, they can take out a hedge for 10 per cent of the portfolio to bring their yen weighting up to EAFE weight, and mitigate the currency risk of only having 30 per cent in Japanese yen. In this way, managers can have equity weights far away from EAFE weights, yet be currency-neutral *vis-à-vis* the index. This is a simple, yet elegant strategy.

- 4. Do not hedge at all. Some managers, particularly long-term value managers, take the view that currency hedging is an unnecessary and potentially expensive diversion from the business of international equity investing. Many currencies are virtually unhedgeable, particularly in emerging markets, so the managers go for real asset growth that is expected to outrun any currency depreciation over the long-term. There is some validity in this view. A glance at a long-term chart of the US dollar shows enormous swings against other currencies. At the time of President Carter and the oil crisis in the late 1970s, the dollar's trade-weighted value fell to a 20th century low. He appointed Paul Volcker as chairman of the Federal Reserve Bank, and the high interest rate policy that followed, combined with the fiscal stimulus provided by President Reagan's policies, led to a long climb by the dollar which culminated in early 1985. The G7[2] meeting in September 1985 conspired to hit the dollar, and accelerated its decline, which continued for the next few years. By 1989, the currency had round-tripped and was virtually back to where it started in 1980. For instance, in January 1981, the dollar/sterling rate was: US$2.43:£1. In January 1985, it was US$1.03/£1. By early 1992, it was around US$2/£1.

Long-term managers oblivious to currency swings would have found that they had a tough time in dollar terms with an international portfolio from 1981 to 1985, and a fantastic run from 1985 through 1988. The ten-year effect was arguably neutral.

---

[2] *G7 is the so-called group of seven industrialized countries: the USA, Japan, Germany, France, Britain, Italy and Canada.*

Conclusion

Currency risk is quite controllable, and the fears of potential international investors are usually unwarranted in the longer term. The key is for investment managers to ensure that they have an understanding of their clients' risk-tolerances and a good grip of the mechanics of currency management.

The use of cash in international equity portfolios

Some managers take the view that they are paid to invest the money fully in the asset class in which they operate. If a large US pension fund allocates money to invest in Europe, measured against a European benchmark, it is fair to presume that the pension fund has already made its own decisions as to cash requirements and that the account should be fully invested. Levels of cash should always be discussed with clients at the outset of a relationship.

Holding cash can be a big risk if the objective is to beat a non-cash benchmark. Having said that, cash needs to be managed in its own right. Factors to be considered are:

- 1. The currency in which the cash is held;
- 2. What the interest-rate is;
- 3. Whether the interest is subject to withholding taxes and if so their rate;
- 4. If the cash is held or a term-deposit, how long is it to be held;
- 5. How to measure the cash component of the portfolio;
- 6. How good is the credit of the bank taking the deposit.

As with every component of a portfolio, cash management should be undertaken with an eye to relative and absolute performance, and done with consummate care.

PART IV

Some administrative considerations

Chapter 14

Global custody

The 'back-office' side of international investing is not glamorous, and tends to be unsung. If investment managers are the combat troops or 'top guns' of the industry, custodians are the logisticians, without whom the war would grind to a halt.

A lot of graduates aspire to be portfolio managers. Few appear to aspire to be global custodians. Perhaps this chapter will help demonstrate the fascination of the subject.

What is global custody?

By law, and certainly by good practice, investment managers must segregate the assets they manage into discrete pools, separate from their own assets and those of other clients. All pension assets in the United States must be held by a custodian appointed by the pension fund itself. The primary relationship is between pension fund and custodian, not between manager and custodian (although this relationship is operationally critical). An investment manager may recommend a particular custodian, but the decision to hire one lies with the pension fund, which is also responsible for paying the custodian for its services. Custody is a more than the simple safekeeping of share certificates. It amounts to the total logistical control of pension assets. Some of the major functions are shown below.

Custody reporting

Pension funds contract to receive periodic accounts from their money managers. The custodian must provide reports to funds, so that they can reconcile figures from all sources. There are often discrepancies between sources, because of timing differences in valuing the portfolios. For example, if the investment manager values the portfolios of equities at the closing time of each stock market in the world, and the currencies in which they are denominated at 3 pm, New York time, the result can be different from that of the custodian who values equities at the market close and currency close in each local market. These discrepancies tend to wash out over several quarters, but it is necessary to understand the nature of discrepancies and provide a fail-safe system so that the pension fund can keep its managers honest. It is one of the reasons why a custodian should be independent from the managers. The custodial function includes the reporting of activity and failed trades in each period, dividend and tax reclaim accruals and collection, corporate actions, proxy notification and securities loaned.

Valuation reporting

For clients such as mutual funds, this function must be done daily. It can entail a complex logistical exercise with a US-based mutual fund, which has a net-asset-value (NAV) that must be calculated daily. A typical procedure could be as follows:

- i) AM European time: close-of-business prices are reported from Japan, Hong Kong, Singapore, Australia and other Far Eastern financial centres.

- ii) PM European time: close-of-business prices are reported from European equity markets.

- iii) PM Central Standard Time (or when available) in the United States: close-of-business prices reported in from the Latin American and Canadian markets.

    These prices are initially reported to the custodian in local currency terms. Close-of-business New York exchange rates are then applied to the portfolio of each country, and a US dollar NAV for the fund is calculated in the late afternoon in the United States for reporting to Nasdaq and publication in the mutual fund columns of the financial press the next day.

How a US$1bn mutual fund portfolio invested in 18 countries around the globe can come up with a dealing price every working day is something to be marvelled at. A one-cent shift in NAV often masks massive underlying market shifts and is the culmination of a daily logistical miracle. Considering it took about a month of number-crunching with a 'comptometer' to calculate the value of a Scottish trust fifty years ago, it should it appreciated how far we have come. This has been accomplished by the unsung heroes of our business: custodian banks and, of course, the processing power of mainframes.

Network management

The way this daily miracle is accomplished is that custodians have built a network of sub-custodians around the world. There are 20 markets in the EAFE Index and 20 markets in the IFC Investable Index. There are at least 20 other markets in the world at various stages of investability, from Nigeria to Poland, in which managers are beginning to invest.

To be credible, the custodian bank must have a sub-custodial arrangement with a bank or an agent in every market in which the manager invests money for clients. This can be a formidable number of relationships, each one of which must be up to scratch technologically to provide the required daily flow of information and enable pricing to be done accurately.

For example, Chase Manhattan Bank has invested hundreds of millions of dollars in developing its global custody network. By 1993, it had agent banks in the following 44 countries:

Argentina	Luxembourg	France	South Korea	UK
Australia	Germany	Malaysia	Spain	USA
Austria	Greece	Mexico	Sri Lanka	Venezuela
Belgium	Hong Kong	Netherlands	Sweden	
Brazil	Hungary	New Zealand	Switzerland	
Canada	India	Norway	Taiwan	
Chile	Indonesia	Pakistan	Thailand	
China	Ireland	Peru	Turkey	
Colombia	Italy	Philippines	Switzerland	
Denmark	Japan	Portugal	Taiwan	
Finland	Jordan	Singapore	Thailand	

Some of these banks are unrelated correspondent banks, such as Credit Lyonnais in Brussels, Toronto Dominion in Canada or Kansallis-Osake-Pankki in Finland. Others are owned by Chase, such as Chase Manhattan, NA Buenos Aires or the Chase Manhattan Bank in Bangkok.

In 1980, Colin Grimsey, who ran Chase Manhattan's global custody network, described the logistics of one typical trading relationship. At that time, US pension fund assets had to be held under US securities law in the vaults of a branch of a US bank. Australian banking law did not permit foreign branch banking, so it was not possible for US-owned pension securities to be held in Australia after a trade. The securities had to be sent to Chase's Hong Kong branch for safe-keeping. Given the difference in settlement times between markets, and given that settlement in some markets can only take place on delivery of stock, such arrangements proved highly cumbersome.

Fourteen years later, settlement is less of a problem—in Australia at least. In the early 1980s, US securities law changed to permit the use of designated sub-custodians where US banks did not have branches. Banks like ANZ in Australia began to take on sub-custodial work for American banks. Then, Australian banking laws changed to allow foreign banks to set up in Australia. Today, Chase has its own branch in Sydney.

The importance of an efficient network is further stressed by different settlement procedures and modes of owning stock in each country. For example, in Argentina, stock is registered in the client's name. In Austria, there are only bearer shares, while in Australia, stock is registered under a custodian bank's nominee name. Each market has its own ownership requirements. In Chile, the stock is registered in the investment company's name. In Denmark, most stock is bearer, but some stock has to be registered in the custodian bank's name. In 44 stock markets there are 44 sets of regulations and 44 sets of practical quirks that must be mastered to operate efficiently. Figure 14.1 shows the number of sub-custodians in 20 markets in 1993.

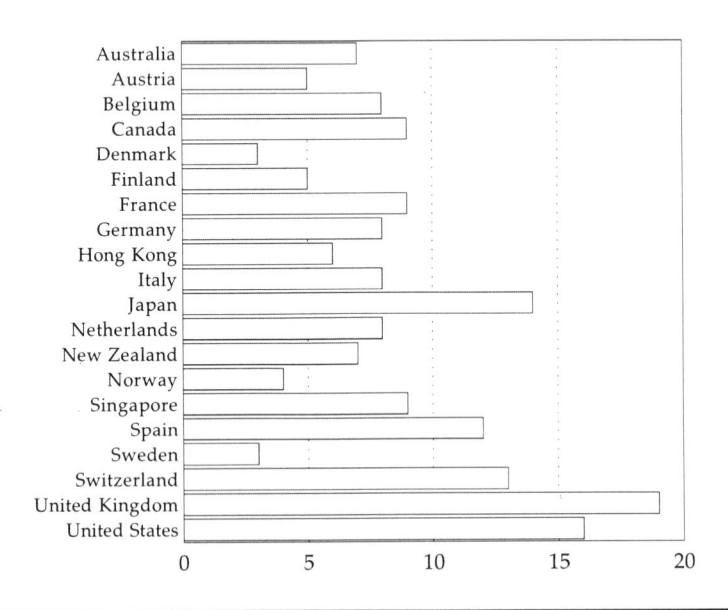

Figure 14.1 Number of sub-custodians by market - 1993
Source: Global Custodian

Settlement

The ease of settlement is one of the greatest concerns of a portfolio manager. Different markets periodically carry the accolade of 'investment roach motel—you can check in, but can't check out.' The Philippines, Italy, Turkey and a variety of new emerging markets have had settlement problems over the years that merit this title.

It is not always just the skills of a custodian bank that determine smooth settlement of trades. It depends on the number of parties to a trade and local conditions. Pre-settlement activity or setting-up the trade is vital, and many questions must be answered, such as:

- 1. When trade instructions have to be received by custodians;

- 2. What procedures are in place for verifying the accuracy of data and communicating information to sub-custodians;

- 3. If a trade fails to settle on the expected date, what procedures are in place for ascertaining why the trade failed;

- 4. How managers are kept up to date with the status of failed trades.

Figure 14.2 shows the percentage of trades settled on time in 1993 in a survey of banks by Global Custodian. No market has a 100 per cent success record, which underlines the degree of frustration that can potentially fly around the investment management community and the importance of custodian banks in tightening up the settlement process world-wide.

It is interesting to see that Italy had such a high settlement rate in 1993. Italy had a reputation for poor settlement procedures in the mid-1980s, when the market began to attract serious investor interest from overseas. Italy was not computerized to handle the surge of trading volume then, but has since addressed the problems. Italy was not a big volume market in 1993, however, and was not attracting the surge of international investors that it attracted in 1984/1985.

Safe-keeping

The safe-keeping process includes dividend collection, tax reclaim notification, proxy voting services and the notification and control of corporate actions. Dividend collection speaks for itself, but dividends become an instant tax event in most countries. The custodian's job is to ensure that clients are correctly registered with local tax authorities so that withholding tax is not greater than absolutely necessary. Appendix D shows the withholding tax

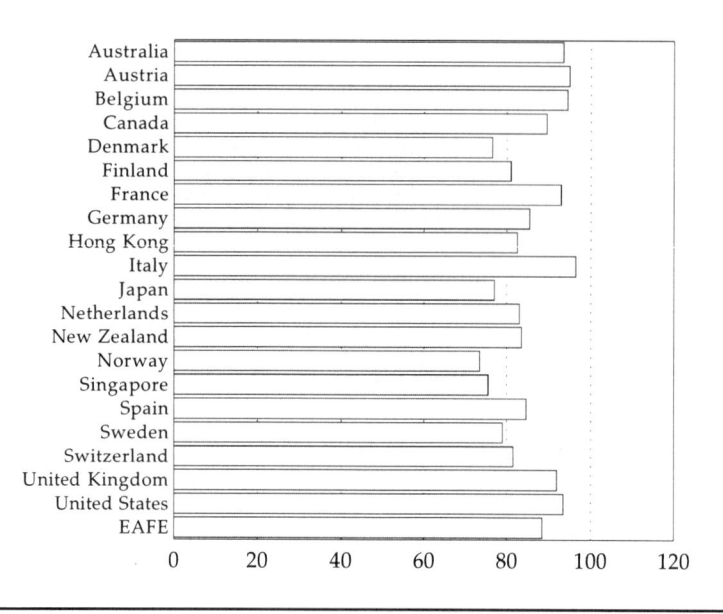

Figure 14.2 Number of trades on settlement date - 1993
Source: Global Custodian

profiles for two broad categories of investor in various markets: taxable and tax exempt.

Proxy voting services are increasingly important in the US pension world. Most large institutions want to know how managers vote proxies on their behalf. Some institutions will direct managers to vote along certain lines on some issues, such as the environment or other aspects of corporate governance. Custodians can monitor this process. The notification and control of corporate actions, keeping on top of rights issues, stock splits, stock buy-backs, underwritings, placings and new offers is a key part of the custodial function. Investment managers advise custodians of their participation and instruct what action is to be taken on behalf of the pension funds.

Cash administration

Even when interest rates are low around the world, huge cash balances exist in portfolios that must be put to work effectively. The performance measurement agencies will judge managers on the effectiveness of their cash management exactly as they are measured on their equity selection in

Australia or Japan. Most custodian banks offer sweep accounts to ensure that cash earns a competitive rate of interest in whatever currency is designated, and ensure that the cash is accessible when managers are ready to invest in equities. Managers are not always obliged to use the cash management services of the custodian bank, so custodians tends to offer competitive rates.

Foreign exchange

Most international custody banks will provide a foreign exchange (forex) function, but again, managers are generally not obliged to use a particular custodian for forex, and must seek 'best execution' wherever possible. Such shopping around often means that the custodian will match competitive bids from elsewhere.

Securities lending

Securities lending is an esoteric practice that is becoming more popular as a way for institutional investors to enhance portfolio returns. Within five years it will probably be the rule rather than the exception among larger investors, because the liquidity and acceptability of the concept will be more universal. In fact, fiduciaries may well be challenged if they do not allow their securities to be lent in this way.

Why do investors participate in securities lending?

- a) As lenders. investors can increase portfolio returns by generating fee income on their otherwise dormant securities.

- b) As borrowers, it offers the convenient use of securities which are not in their possession when required. For example: (1) If they wish to sell short (sell securities they don't own) to take advantage of an anticipated price drop. (2) If they need to avoid settlement defaults on securities already sold by the borrower to effect a timely settlement. (3) If they wish to participate in various arbitrage and hedging strategies, such as index arbitrage, options or warrant trading.

Typical securities-lending structure

Typically, the lending institution enters into a securities lending programme managed by an intermediary (usually a custodian bank). It is advisable to go with an intermediary with size and experience, which can monitor and control the quality of the borrowing institution and manage the collateral in each deal. The list below shows the top equity lenders in a poll by International Securities Lending in June 1993:

1. State Street
2. Wells Fargo
3. UBS
4. London Global Securities
5. JP Morgan
6. Barclays Cater Allen
7. Paribas
8. SBC Zurich
9. Paine Webber
10. Bankers Trust Company

Ideally, the intermediary bank should also be the custodian of the institutional assets that it lends.

Once an institution signs up for a programme, the intermediary is entitled to borrow securities from the pool of securities of the lender, against provision of collateral and payment of a fee. The intermediary then offers its lending programme to potential borrowers.

Borrowers must put up collateral for the transaction. Cash, securities or irrevocable letters of credit issued by approved banks are the accepted form of collateral. Collateral requirements vary around the world, but they are usually from 102 per cent to 110 per cent of the amount borrowed.

The intermediary should mark to market the collateral on outstanding loans on a daily basis, preferably requiring a same-day settlement requirement on the part of the borrower. This is to protect the lender against complications.

During the period of the contract, the lender is entitled to dividends, interest and other distributions relating to the securities on loan. The borrower is entitled to the benefits generated by the collateral.

For international securities lending to operate effectively, the intermediary should be well represented in the major financial centres. Chase Manhattan, for example, has an agent network in over 100 countries. This would minimize operating errors, against an intermediary which does not have a well-tried network.

Figure 14.3 shows the typical flow of a transaction, with the intermediary in the centre, controlling the relationship between lender and borrower, managing the collateral, collecting and disbursing fees.

There are many tax and legal implications in the practice of securities lending, and it is the job of the custodian bank to lead practitioners through

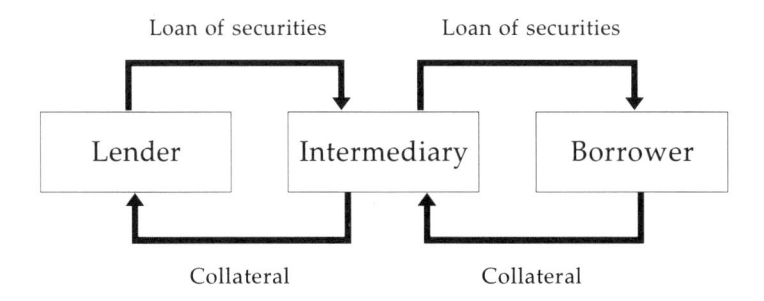

```
                Loan of securities        Loan of securities
          ┌──────────────────┐      ┌──────────────────┐
          │                  ▼      │                  ▼
   ┌──────────┐        ┌──────────────┐        ┌──────────┐
   │  Lender  │        │ Intermediary │        │ Borrower │
   └──────────┘        └──────────────┘        └──────────┘
          ▲                  │      ▲                  │
          └──────────────────┘      └──────────────────┘
                 Collateral                Collateral
```

Figure 14.3   Typical flow of a transaction
Source: Baker & MacKenzie

the maze. One risk in cross-border transactions is that withholding taxes, which might not be reclaimed by the lender, may be imposed on payments.

The acceptability of securities lending varies around the world. In Italy, for example, many banks are reluctant to act as intermediaries because securities lending is unregulated. They fear that they could be caught retrospectively for violating banking laws. Foreign banks with international securities lending experience operate freely in Italy, although the greatest volume of lending is with Italian government bonds, not equities. The Italian tax consequences of lending is unclear, because the Ministry of Finance, tax courts, and politicians have not addressed them. Once the practice is more widely accepted, it is likely that the Italian tax treatment of securities lending will become similar to that in the UK, where the practice of securities lending has a distinct body of law under which it operates. English law tries to ensure that the outright transfer of assets which a securities lending transaction creates, should put each party in the same position as they would have been in if they had a security interest over the asset transferred, without actually creating such an interest. Protection is given to each party by the rules of set-off and the terms of the securities lending agreement.

Persons engaging in securities lending in the UK are covered either by the Securities and Futures Association (SFA) or the Investment Management Regulatory Organization (IMRO). Conduct of business rules are clearly defined for operators in this market-place. Unlike Italy, there is also detailed legislation relating to the tax treatment of securities lending transactions.

Most countries have their own rules relating to securities lending, and it is the custodian's job to ensure that the process is undertaken correctly for each client, with regard to all the relevant legislations around the world.

Who is eligible?

The securities lending institution should have securities that someone else wants to borrow. An intermediary would normally be interested only in larger institutions, probably in excess of US$100m. The reason is that at any one time only 25 per cent of the portfolio may be on loan, and the fees generated by smaller portfolios (a) may not be interesting to the intermediary relative to the paperwork, and (b) may not be interesting to the lender relative to the risk. Typically, a lender should expect a fee of 0.25 per cent to 0.50 per cent for the loan of its securities. One quarter of a per cent on 25 per cent of the portfolio is not of great interest to many clients, unless they are 'indexers', in which case a small pickup of this size over index returns could be a very useful piece of extra return. This is probably why State Street and Wells Fargo are considered the top equity lenders. They are also the largest index managers in the business.

Client servicing

The top global custodians are mainly American world-wide banks which have parleyed the position they have as US custodians into a world-wide dominance. They will only retain that position through servicing their clients. This ranges from keeping their clients up to date with technology advances, sending newsletters, setting out developments in markets around the world and being generally creative to meet the challenges of evolving and emerging markets. In a business where large chunks of pension money are at stake, custodians must always demonstrate that they are on top of the assets entrusted to them. Many have set up enquiry control centres, which guarantee a client response within 24 hours.

Conclusion

Figure 14.4 shows the results of the Global Custodian 'Roll of Honour' survey for 1992 and 1993, showing the performance of 15 custodian banks in 12 categories.

☆ = 1992; ★ = 1993	Experience organization control	Client service	Custody reporting	Valuation reporting	Network management	Settlement	Safekeeping	Cash administration	Foreign exchange	Securities lending	Operations technology	Client technology	
ABN-AMRO	★	☆				☆	★		★				ABN-AMRO
Bank of New York	★			☆	★		☆★	★	☆	☆★		☆	Bank of New York
Bankers Trust	☆	☆★	★	★	☆★			★			☆	★	Bankers Trust
BBH		★	☆	☆★	★								BBH
Boston Safe							★		★	☆		☆★	Boston Safe
Chase Manhattan	☆★	☆★	☆★			☆★					☆★	☆	Chase Manhattan
Chemical					☆		★						Chemical
Citibank	☆★		★			★			☆★		☆★		Citibank
Midland		☆	★		☆			☆					Midland
JP Morgan	★								☆★		☆★		JP Morgan
Northern Trust			☆	☆		★	☆★	☆★	☆	☆★		☆	Northern Trust
RB of Scotland								☆★					RB of Scotland
Royal Trust		★											Royal Trust
State Street		☆★	★	☆★	★	☆		☆		★		★	State Street
SG Warburg						★	☆				★		SG Warburg

Figure 14.4 Global Custodian 'Roll of Honour' survey for 1992 and 1993
Source: Global Custodian

Chapter 15

Corporate governance and social screening

There is increasing awareness and pressure among the trustees of major US and UK pension funds, foundations and mutual funds (unit trusts) to subscribe to 'good corporate governance.' This is an expression that describes the relationship between a company's owners (shareholders) and its management. In the UK the Cadbury Committee on the Financial Aspects of Corporate Governance urged pension funds to exercise their voting rights in relation to the shares of the companies they own to ensure the desired stewardship of their assets. It could be argued that if you do not like the management of a company, you should sell your shareholding. This is fine for a small shareholder, but once a pension fund reaches a few billion in size, it is not easy simply to sell out of a position. It could severely prejudice the value of a shareholding if a sizeable sell order were made. So shareholder voting is being increasingly encouraged to influence the desired changes in companies.

The Cadbury Committee produced a 'Code of Best Practice' for company managements to follow (see Appendix B for the text). Not least, the recommendations of the committee were intended to prevent future episodes such as the one when Robert Maxwell treated a public company and its pension fund as his personal fiefdom.

In the United States, many pension funds insist on knowing how their managers vote proxies. Sometimes, funds issue guidelines for the managers to follow. In 1990, there were 170 social proxies on the ballot of major corporations. In 1991, there were 210. The number was threatening to explode, so the US Securities and Exchange Commission (SEC) applied the rule that resolutions pertaining to less than 5 per cent of a company's activities are not significant, and can therefore be excluded from the proxy ballot (Rule 14a-8). This discourages activists who feel strongly about a tiny aspect of a corporation's business from disrupting annual meetings

Social proxies can relate to a wide range of issues, from South Africa to minority rights, the environment and the manufacturing of weapons systems. Fortunately the South African issue is now less important, with the dismantlement of apartheid.

In the UK, a leading consulting group which advises on corporate governance is Pension Investment Research Consultants (PIRC). They have issued a 'PIRC Statement of Principles', the text of which is given below:[1]

> 1. Shareholders should assume the responsibilities of ownership. This does not entail intervening in daily management tasks but in setting standards and guidelines for corporate activity.
>
> 2. Shareholders have three primary interests. The first is to protect their rights as shareholders. The second is to ensure that corporate governance practice is consistent with protecting shareholder assets. The third is to promote good governance in order to enhance long-term value.
>
> 3. Shareholder voting rights are an asset. They need managing with the same duty of care as any other asset. Exercising the rights attached to shares is essential to protect the long-term interests of the beneficiaries.
>
> 4. Shareholder voting rights should be exercised on an informed and independent basis. Voting guidelines should be developed in order to establish a consistent approach on both routine and exceptional issues so that management fully understand shareholder intentions.
>
> 5. A company's success in the long-term is dependent upon it fully addressing its responsibilities to all stakeholders including employees and the communities within which they operate. This gives shareholders an interest in companies adhering to high standards of excellence in social, ethical and environmental matters.

The area of social screening of investments remains in its infancy, and the ethical assumptions under which economic activity takes place are evolving continuously.

Many of Britain's great country houses were built from the proceeds of piracy, looting, corruption or slavery. In the 16th century, national heroes like Sir Francis Drake caused great amusement in England by 'singeing the King of Spain's beard', but in today's terms he would be on the CIA's 'Most Wanted' list for piracy, terrorism and general mayhem. They would at least be able to rap him for tax evasion, or under RICO. At the time, his activities were considered fair game—by the English, at any rate.

---

[1] *Source: Pension Investment Research Consultants.*

In the 18th century, it was considered fashionable for a young man to make his fortune in the West Indies sugar trade on the back of slave labour. He would return to rural Scotland in mid-life and commission a Palladian house from Robert Adam, Playfair or Craig and lead a God-fearing life on his estates. Times were harsher then, but there was little comment given to the contradictions of such behaviour at the time.

In the 19th century, slavery was abolished in the Anglo-Saxon world, to be replaced by a form of indentured slavery in the factories of the Industrial Revolution. There were voices, such as JS Mill, Karl Marx and William Blake speaking against the inhumanity of conditions, but the social and environmental mess was generally accepted as a concomitant of doing business.

Wars tend to brutalize attitudes. The deadly urgency of producing industrial weapons and material, from the American Civil War through the First World War, created the vast military-industrial complex that fuelled the Second World War. It is only in the 1990s that the relative scale of production of weaponry is decelerating, and, just perhaps, national industrial machines can be turned to peaceful purposes.

The underlying rivalries and political tensions of the world in the last century have often precluded the delicacy of social investing.

In 1992, it was estimated that over US$500bn of US institutional money was invested according to some ethical screen or other.[1] Most of it was invested in the United States, but a significant portion was being earmarked for international investing. In 1992, The Calvert World Values Global Fund was launched in the United States. It was among the first US mutual funds to apply social screens to investments outside the United States and divided screens into two categories: 'aspirational screens' and 'avoidance criteria'.

Aspirational screens

Aspirational screens are those that investors might aspire to include in a portfolio. Three areas were singled out for investment.

- *1. The environment*
  Companies providing innovative solutions to environmental problems through products, processes and services, as well as companies with clear policies in support of sustainable development, environmental preservation, energy conservation, renewable or alternative energy sources.

---

[1] *Source: Blairlogie Capital Management.*

- *2. Healthcare*
  Companies providing their employees or 'a segment of the global population' with quality, affordable healthcare.

- *3. Human rights*
  This is a somewhat nebulous criterion, but includes such areas as minority enhancement, 'promoting social and economic justice', community outreach and equal rights for women.

Avoidance screens

- Companies providing strategic goods to repressive regimes;

- Companies deriving over 10 per cent of their revenues from tobacco, alcoholic beverages, or weapons systems;

- Companies deriving income from any aspect of nuclear weapons or the nuclear power industry;

- Egregious polluters or businesses not subscribing to 'generally accepted environmental standards'.

South Africa was on most avoidance screens until the Mandela/de Klerk accord was signed in 1993 committing that country to free elections. Many pension funds that prohibited any form of investing in South Africa then began to loosen investment restrictions. The Investor Responsibility Research Centre (IRRC) in Washington DC monitors companies world-wide with South African revenues, direct or indirect. It was the IRRC criteria that US pension funds would follow most assiduously when avoiding South African investment.

It is questionable how effective the South African investment ban actually was in bringing down apartheid. Some would argue that the Sullivan Principles, and ultimately, full sanctions, accentuated the pain at the bottom of the social scale, and that it was demographic pressures that forced political change, not sanctions.

Making a moral judgement about a country and tilting a portfolio accordingly is a treacherous path to take. It would not be difficult to find many other candidates for exclusion, such as companies doing business in Northern Ireland (The MacBride Principles) or the former Soviet Union (Slepak Principles). Why not exclude Norway, because it has resumed whaling, or Japan for the same reason? Why not exclude France for occupying Tahiti and French Guyana? Indeed, why not castigate the United States and Canada for their treatment of Native Americans? Or Germany, Italy and Russia for their re-nascent fascism?

There is a potential *reductio ad absurdum* in this line of thought so it is probably advisable to avoid being drawn into the debate.

Social screening and international investing

It takes a brave investor to take on all the screens described above and attempt to construct a portfolio that has a good chance of beating a recognizable Index. It could turn out to be a ragbag portfolio of environmental stocks and high P/E companies in the few industries that qualify. Nonetheless, the trend towards social screening is picking up, and many US and UK pension funds now insist on a degree of social screening from their managers.

What has been observed is selectivity in the choice of screens. Some pension funds want screens relating to 'sin stocks', others want a pro-active environmental approach. It is rare to find funds that want more than a handful of screens. For instance, there is a US religious charity that specifically excludes tobacco stocks and companies not subscribing to the MacBride Principles, but 'you can have as much alcohol as you like' in the portfolio.

Many screens are culturally biased, and it is not realistic to expect companies around the world to subscribe to norms devised according to American political correctness. Suggesting minority or female representation on Japanese boards might be met with puzzlement, as it might in other culturally and racially homogeneous countries. It is more realistic to see how companies operate within their domestic cultural norms, before insisting on the application of American values to their activities.

Environmental investing

Of all the social screens, environmental ones cause the least controversy. There will always be utilities or chemical companies which claim they are over-regulated, but generally it is agreed that clean air, clean water and safe working conditions are desirable.

The trend among institutional investors towards environmentally-sound or 'green' international investing is going to become increasingly important as the 1990s progress. In April 1992, a 'Tokyo Declaration' was released by a group of statesmen in Japan, at a meeting hosted by former Prime Minister Takeshita. The Declaration called for a 're-evaluation of the thinking which underlies our present society' and the adoption of 'new environmental ethics.' The Japanese are beginning to take a lead in this area, and are becoming more conscious of destructive fishing techniques and the environmental cost of economic success.

The June 1992 Earth Summit, in Rio de Janeiro, attempted to codify acceptable environmental behaviour and recommended world-wide carbon taxes to reduce emissions, as well as penalties for pollution on companies and communities that have unacceptable behaviour (as defined).

In 1994, the British government raised gasoline taxes and imposed value-added tax (VAT) of 17.5 per cent on domestic heating fuel; citing it as a contribution to carbon dioxide (CO_2) reduction. Although the government claims the tax is environmentally motivated, cynics might argue that they have a conveniently 'green' excuse for adding yet another tax. With a budget deficit of 6.9 per cent of GNP and a record of dubious economic husbandry, the British government is strapped and no doubt would welcome the excuse to tax anything on socially-acceptable grounds.

If anything positive came out of the Exxon Valdez incident when an Exxon oil tanker was wrecked on the Alaska coast in 1989, it was the Valdez Principles, drawn up by a group of social investors and environmentalists. It seems clear that an increasing number of socially-conscious investors will begin insisting on corporate adherence to these principles in the United States, and to something similar in the foreign companies that they invest in. The Valdez Principles were soon re-named the CERES Principles, for the Coalition for Environmentally Responsive Economies.

Many of the CERES Principles relate to simple, good corporate husbandry. They are not necessarily onerous requirements, but courses of action that could help a company tighten up its operations and get more mileage from limited resources than it did before. A company that conserves non-renewable materials, becomes more energy-efficient, and reduces hazardous wastes is more likely to be innovative and more productive over time—and therefore viable for the long-term—than a company that has a more profligate approach to its resources.

The CERES Principles are set out below:[1]

- 1. *Protection of the biosphere*
  Signatories will try to eliminate pollutants that damage the air, water, or earth.

- 2. *Sustainable use of natural resources*
  They pledge to use renewable resources, conserve renewable materials, and preserve biological diversity.

- 3. *Reduction and disposal of wastes*
  They pledge to minimize and safely dispose of hazardous wastes.

---

[1] 'The Socially Responsive Portfolio', by James Melton & Matthew Keenan, Probus Publishing.

Corporate governance & social screening 165

- *4. Wise use of energy*
  They call for energy-efficient products and processes.

- *5. Risk reduction*
  They pledge to reduce environmental risks and prepare for emergency action in the event of accidents.

- *6. The manufacture and sale of safe products and services*
  They pledge to disclose the environmental impact of products and services.

- *7. Damage compensation*
  They pledge to make good environmental damage and compensate for human injury.

- *8. Disclosure*
  They pledge to disclose accidents and hazards and to protect employees who report them.

- *9. Environmental directors and managers*
  Corporate signatories agree to at least one board member being an environmental expert. A senior executive for environmental affairs should also be appointed.

- *10. Assessment and annual audit*
  They pledge to carry out an environmental audit of their world-wide operations which will be made public.

The CERES Board of Directors added a Disclaimer to the Principles, that was adopted in April 1992. It stated: 'These Principles establish an environmental ethic with criteria by which investors and others can assess the environmental performance of companies. Companies that sign these Principles pledge to go voluntarily beyond the requirements of the law. These Principles are not intended to create new legal liabilities, expand existing rights or obligations, waive legal defences, or otherwise affect the legal position of any signatory company, and are not intended to be used against a signatory in any legal proceeding for any purpose.'

Portfolio consequences of social investing

It is useful to be able to quantify, at the outset of the relationship, the benchmark risks of taking a social stance in a portfolio so that clients know managers are doing a good job, even if they should underperform a more conventional benchmark.

In the United States, the Domini Social Index (DSI) is the leading equity index against which to measure portfolios with social constraints. It consists of 400 stocks which have passed social screens, including product quality, corporate citizenship and treatment of women and minorities. Using BARRA's Performance Analysis package, the DSI outperformed the S&P 500 from 1 May 1990 (inception) to 30 September 1992 (period of study). BARRA's conclusion over this short period was that social investing can provide above average returns, but that the portfolio risks are quite high: the DSI had a beta of 1.06 against the S&P 500.

Another point to consider is how an international manager can get the information on companies to construct an adequately screened portfolio.

Firstly, many companies have 'corporate affairs' policies which are stated in their annual reports or in separate documents. Nestlé, Fisher and Paykel, Glaxo and many others are in this category.

Secondly, an increasing number of companies are voluntarily producing environmental reports on their activities. They are not legally obliged to do so, but KPMG found that 15 per cent of 690 companies world-wide which responded to their recent survey published environmental reports.

Thirdly, some stock broking firms will carry out social screening to supplement their financial analysis of companies, in response to increasing investor demand.

Fourthly, each investment firm must satisfy itself as to the quality of screening it does. This can be helped by sending a 'corporate governance questionnaire' to companies, supplemented by asking questions when they meet company managements.

Fifthly, it pays to keep an eye open for public declarations and statements by companies, which help to define their activities to corporate governance. Appendix C contains the text of a splendid Declaration by 30 banks from across the world, sponsored by National Westminster Bank plc. The accompanying statement by the Royal Bank of Scotland is worthy of note, and confirms its interest in environmental matters.

Chapter 16

International performance measurement

International investment managers and their clients need to know how well their portfolios are performing. This is one of the differences between a professional and an amateur. Amateurs may just be pleased to be in the game and enjoy the reflected light of a bull market. Professionals should demand to know how they are doing—relatively and absolutely.

The investment arena is intensely competitive and attitudes to performance measurement are becoming increasingly sophisticated. There are three questions that institutional clients should pose at the end of each reporting period. These are:

- 1. Did the account beat the agreed benchmark?

- 2. Did the manager beat his peer group?

- 3. How was that performance achieved?

Benchmark

At the beginning of an investment management relationship, an agreement letter or contract should stipulate the benchmark against which the manager will be measured. For example, a US pension fund investing overseas will tend to stipulate that the manager should beat the MSCI EAFE Index. Emerging market mandates are expected to beat the IFC Investable Index, and so forth. I have been involved in managing assets for clients in the past who have given us American money to invest overseas and stipulated that we should beat the S&P 500 or the US inflation rate (CPI) by 5 per cent in real terms each year. One of these was funded in 1984, just before the US dollar collapsed against the major European and Japanese currencies, inflation was low and the world was in a bullish mood, so beating inflation in the late 1980s was easy. Nevertheless, it is a risky proposition taking on business in Asset Class A which has the objective of beating an index that represents Asset Class B.

There are many single-country mandates being made by European pension funds and insurance companies. For instance, a Swedish insurance company wishing to invest a defined percentage of its assets in the UK will tend to hire a British fund manager with the objective of beating the FTSE All Share Index. Or a Dutch pension fund investing in the United States will tend to hire an American manager to beat the Standard & Poor's 500 Index.

It does not much matter what clients stipulate, but it is critical that managers invest with an eye to the relevant index. As mentioned earlier in the book, expecting managers to beat one benchmark by restricting them to the assets of another is not scientific; it is like real estate managers who spice up performance by investing in pork belly contracts—they may beat the real estate index handsomely, but run a great risk both to themselves and, more importantly, to their clients. The Financial Times has a daily listing of the world's equity indices, and more esoteric indices can be obtained from stockbrokers dealing in individual markets. Some representative indices are listed below.

- *World Index:*
  Morgan Stanley Capital International World Index (MSCIWI)

- *Europe, Australia, Far East:*
  Morgan Stanley Capital International Europe, Australia, Far East Index (MSCI EAFE)

- *Emerging Markets:*
  International Finance Corporation Investable (IFC Investable)

- *Latin America:*
  International Finance Corporation Latin America (IFCL)

- *Smaller Asian Markets:*
  International Finance Corporation Asia Index (IFCA)

Note: MSCI also have indices which cover other market areas, including in Latin America and smaller Asian markets.

It should be further noted that indices have many imperfections relative to the real world. Firstly, an index is always fully invested. The EAFE Index has no cash in it, so a manager holding cash is taking an automatic, explicit, risk against the index.

Secondly, there are no imputed trading costs in an index. If Japan falls relative to Germany and France, the index is automatically readjusted. In the real world, such adjustments cost money, in the shape of broking and custodial transaction costs.

Thirdly, there are no taxes levied in an index. It will not reflect dividend withholding taxes or the expenses of reclaiming them incurred by the custodian. There are no stamp duties imputed on weighting shifts in an index, or capital gains levies.

Fourthly, there are no investment management fees levied against an index.

At this point, readers should note that Appendix D contains representative indices in the world markets.

Country indices tend to be capitalization-weighted, which is to say that they are the aggregate of the market capitalization of the companies listed in the underlying markets. For instance, the Belgium 20 is the largest 20 companies listed on the Brussels Stock Exchange, by market capitalization.

Some managers are distrustful of capitalization-weighted indices because they may not reflect the productive capacity of the underlying economy accurately. When the Tokyo stock market represented 64 per cent of the EAFE Index in late 1989, many managers switched to a GDP-weighted index because it reflected Japan's relative economic position—about 34 per cent of the EAFE countries' economic power, instead of 64 per cent. The risk of capitalization benchmarking is that managers end up owning more of a market as it rises.

When a manager takes on a new client and agrees to work against a particular benchmark, it is fair to assume that the manager has the wherewithal to beat that benchmark. It is common to hear managers, justifying under-performance in a market and saying 'I am a value manager and the market was in a growth phase, so I under-performed the index.' Perhaps that manager should have more clearly defined the sub-index against which he was managing assets. If he was only investing in part of the index—the 'value' component—he should have defined that component in advance, and not subsequently complain that beating an index was difficult.

The peer group

Ostensibly, a peer group is all of the managers who compete in the same market-place, managing assets with the same objective and investing towards the same benchmark. International investing has many different peer groups:

- *Global managers*
  Those who invest everywhere in the world on a discretionary basis. including the United States, and who would typically be measured against the MSCI World Index.

- *International managers*
  Those who invest everywhere in the world on a discretionary basis, excluding the United States, and who would typically be measured against the MSCI EAFE Index.

- *Regional managers*
  Those who invest in a designated region, such as Europe, (including the United Kingdom) and who are measured against an index which covers that region.

- *Country managers*
  Those who invest in a particular country and who are measured against that country's index: e.g. someone investing in Hong Kong would be expected to beat the Hang Seng Index.

- *'Style' managers*
  Those who are grouped into a particular style—active, passive, growth, value, balanced, small-capitalization, micro-capitalization, large capitalization are but a few. It is not much to brag about if one is a 'Mid-250' investor in the United Kingdom and beats the FTSE All-Share Index, when the 250 Index has been roaring upwards and the FTSE All Share Index has been flat. The key question is: 'How did you do against your peer group operating in the 250 Index?'

It is important for pension funds to hire managers for specific purposes. If they hired a manager to beat the EAFE Index, they should not be disappointed if EAFE is flat and emerging markets have risen by 60 per cent: that is not the benchmark, nor the peer group, against which the manager should be measured.

Technically, managers hired to manage assets in the EAFE Index should not be included in the EAFE peer group for measurement if they invest 20 per cent of those assets in emerging markets. Unless, of course, the EAFE component is segregated from the merging markets component and measured separately, otherwise it is not comparing like with like.

There is a lot of fuzzy thinking on this subject. In the annual report of a large number of mutual funds, there is cross-pollination on a grand scale: US growth stock funds with 30 per cent overseas being measured against the S&P500 Index, international funds investing 25 per cent in emerging markets being measured against the EAFE Index, and so forth. There is nothing wrong with investing anywhere in the world in pursuit of all profitable asset classes. What is wrong is applying the performance generated by doing so to a peer group that is not accurate: it gives a misleading impression of a manager's prowess.

For mutual funds, it is not difficult to find an ostensible peer group. A cursory look in the mutual fund columns of a daily newspaper lists their investment category—global, international, growth, balanced, etc. Finding your peer group in institutional/money management is more difficult. For this, it is necessary to subscribe to one of the performance measurement services in order to get a ranking of performance against the peer group.

Steps were taken in peer group categorizing by InterSec Research Corporation. In late-1992, InterSec created an investment industry task force to produce guidelines for international portfolio composite creation. It was in response to the Association of Investment Management Research (AIMR) Performance Presentation Standards that had to be in place by 1 January 1993. InterSec applied broad guideline principles; including 'discretion' and 'carve-out', explained more fully below.

Discretion

All portfolios in international composites should be discretionary. The InterSec Task Force recognized that 'discretion' is a variable term and broke it into three categories:

- a) Portfolios subject to normal restrictions common to prudent management, such as the investment quality of securities. These are discretionary portfolios.

- b) Portfolios with restrictions in addition to those in (a), such as 50 per cent hedged requirements. These are discretionary, but should probably be excluded from standard composites.

- c) Portfolios that are heavily restricted so as to be unrepresentative of a manager's style or skills. For example, if the client fixes weights in countries, industries or in securities of a particular duration. AIMR standards exclude such portfolios from performance presentation.

Carve-outs

A carve-out is measuring part of a portfolio as if it were a discrete portfolio in its own right. As long as managers observe the guiding principles of representativeness, materiality and full disclosure, it is acceptable. Managers must be able to demonstrate that such sub-portfolios are representative of portfolios they would have created on a stand-alone basis.

Ideally, the carve-out should be set alongside the larger portfolio from which it came, so that there is no misunderstanding. Going back to the example, above, of the US growth stock mutual fund with 30 per cent overseas, it should consider presenting its performance in two tranches: its US equity component against the chosen US index, and the overseas component against the EAFE Index. It would certainly give a more accurate picture of the manager's skills.

How was performance achieved?

This question is at the heart of the science of performance measurement and of the entire investment industry. A typical international portfolio has three components to its returns:

- 1) Country/market
- 2) Currency
- 3) Security

Managers can provide information about the relative contribution of these three elements fairly accurately, but it is best to use an independent third party with a systematic methodology applied to all managers to obtain the fairest picture. There are many performance measurement services for international managers. Three of the most widely-used are:

> InterSec Research Corporation, of Stamford Connecticut;
> Frank Russell, of Tacoma, Washington; and
> The WM Company, of Edinburgh, Scotland.

A typical performance measurement analysis should contain at least the following data:

- 1) Performance of the portfolio, by percentile ranking, relative to the composite;

- 2) Attribution of performance between currency, market selection and security selection, relative to the composite;

- 3) Country weightings, relative to the composite;

- 4) Ranking of performance within each stock market;

- 5) Returns versus standard deviations, relative to the composite.

- (6) Risk analysis relative to peer group. Typically, this would show the standard deviation of the portfolio: R^2 versus benchmark (IFC, EAFE, S+P500, etc.); beta versus benchmark; market risk and specific risk.

International performance measurement 173

The data should relate to the most recent reporting period—usually one calendar quarter—and link it to past periods. Figure 16.1 is of a 'model fund' such as might be produced by a performance measurement firm. It illustrates the way in which the relative performance contribution from currency, market weightings and investment selection is broken down for one quarter, then for one, two, three, four and five years.

Similar graphics will show the ranges of return and rankings relative to the composite, category analysis by market, and so forth.

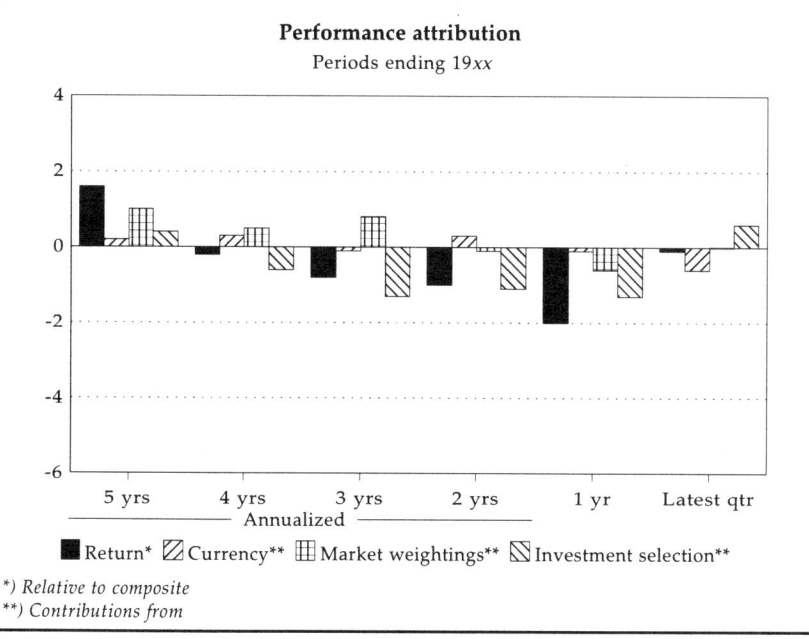

Figure 16.1 A model fund such as may be produced by a performance measurement firm

Every investment manager should read the report of the Performance Presentation Standards Implementation Committee of the AIMR dated December 1991. Among other issues, it sets out detailed standards on performance presentation. These standards include the following requirements that relate to typical international equity managers:

- The standards require use of a time-weighted rate of return calculation that minimizes the effect of contributions and withdrawals. The committee encourages the use of the exact time-weighted rate of return formula if possible but supports the use of an appropriate approximation method if daily market valuation is not feasible. The exact formula is left to the manager.

- Total return is mandatory.

- Performance calculations should include all discretionary, fee-generating accounts in at least one composite.

- Compound annualized performance returns should be presented for all presentation periods exceeding one year. Non-annualized performance data should be presented for periods of less than a year.

- Investment returns should be presented before the deduction of fees, and the fee schedule should be disclosed along with other SEC-required disclosures, except in cases requiring net-of-fees presentation to comply with the SEC advertising rules.

- Managers and their clients should agree in advance on the starting date for performance calculation.

- Investment income should be included on a full-accrual basis. The guiding premise should be to include that income to which the portfolio was truly entitled if the security were sold at the end of the performance interval. Stock dividends do not become payable unless the stock is owned on the ex-dividend date. Dividends should therefore be accrued as income as of their ex-dividend date. Interest on most fixed-income securities becomes payable pro rata as long as the security is held. Interest should therefore be accrued according to what ever method is appropriate for the specific issue. The accrual of income is included in the market price for Treasury bills and zero-coupon bonds, therefore no accrual is needed. If, however, in the presentation of performance, principal changes—including gains and losses—are shown, an acceptable convention for calculating accretion should be used.

- Portfolios should be valued at least quarterly. The standards state that monthly valuation and geometric linking is the preferred frequency when practical. If a true time-weighted rate of return, which is the most accurate calculation method, is used, daily valuation would be required.

- Performance results for any one asset class should include cash and any other securities held by the manager in place of that asset.

- Exclusions from account-performance calculations and presentations should be clearly stated. AIMR feels strongly, however, that disclosure of such exclusions cannot be used to circumvent the standards.

(From the Report of the Performance Presentation Standards Implementation Committee, AIMR, December 1991.)

Investment managers should also be aware of the SEC's regulations on the advertising of investment performance under Section 206 of the Investment Advisors Act. They define 'advertisement' as any written communication addressed to more than one person, or a communication with the media. IMRO, in the UK, have similar guidelines on the dissemination of performance figures.

Chapter 17

Investment vehicles

Previous chapters have discussed direct investment in international equities in some detail. This chapter discusses some other ways in which an investor may participate in international markets. It briefly covers the following areas:

1. Multinational companies
2. Mutual funds
3. Investment trusts
4. American Depository Receipts (ADRs)

Multinational companies

By definition, a multinational company is one which has activities in, and presumably derives revenues from, many countries. How many countries need to be included in the 'multi' to qualify for the name is open to conjecture. We do not hear too much about *bi*nationals, *tri*nationals or *quadri*nationals, so perhaps any company with operations outside its own country is entitled to call itself a multinational.

A multinational company offers its share holders an exposure to international economies that a purely domestic company cannot. It is a haphazard way of getting involved in international investing, but for some reason many people feel it is a 'safe' way of getting their feet wet internationally. In the early 1980s, there were several managers in the United States who touted multinational stock selection as the best route to international investing. There are several observations to be made on this mode of investing:

   a) Shareholders in a multinational have little way of knowing what their international exposure is at any one time. There are different economic growth rates around the world, and the earnings of the company may be distorted by a sudden growth spurt in one economy. A single large contract in one country could have the same effect, and it may not be repeatable.

   b) The multinational may be overexposed to mature economies and not give exposure to the rapid growth that the shareholders thought they were getting. Shareholders should ascertain in which countries the company operates.

c) Shareholders have no influence over the multinational's currency management. There are many instances of multinationals which have mis-hedged on a Napoleonic scale: One UK food company lost the equivalent of its entire earnings in the United States one year because of a series of misjudgements on currency hedges; maverick forex dealers at certain banks have, in the past, created huge holes in their companies' earnings by unauthorized trading from places like Chiasso and Lugano. It is fair to assume that for every unauthorized foreign exchange disaster in the market-place, there is an unauthorized foreign exchange coup, a lucky break which artificially boosts revenues at great risk to the shareholder. These risk tend not to come to light because the gamble paid off.

Associated disasters also occur in commodity hedging. The near-bankruptcy of Metallgesellschaft was caused by margin calls on oil futures contracts traded on the New York Mercantile Exchange in 1993. A futures hedge was not stopped out as the oil price went the wrong way, and Metallgesellschaft could not meet a DM 1.1bn margin call (approximately US$640m).

Aside from these objections, multinationals can provide good diversification away from the vagaries of their home economies. Sometimes, companies saturate their home market and can only expand abroad. Winterthur is one of the leading Swiss direct insurers. Some 30.1 per cent of their non-life premium income came from Switzerland in 1992, while 45.2 per cent came from the rest of Europe, 18.8 per cent from North America and 5.9 per cent from elsewhere. In the reinsurance market, less than 10 per cent of premium income of all Swiss insurance companies came from Switzerland: 64 per cent of the overall premium income of Swiss insurance companies was sourced overseas. These companies have simply outgrown their home market.

Electrolux is a Swedish company which is the world leader in white goods. Only 13 per cent of its sales in 1992 were in Scandinavia, 51 per cent in the rest of Europe, 28 per cent in North America and 8 per cent elsewhere. For Swedish investors who felt the Swedish krone was vulnerable and who wanted to diversify using the multinational route, Electrolux would be a good place to look.

Similarly, an Italian investor wanting to tap global growth should look at Benetton, the textile company. Approximately 33 per cent of sales are in Italy, 39 per cent in the rest of Europe, 10 per cent in the Americas and 17 per cent elsewhere. It is that 'elsewhere' which could provide the long-term growth surge of the company. In the Middle East and Far East the company has been expanding its outlets aggressively in the last few years.

There are hundreds of similar examples in the world's major stock markets. In the United States, companies like 3M, McDonalds, Ford and Boeing are major non-dollar earners and should be considered in a multinational strategy.

Mutual funds

A mutual fund is an investment management company that combines the money of its shareholders and invests it in a wide variety of securities. It provides investors with professional management of funds and a diversification of investments that they would probably not achieve as direct investors in equity markets. Most mutual funds are open-ended, which means that the fund will redeem outstanding shares on request. The number of shares of mutual funds is not fixed, but fluctuates as new shares are sold to investors and outstanding shares are redeemed. In the United States, they are simply known as mutual funds, in the United Kingdom, they are unit trusts, and in the French-speaking world, Sicavs (*Société d'Investissement à Capital Variable*). Below is a brief description of the type of international exposure that an investor may achieve through investing in mutual funds.

Global mutual funds

In the parlance of the industry, a global fund is one which invests anywhere in the world, including the United States (or if it is UK-based, it will include the United Kingdom, and so forth). They are a well-rounded approach to investing, and many investors favour global funds because the fund managers make their country equity weighting decisions for them. A fund which may invest anywhere in the world provides greater overall diversification potential than one which focuses on a smaller part of the world.

If investors already have a portfolio of equities within their home country, there is little point in investing in a global fund, because they have no way of controlling their exact percentage exposure to international markets at a given time. Fund managers may decide to have 50 per cent in US equities at precisely the time investors want 100 per cent of their investment overseas.

Global funds used to have a universe consisting of the US stock market and all the markets represented in the EAFE Index. Today, an increasing number of global managers are including emerging markets in their universe, to take account of opportunities presented everywhere. Each fund manager has a different approach, so it is incumbent on potential investors to check out the methodology of each fund before investing.

The doyen of global funds in the United States is undoubtedly the Templeton Growth Fund. It has been in existence since 1954, and has always had the objective of investing in values wherever they may be found in the world. From its launch in November 1954 to April 30, 1986, the fund produced a total return of 4586 per cent, compared with a Dow Jones Index return of 359 per cent over the same period. In the three years to December 31, 1993, the fund rose 81.6 per cent and the DJIA index rose 27.14 per cent.

International mutual funds

This group of funds invests exclusively outside the United States (or an investor's home market). The advantage of these funds is that investors know that the assets are, at all times, invested outside their home country, so they can make asset allocations on the basis that there will be no dilution of international exposure by their fund managers.

Until recently, an international fund was one which invested in the EAFE markets. Today, it can include emerging markets and may invest in a universe of over 40 markets. However, some mutual fund groups like to differentiate and have an EAFE-targeted international fund and an emerging-market-targeted international fund. Again, it is up to all potential investors to study the manager styles available to ensure that the right mix exists in the portfolio in which they are investing.

The PFAMCo group of funds in Newport Beach, California, has two international funds managed by Blairlogie Capital Management in Edinburgh. One is called the PFAMCo International Active Fund, and invests solely in countries represented in the EAFE Index. The other is called the PFAMCo Emerging Markets Fund, and invests solely in countries represented in the IFC Emerging Markets (Investable) Index. These funds were designed to be 'core' international funds in their fields, so that an investor could get wide exposure in a defined country universe at all times. Investors often do a 'split-ticket' whereby they devote money to each fund in proportion to their risk profile. An aggressive investor may want to have 50 per cent in emerging markets and 50 per cent in EAFE markets. A more conservative investor 20 per cent in emerging markets and 80 per cent in EAFE. The advantage of this product design is that investors have undiluted exposure in whatever pool they invest. Figures 17.1 and 17.2 show the market breakdown for each fund in February 1994. It should be noted that the percentage allocation to each market was relevant to a specific moment in time, and that these tables are not a recommended investment position. They are purely illustrative.

At that time, the investor had exposure to a broad number of markets—15 in the case of the International Active (mature market) Fund and 20 in

	Fund weight (%)	February 1994 EAFE Index weight (%)
Australia	5.41	2.9
Belgium	2.04	1.1
France	5.61	6.2
Germany	6.22	6.4
Hong Kong	1.63	4.6
Ireland	1.33	0.3
Italy	0.56	2.2
Japan	43.60	42.8
Netherlands	3.62	3.2
New Zealand	2.58	0.4
Norway	1.64	0.4
Singapore	2.85	1.1
Spain	2.84	2.0
Switzerland	4.89	4.3
UK	13.13	16.9
Cash/Other	2.05	5.2
Total	100.00	100.00

Figure 17.1 PFAMCo International Active
Source: Blairlogie Capital Management

the case of the Emerging Markets Fund.

All mutual funds have their own unique cost structure. These PFAMCo funds were designed for institutional investors. They are no-load funds, which is to say that an investor does not pay a charge to invest, nor a penalty to redeem shares.

A fund can be 'front-loaded', which means that investors are charged when they invest in the fund, or 'back-end', which means that they are charged if they sell the shares within a certain period, often a minimum of one year. Loads are also known as 'charges'. They are nearly always on a sliding scale, depending on the sum invested. For example, with some mutual fund groups, the first US$10,000 investment may attract a load of 8½ per cent and from US$10,000 to US$20,000, 7½ per cent. Amounts over US$1m often attract a very small load, such as ¼ per cent. Mutual fund companies often waive loads for 'qualified' investors, such as pension funds or foundations. Part of the load goes towards paying the introducing agent (stockbroker or financial planner) and part will go towards the distribution costs of marketing the fund.

PFAMCo's International Active Fund has an annualized expense ratio of 1.32 per cent and the Emerging Market Fund has an annualized expense

	Fund weight (%)	February 1994 IFC Investable index weight (%)
Argentina	7.40	6.8
Brazil	12.24	11.9
Chile	3.55	1.8
China	1.25	-
Colombia	2.51	1.8
Greece	4.06	1.8
India	1.32	2.8
Indonesia	2.55	2.2
Jordan	0.73	0.2
Korea	3.43	2.5
Malaysia	1.27	20.0
Mexico	24.53	27.7
Pakistan	1.23	0.5
Peru	2.62	0.6
Philippines	0.76	2.4
Portugal	3.81	1.5
Sri Lanka	0.97	0.1
Taiwan	2.59	1.8
Thailand	1.59	4.2
Turkey	2.92	4.7
Cash/Other	7.21	4.7
Total	100.00	100.00

Figure 17.2 PFAMCo Emerging Markets

Source: Blairlogie Capital Management

ratio of 1.44 per cent (at the time of writing). It is believed that these expense ratios, which include management and administrative fees, but not transaction costs, are among the lowest in the industry for these categories of fund. The minimum investment of US$200,000 ensures a more sophisticated clientele and does not clog the company's administrative systems with smaller trades.

All fund groups have their own philosophy and some actively encourage small retail investors, with sums as low as US$1000. Some will even take monthly salary deductions as low as US$50 on long-term savings plans. Expenses vary from one mutual fund company to another and every potential investor should satisfy himself that expense ratios are under control and worth paying.

Eight and one-half per cent front-end loads used to be common in the US mutual fund industry, but the trend is moving towards lower loads today.

A brief scan down the mutual fund pages in the Wall Street Journal will reveal the presence—or absence—of front-end loads for each mutual fund. The Journal has a number of columns, from left to right—the name of the mutual fund company, its investment objective, NAV (net asset value) and offer price. In the case of Merrill Lynch funds, for example, there is a difference between the NAV and offer price. The difference is the front-end load for each fund. Where it says NL under the offer price column, this means no load, and a purchaser can buy the fund at net asset value, which is the market value of the underlying assets in the fund, divided by the number of shares.

Regional mutual funds

In the early 1980s in the United States, mutual funds that invested in a particular region of the world were relatively rare. Today they are quite common. US investors can invest in Latin America, Japan, the Pacific Basin excluding Japan, Europe and Canada by using mutual funds that are specifically targeted on those regions. They are a useful vehicle for the more sophisticated investor who has a clear idea where in the world he wishes to focus non-domestic investments. For historical reasons, British investors have had a wide-selection of regional mutual funds available for many years. Funds targeting Australia, America, Hong Kong, Canada, Japanese smaller companies, etc. have long been available to British investors through firms like M&G and GT.

Among the premier US purveyors of regional mutual funds are GT Global, who offer Europe, Japan, Latin America and the Pacific Basin as separate investment destinations, and Fidelity, who offer Europe, Japan and Latin America.

An investor always should ask when investing in a regional fund, how performance is measured. What is the fund's benchmark? Often, investors are happy enough if their South East Asian fund has better returns that US money market funds, Treasury bills or the S&P 500. But they should look beyond these benchmarks to ascertain if their mutual fund manager is actually doing a good job. A mutual fund prospectus should clearly state what its performance objectives are. In the case of South East Asia, for instance, it should set a benchmark of the IFC Asian Index or Morgan Stanley Capital International Asia ex-Japan Index. A professional investment manager will work against such an index and attempt to outperform it over time.

In February 1994, a country allocation model for Europe including the United Kingdom assigned the weightings set out in Figure 17.3.

A European portfolio such as this has the objective of beating a defined benchmark. It is always cognizant of the benchmark weights of each country, but at the same time takes bets away from those weights. It is sug-

	Portfolio (%)	Index weight (%)
Belgium	2.82	2.3
Finland	0.47	1.0
France	14.58	13.5
Germany	13.35	13.1
Ireland	0.89	0.4
Italy	3.33	4.8
Netherlands	7.81	7.9
Norway	2.09	0.8
Spain	5.71	4.2
Sweden	2.05	3.3
Switzerland	11.63	10.3
United Kingdom	35.15	36.9
Cash/Other	0.15	1.5
Total	100.00	100.00

Figure 17.3   European allocation model
Source: Blairlogie Capital Management

gested that investors should look for similar characteristics in their regional funds, so that they can reasonably expect to beat a given index without assuming excessive risk.

Closed-end funds/investment trusts

Closed-end funds generally have a fixed number of shares outstanding and are traded on a stock market. Shares are traded at the market price, plus a commission. They may sell at a premium—that is, above the value of their assets, or at a discount, below the value of their assets.

Such funds have proliferated in the United Kingdom and the United States since the mid-1980s. In February 1994, there were at least 64 international closed-end funds listed on US stock exchanges. Some were regional, but most were targeted on individual countries. Countries represented by these funds were:

> Argentina   Korea
> Australia   Malaysia
> Austria   Mexico
> Brazil   Pakistan
> Chile   Portugal

China	Singapore
France	Spain
Germany	Switzerland
India	Taiwan
Indonesia	Thailand
Ireland	Turkey
Israel	United Kingdom
Japan	

Source: Barron's

There were many others, such as Asia Pacific and Global Growth, that had a wider objective.

Single-country funds represent the highest risk category of overseas funds because of their relative lack of diversification for US investors. If investors have portfolios of many single-country funds, they may accomplish good risk diversification *vis-à-vis* a US portfolio, but they may as well own diversified international funds rather than cherry-pick countries themselves. It would certainly save on the transaction brokerage.

Closed-end fund shares typically trade at a price different from their net asset value. This is a very different characteristic from open-ended mutual funds which always trade at NAV. When they trade at a premium to their underlying value, it is probably advisable to sell them. It makes no sense to own an asset that is worth US$100 which has a price of US$110. Similarly, there is every reason to own a share that has an underlying value of US$100, at a price of US$90.

Thomas J. Herzfeld Advisors, Inc. of Miami, Florida, produces *The Investor's Guide to Closed-End Funds*, which keeps track of discounts and premiums in such funds.

In mid-February 1994, there were many funds which traded at a premium. Among them were:

Argentina Fund	+12.7%
Brazilian Equity	+16.7%
China Fund	+23.5%
First Israel	+18.3%
Indonesia Fund	+23.6%
Japan OTC Equity	+31.7%
Korea Fund	+35.5%
Taiwan Fund	+21.5%
Turkish Investment Fund	+36.8%

Source: Barron's 14 February 1994

There was also a handful of funds trading at a discount to their net asset value, such as:

First Philippine	-14.4%
New Germany	-9.9%
Growth Fund of Spain	-8.0%
Irish Investment Fund	-6.1%
Mexico Fund	-4.3%
Pakistan Fund	-3.2%

Source: Barron's 14 February 1994

Buying a fund for less than its liquidation value is appealing, and for the value investor, it can be easily justified. Buying the Turkish Investment Fund for 36.8 per cent more than it is worth is ill-advised: gravity will eventually assert itself.

Investment trusts in the United Kingdom

The development of Scottish investment trusts in the 1870s has been described in an earlier chapter. Today, investment trusts represent one of the most important components of British stock market capitalization. There are approximately 260 quoted investment trusts on The London Stock Exchange, which include some old established giants like the Alliance Trust (market capitalization of £992m/US$1.5bn), Foreign and Colonial Trust (market capitalization of £1518m/US$2.28bn) and Edinburgh Investment Trust (market capitalization £918m/US$1.5bn).

It is common to find discounts to net asset value among the older UK investment trusts. Of the three featured earlier in this book, in February 1994, the Alliance Trust had a discount of 6.4 per cent, Edinburgh Investment Trust, 8.3 per cent and Scottish American, 10.1 per cent. In the 1970s, average discounts fell as low as 40 per cent, but they have steadily narrowed as a result of popular tax efficient investment plans, and the threat of take-over and liquidation. Having said that, premiums to NAV are still quite rare in the UK, even treated with suspicion. More sophisticated investors balk at the idea of paying more than one dollar for one dollar.

American Depository Receipts (ADRs)

An American Depository Receipt is a certificate issued by a US depository (generally a bank) which evidences the ownership of a foreign security held by the bank on behalf of the ADR holder. They are negotiable receipts traded on the New York Stock Exchange, American Stock Exchange or

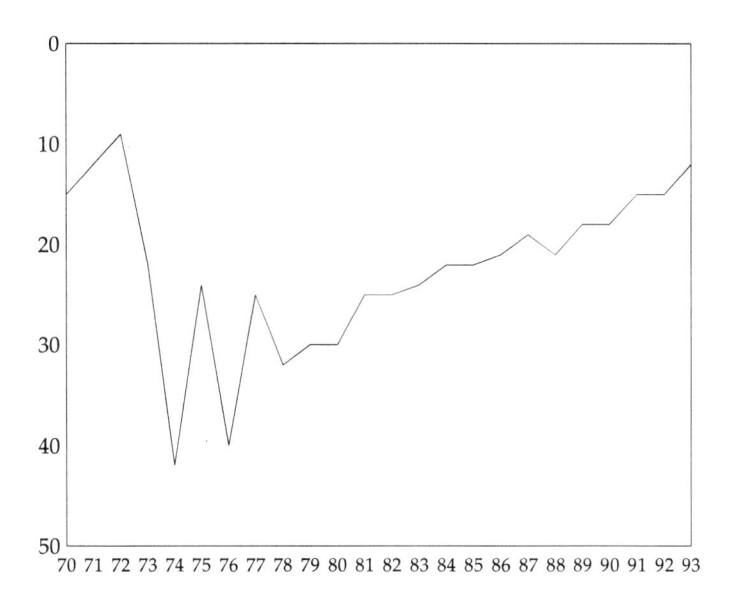

Figure 17.4 British investment trusts: average discount
Source: Datastream

over-the-counter markets certifying that a stated number of shares of a foreign company have been deposited with the US depository's overseas branch or a designated sub-custodian. ADRs are interchangeable with such shares and serve as a receipt of ownership. ADRs can either represent the underlying shares on a one-for-one basis, for example, one Philippines Long Distance Telephone common share equals one ADR, or they can represent a multiple of underlying shares, such as Kobe Steel in Japan, where one ADR equals five underlying common shares.

There are certain advantages to ADRs:

- The time involved in buying and selling the security is shortened, since the transfer of the ADR on the depository's books is all that is necessary. When ADR owners sell, they merely deliver the endorsed ADR to the depository, which instructs the foreign custodian to release the shares to the transferee.

- Dividends are paid in US dollars and the depository takes care of the foreign exchange transactions.

- Certificates are in English and subject to US transfer regulations. A holder does not need to worry about settlement procedures overseas—these are dealt with by the depository.

- The depository must keep ADR holders informed of recapitalization plans, stock exchange offers and noting issues pertaining to the underlying shares.

- Liquidity: It is fairly common to see companies like Glaxo or Telefonos de Mexico with high daily trading volume alongside leading US stocks. The institutional and private following of foreign stocks by Americans is creating a large, liquid market in the United States.

There are also some disadvantages, such as:

- Cost: An investor pays a brokerage fee to his own broker, a fee to the depository and sometimes a fee to the foreign custodian. Each issuing bank has its own fee schedule, but the table below is quite typical of the cost of buying ADRs:

1. The $2—$3—$4 basis:

    $2 per 100 when selling at $5.00 or less
    $3 per 100 when selling between $5.01 and $10.00
    $4 per 100 when selling over $10.00

2. The $3—$4—$5 basis:
    As above, but scaled up to provide a higher return to the bank and a higher cost to the investor.

There are often other charges, such as telex costs, stamp duties, and transfer and stock-splitting fees which may be appropriate.

Many foreign companies with ADRs tend to be large international blue chips whose rapid growth phase has already passed. A listing on a US exchange is often done to give the company access to US capital markets rather than to give shareholders the benefit of a superior investment.

ADRs are becoming increasingly popular among American investors. There are over 1400 companies with ADRs available in the US and while they have the tradeability of US equities, can often produce greater returns. Merrill Lynch's index of ADRs rose 29.9 per cent in 1993, versus a 9.1 per cent gain in the S&P 500 Index. The volume of trading in ADRs has grown substantially, with annual volume rising from US$41bn in 1988 to US$200bn in 1993, for ADRs listed on exchanges, according to the Bank of New York.

Chapter 18

Research, technology and data sources

When international equity investment began to flourish in the last quarter of the 19th century, managers had little choice but to do their own original investment research. The powerful network of research houses and intermediaries that exists today was not yet in place. Granted, City of London and Wall Street connections were invaluable as sources of deals that had been researched or syndicated by other reputable firms, but the onus of original research lay strongly on each investment manager. Today, a manager should be able to safely trust the research work done by leading stockbroking and research firms in each country. Facts and financial data are generally accurate, and although one may disagree with a broker's conclusions or recommendations, the quality of data provided, say, by Baring Securities on Telekom Malaysia, is unlikely to be superseded by an investment firm doing its own research on that company.

An investment firm doing original research on quoted securities is probably wasting resources and time in an area which is better covered by people whose entire business hinges on the quality of their research—stockbrokers and professional research intermediaries. Their information can be purchased at a fraction of the cost of setting up an in-house research capability. Investors should beware of international investment firms that describe their office network in glossy brochures from Hong Kong to Paris to Tokyo to Djakarta. These operations are unnecessary for the provision of long-term outperformance for US investors, and entrench a high cost structure that has to be paid for by their clients, often in the form of high expense ratios in mutual funds. There is no evidence that international firms with glamorous-sounding multi-country offices can systematically outperform their peers who operate on one floor in San Diego or Edinburgh.

Today's challenge is not one of performing original research. There is a multitude of research services available around the world whose databases of expertise can be tapped by using computers. It is thus important for investment firms to hire the brightest individuals who are computer-literate to a high degree, who can sift through and evaluate the most useful information towards building and validating their investment process.[1]

The *raison d'être* of most investment processes is to beat a benchmark. It may be the S&P 500 Index, it may be the EAFE Index, it may be the DAX Index in Germany. There are many ways of approaching the problem of beating an index, as discussed throughout this book. One way is to look at the constituent parts of the index and make small, but significant, investments in preferred securities above their index weighting. How can a manager decide which is the cheapest investment with the greatest potential for total return in a sector? One way might be to design a spreadsheet that minutely examines the leading financial ratios that define a bank's potential for current investment. This information can be gleaned from a supplier of international databases, such as Randall-Helms, whose proprietary software, DataScreen II, gives access to a variety of data sources.

One of the databases on DataScreen II is Morgan Stanley Capital International Perspective. It has fundamental information on 2500 companies in 21 countries, with over 1100 data items on each company, including seven years of monthly price and valuation factors, and the last 12 months of daily prices. So if one wished to compare price/earnings ratios, price to book value, price to cash earnings and the yield of the leading German banks on a historic basis, the data is readily available. The database can be accessed to quickly point to the best value according to these criteria.

Randall-Helms also provides access to I/B/E/S, the Institutional Brokers Estimate System, which gives earnings estimates and projections for 8500 companies around the world in 29 countries outside the United States, to a detailed level.

If a manager required further analysis, he could tap into the EuroEquities database on DataScreen II, for fundamental data on 2600 companies in 18 European stock markets, that provides eight years of historic income statements, balance sheets, data per share and key ratios, 12 months of price graphs, company profiles and 2 years of estimates.

Yet a further cut can be made by using Worldscope, which provides financial information on nearly 9000 of the world's largest companies in 32 countries and 27 industries. Ten years of financial data is available, as well as a written text detailing accounting practices and each company's auditor.

---

[1] *For further reading: 'Simulation, Optimization and Expert Systems', by Dimitus N. Chorafas, Probus Publishing ISBN 1 555738 231x.*

There are many other data services, some of which provide historic information on companies, some providing current price information. Some provide both.

Reuters have a service called Securities 2000, which gives prices for over 100,000 instruments around the world, including equities, derivatives, corporate bonds and equity-linked debt. Prices are sourced from 113 stock exchanges and from over 1200 contributors in over-the-counter markets. As with Randall-Helms, users can customize their displays so that only the relevant data is regularly on-screen. There is also a graphical application to enable charting and technical analysis. For many years, Reuters had a strong hold on computer-based information services, from eurobond prices to news flashes as they broke across the world. This near-monopoly has been challenged by many newcomers.

Bloomberg offers over 2000 functions, from current market information with a 15-minute delayed exchange feed on a large number of stock markets, to historical functions, such as price/yield history on cash instruments from 2 to 22 years, depending on the product and price source. An increasing number of managers also use the Bloomberg Portfolio System which stores an unlimited number of portfolios. A detailed display shows all the holdings in the portfolio and summarizes the profit and loss position for the entire portfolio. News files from Bloomberg's own news-gathering team, as well as combined new wires from outside providers, such as Tass and Agence France Presse, are included in the basic service.

Datastream covers 40,000 equities, 65,000 bonds and warrants, 50,000 economic series, indices, 11,000 company accounts, as well as futures, options and other derivatives. Aside from their vast coverage, from 210 Danish government economic series, to warrants on 520 Japanese Swiss Franc warrants, they have the Datastream Data Guarantee, which offers money back for qualifying errors in the Datastream databases. It is easy to use: Datastream has a software package which can be accessed through Microsoft Windows™. All the facilities and functions of Microsoft, from windows, icons, and mouse, can be used in conjunction with Datastream.

The Extel Financial Workstation is a database which covers around 12,000 companies in 48 countries. Its company research offers detailed information on all aspects of companies' accounts. The service includes over 900 indices, 140 currency exchange rates and economic data.

While it is not the purpose of this book to attempt a technology/data comparison between the many purveyors of research and price information, it is sufficient to point out that hundreds of research services are available around the world. Each manager must come to his or her own conclusion as to which service most suits their need. American and British addresses of some key data-providers are set out in Appendix E.

Soft commissions

Often, information services and research are provided on condition that commissions on trades are directed towards the payment of those services. 'Soft commissions' or 'soft dollars' refers to the practice by which investment managers direct a defined amount of commission-generating business to a broker, in return for which the broker will pay for services from third parties to be supplied to the investment manager.

The amount which the soft commission broker keeps, and passes out for payment to a third party, is determined at the outset by an agreed conversion ratio. In the 1980s, it was typically two to one. In other words, if the investment manager had to pay US$10,000 for a service, he would need to generate US$20,000 of trades through a soft dollar broker for the payment to be met in full.

Competition is strong in the United States and United Kingdom, where conversion ratios have fallen sharply in the 1990s. The US ratio is typically 1:6 and has been quoted as low as 1:2 in some cases in the United Kingdom. In other words, 80 per cent of the commissions on each trade go to paying for services, and the rest goes to the broker to cover the cost of the trade.

The concept of soft dollars began to get into disrepute as international investment burgeoned in the United States in the late 1980s. 'Financial tourism' became a major industry, whereby stockbrokers or public relations firms would organize trips from America to the Far East, Europe, the Eastern Bloc, or wherever, with all expenses paid, in the name of research and fact-finding, for considerations up to US$25,000 soft.

While these trips were usually informative and often arduous, they began to raise ethical questions and compliance issues. Many international investment firms will not use soft dollars today, except for the specific provision of research or systems that can be demonstrated to enhance the investment service to their clients. Indeed, it is essential for firms to have commission patronage at their disposal, because it attracts the service of the best brokers and encourages them to 'go the extra mile', providing information and customizing their services.

'Commission recapture programs' are beginning to grow in importance in the United States. Institutional clients of investment firms instruct them to direct trades through designated soft-dollars brokers, who then pay the clients back with a proportion of the trades. Typically, these programs aim to recapture commissions on 25-30 per cent of trades, although some public funds insist on a higher percentage. The key is that managers should be able to demonstrate 'best execution' on these directed trades, and to that end they are usually given a list of brokers with whom to trade.[1]

---

[1] *For further information: Thamesway Inc., 1177 High Ridge Road, Stamford, CT 06905. Tel: (203) 321-1212; Fax: (212) 412-1953.*

Glossary

Author's note: The terms and definitions noted in this glossary are generally common to the financial sectors of all English-speaking countries. Where applicable, however, local variations are shown. Unless otherwise stated, references to legislation apply solely to the United States.

A

actuarial assumption
The assumptions—about such matters as mortality rates among employees and pensioners of a pension-sponsoring organization, turnover rates among employees, rates of wage inflation, and investment return on pension fund assets—used by actuaries in reckoning the cost of, and required annual contributions to, a particular pension plan.

ADR
See **American Depository Receipt**.

AG
Aktiengesellschaft, a joint stock company in Germany and Austria.

agent
Someone who has the authority to represent another person, called a principal.

AIMR
Association of Investment Management Research (USA).

alpha
Alpha is the constant term in the equation relating risk premium on an asset to the risk premium on the market. Its expected value is zero, but its actual value may differ from zero. It is this possibility that explains investors' efforts to identify undervalued or overvalued securities, i.e., those with non-zero alphas.

American Depository Receipt (ADR)
An ADR is a certificate issued by a US depository (generally a bank) which evidences the ownership of a foreign security held by the bank on behalf of the ADR holder. They are negotiable receipts traded on the NYSE, American Stock Exchange or over-the-counter markets, certifying that a stated number of shares of a foreign company have been deposited with the US depository's overseas branch or a designated sub-custodian. ADRs are interchangeable with such shares and serve as a receipt of ownership. ADRs can either represent the underlying shares on a one-for-one-basis (for example, one Allied Lyons (United Kingdom) share equals one ADR). Or they can represent a multitude or fraction of underlying shares, such as South Pacific Petroleum (Australia), where two underlying shares make up on ADR.

amortization
Accounting for expenses or charges as applicable rather than as paid. Includes such practices as depreciation, depletion, write-off of intangibles, prepaid expenses and deferred charges.

annuity
A contract, usually issued by an insurance company, that provides an income for a specified period of time such as a number of years or for life.

arbitrage
A technique employed to take advantage of differences in price. If, for example, XYZ stock can be bought in London for $10 a share and sold in Tokyo at $10.50, an arbitrageur may simultaneously purchase XYZ stock in London and sell the same amount in Tokyo, making a profit of 50 cents a share, less expenses.

AS or Akts
Aktieselskabet, a joint stock company in Denmark and Norway.

Asean
Association of South East Asian Nations, including Singapore, Malaysia, Philippines, Thailand, Indonesia and Brunei.

asked
The price at which securities on certain markets and commodities are offered to potential buyers; the price sellers offer to take; the asking price.

asking price
The price at which commodities and securities on certain markets are offered to potential buyers; the price sellers offer to take.

asset
Anything one owns that another would buy; something one owns that has commercial or exchange value.

B

balanced portfolio
Generally meant to describe a portfolio with a mix of bonds and equities in it—balanced as to income and long-term capital protection.

basis point
See **point**.

bear market
A condition in which a market for securities is in a persistent decline, usually for a period of months.

bear
A person whose behaviour on the securities markets indicates that he expects the markets to decline generally or the price of a particular issue to fall.

bearer security
A security whose owner is not registered on the books of the issuer. A bearer security is payable to the holder.

beneficiary
A person receiving or who is designated to receive an interest or a benefit, as under a trust, a will, or an insurance policy, one for whose benefit property is held in trust.

best-efforts basis
Securities dealers do not underwrite a new issue, but sell it on the basis of what can be sold. In the money market, it usually refers to a firm order to buy or sell a given amount of securities or currency at whatever best price can be found over a given period of time; can also refer to a flexible amount (up to a limit) at a given rate.

beta coefficient (β)

The beta coefficient measures sensitivity of rates of return on a portfolio or on a particular security to general market movements. If the beta is 1.0, a 1 per cent increase in the return on the market will result, on average, in a 1 per cent increase in the return on the particular portfolio or asset. If beta is less than 1.0, the portfolio or asset is considered to be less risky than the market. An estimate of the beta coefficient of a portfolio is a weighted average of the betas of the portfolio's component assets.

beta factor

In the capital asset pricing model, the expected risk premium on an asset depends on the expected risk premium on the market multiplied by the asset's beta coefficient. In a more elaborate model (attributable to Black, Jensen and Scholes), the expected return on an asset depends also on the expected return on a portfolio not correlated with the market multiplied by one minus beta. This second factor is called the beta factor.

bid-offer spread

The difference between the selling bid and buying (offer) prices of a unit in a unit trust or an investment trust that accounts for the dealing and administration expenses, including the initial charge, of a unit trust or investment trust.

bid^1

An offer to buy at an auction or on an auction market as for securities or commodities.

bid^2

The price at which sellers may dispose of securities or commodities on an auction market.

bid^3

The price offered by a unit trust to a unitholder in the cashing in of his or her units.

billion

1000m.

blue sky laws

Laws of the various states governing the sale of securities, including mutual fund shares, and the activities of brokers and dealers within the particular state.

bond
A security evidencing a loan to a company or to a government unit that contains a written promise by a borrower to repay a fixed amount on a specified date and, usually, in the meantime to pay a set annual rate of interest at semiannual intervals.

book value
An accounting term. Book value of a stock is determined from a company's records, by adding all assets then deducting all debts and other liabilities, plus the liquidation price of any preferred issues. The sum arrived at is divided by the number of common shares outstanding and the result is book value per common share. Book value of the assets of a company or a security may have little or no significant relationship to market value.

break-point
Dollar-value level of a purchase of mutual fund shares at which the percentage of the sales charge becomes lower. Typically, a sales charge schedule contains five or six break-points.

broker
A person acting as an agent for buyers and sellers.

bull market
A condition in which a market for securities is rising generally for a period of months.

bull
A person whose behaviour on the securities market indicates that he expects the markets to rise generally or the price of particular issue to rise.

C

call money
Interest-bearing bank deposits that can be withdrawn on 24-hours notice. Many euro-deposits take the form of call money.

capital asset pricing model
The capital asset pricing model describes the way prices of individual assets are determined in markets where information is freely available and reflected instantaneously in asset prices—that is, efficient markets. Prices are determined in such a way so that risk premiums are proportional to systematic risk, which is measured by the beta coefficient.

capital gains distribution
A distribution to investment company shareholders from net long-term capital gains realized by a regulated investment company on the sale of portfolio securities.

capital gains tax
A government tax on asset inflation generally caused by government policies.

capital^1
Wealth; assets that produce income.

capital^2
In banking, the difference between the market price of a bank's assets and the market cost of its liabilities.

capitalization
See **market capitalization**.

cash equivalents
Assets that are essentially as liquid as cash.

cashflow
Reported net income of a corporation plus amounts charged off for depreciation, depletion, amortization, extraordinary charges to reserves, which are bookkeeping deductions and not paid out in actual dollars and cents.

CD
See **certificate of deposit**.

cellular telephone
Radio communication based on a network of transmitters serving a small area known as a 'cell'. Used in personal communications systems in which the mobile receiver switches frequencies automatically as it passes from one cell to another.

certificate of deposit (CD)
An interest-bearing negotiable promissory note issued by a bank (the maker) to a customer (the payee) against funds deposited in the bank for a definite period. The minimum maturity is fourteen days at commercial banks. Interest rates are in line with money market rates current at the time of issuance.

CFCs
Chlorofluoro carbons. Chemicals widely-used as coolants for refrigerators, air conditioning units and as aerosol propellants. Widely regarded as destructive to the earth's ozone layer.

clear
A trade is carried out by the seller delivering securities and the buyer delivering funds in proper form. A trade that does not clear is said to fail.

closed-end investment company
An investment company with a relatively fixed amount of capital, whose securities are traded on a securities exchange or in the over-the-counter market, as are the securities of operating business corporations.

close
The end of the trading session. On some exchanges, the 'close' lasts for several minutes to accommodate customers who have entered buy or sell orders to be consummated 'at the close'.

closed-up fund
An open-end investment company which for one reason or another has discontinued the sale of its shares to the general public, but still stands ready to accept redemptions.

collateral
An asset a borrower pledges to a lender which the lender may seize and sell if the borrower defaults.

commercial bank
A financial institution that accepts demand deposits and makes commercial loans. Its principal banking functions are the collection of deposits, lending, and the servicing of checking accounts, and its principal source of funds is deposits. It uses these funds for commercial, consumer, and residential loans. Its principal source of income is the interest on these loans and fees for its services.

commercial paper
Unsecured promissory notes issued to finance short-term credit needs in conjunction with bank loans. Commercial paper is generally backed by unused bank credit lines to refund the notes in the event of an adverse market. Commercial paper is usually bought and sold on a discount basis figured for the actual number of days to maturity on a 360-day basis, in the same manner as Treasury bills and bankers' acceptances.

commission
The fee charged by a broker for making a trade on behalf of customers.

common stock
Equity securities, shares in a corporation that typically have voting rights, but have the lowest priority when the corporation make distributions of earnings or in liquidation.

company^1
A term used to indicate a for-profit enterprise.

company^2
UK: An enterprise formed and registered in accordance with the Companies Act that has a legal identity separate from that of its members.

compounding
Compounding is the arithmetic process of finding that final value of an investment or series of investments when compound interest is applied. That is, interest is earned on the interest as well as on the initial principal.

contract
In the case of futures, an agreement between two parties to make and in turn accept delivery of a specified quantity and quality of a commodity (or whatever is being traded) at a certain place (the delivery point) by a specified time (indicated by the month and year of the contract).

contributory plan
A pension plan under which employees contribute some stipulated part of the funding of the benefits they are to receive.

control
In a corporation, the ability of a shareholder or a group of shareholders to run a corporation.

core manager
An investment manager who handles the portfolio representing the core of a client's investment policy. *See* **speciality manager**.

correlation coefficient
A correlation coefficient is a measure of the degree to which two variables move together. If the relationship is causal, it can be interpreted as a measure of the degree to which knowing the value of one variable helps to predict the value of the other.

correspondent
A securities firm, bank or other financial organization which regularly performs services for another in a place or market to which the other does not have direct access. Custodian banks may have correspondents in foreign countries where they have no direct representation.

coupon
Evidence of interest due to a bond. The coupon is detached from the bond and presented to the issuer's agent or the bondholder's bank for payment of interest.

covariance
Covariance is a measure of the degree to which two variables move together. A positive value means that on average, they move in the same direction. The covariance is related to, but not the same as, the correlation coefficient. It is difficult to attach any significance to the absolute magnitude of the covariance.

cover
Buying futures contracts to offset previous selling. 'Short covering' often results in market prices rising despite what appear to be sufficient reasons for prices to fall.

cumulative preferred
A stock having a provision that if one or more dividends are omitted, the omitted dividends must be paid before dividends may be paid on the company's stock.

current yield
Coupon payments on a security as a percentage of the security's market price. In many instances the price should be gross of accrued interest, particularly on instruments where no coupon is left to be paid until maturity.

custodian
A person or institution holding funds on another's behalf.

D

dealer
A person or firm acting as a principal in buying and selling securities.

debenture
A bond that is not secured by a particular asset but rather is backed by the general credit of the issuing corporation.

delivery month
The specified month within which a futures contract matures and can be settled by delivery.

delivery
The tender and receipt of the actual (cash) commodity, or of warehouse receipts covering such commodity, in settlement of a futures contract.

depository trust company (DTC)
A central securities certificate depository through which members effect security deliveries between each other via computerized bookkeeping entries thereby reducing the physical movement of stock certificates.

depression
A protracted period characterized by deflation of assets, when money supply usually contracts, unemployment rises and business conditions are slow.

derivative
A producer derived from a type of securities or another financial vehicle, such as an option, future or warrant.

deviation, residual
A deviation is the amount by which a particular value differs from some other value such as the average, or mean. Deviations can also be related to values, such as normal trend values, or to theoretical values one would expect on the basis of an historical relationship among the variables. This type of deviation is usually called a residual.

diminishing marginal utility of wealth
Marginal utility is the amount of additional satisfaction associated with an additional amount of something such as money or wealth. If successive increments in satisfaction decline as the level of wealth increases, there is diminishing marginal utility.

discretionary management
An investment account in which the customer puts up the money but the investment decisions are made at the discretion of the manager.

diversification
Diversification is the spreading of investments over more than one company, industry or country to reduce the uncertainty of future returns caused by unsystematic risk.

dividend yield
Total cash dividends paid as a per cent of market capitalization at the end of the period. The yield for an index is the total of all dividends paid divided by the total market capitalization.

dividend
A portion of a corporation's earnings distributed pro rata among the share outstanding in a class of stock.

dollar cost averaging
An automatic capital accumulation method that provides for regular purchases of equal dollar amounts of securities and results in an average cost per share lower than the average price at which purchases are made.

dollar premium
The premium that British investors had to pay to own dollars when exchange controls were in place. Exchange controls were abolished when the Conservatives came to power in 1979.

E

EAFE
Acronym for the Morgan Stanley Capital International Europe, Australia and Far East Index.

EC
European community, a burgeoning political/economic entity comprising 10 countries and considering the addition of many more.

economic risk
The probability that economic conditions will deteriorate and thereby affect the safety of the company.

EEC
See **European Community**.

efficient frontier
The efficient frontier is the locus of all efficient portfolios.

efficient market
An efficient market is one in which prices always reflect all available, relevant information. Adjustment to new information is virtually instantaneous.

efficient portfolio
An efficient portfolio is one that is fully diversified. For any given rate of return, no other portfolio has less risk, and for a given level of risk, no other portfolio provides superior returns. Efficient portfolios are perfectly correlated with a general market index.

equity securities
Ownership interests in a corporation; stock; intangible personal property, ownership of which usually is represented by a share certificate or stock certificate.

equity
Ownership.

ERISA
The Employee Retirement Income Security Act 1974. This statute governs the investment activities of private US pension plans and their outside investment managers. It is administered by the US Department of Labor.

ethical investment
A social investment.

eurobonds
Bonds issued in Europe outside the confines of any national capital market. A eurobond may or may not be denominated in the currency of the issuer.

eurocurrency deposits
Deposits made in a bank or bank branch that is not located in the country in whose currency the deposit is denominated. Dollars deposited in a London bank are eurodollars. German marks deposited there are euromarks.

event risk
The probability that an event will affect the value of a company.

ex-dividend
A synonym for 'without dividend'. The buyer of a stock selling ex-dividend does not receive the recently declared dividend. Every dividend is payable on a fixed date to all shareholders recorded on the books of the company as of a previous date of record.

exchange privilege
The right to exchange the shares of one open-end fund, or class of fund, for those of another under the same sponsorship at nominal cost or at a reduced sales charge. For tax purposes, such an exchange is considered a sale and new purchase.

exempt securities
Instruments exempt from the registration requirements of the Securities Act of 1933 or the margin requirements of the Securities and Exchange Act of 1934. Such securities include governments, agencies, municipal securities, commercial paper, and private placements.

expected rate of return
The expected rate of return on an asset or portfolio is the weighted arithmetic average of all possible outcomes, where the weights are the probabilities that each outcome will occur. It is the expected value or mean of a probability distribution. For example, the expected return on a portfolio, is the weighted average of all possible returns, each weighted by its probability.

F

fail
A trade is said to fail if, on settlement date, either the seller fails to deliver securities in proper form or the buyer fails to deliver funds in proper form.

Federal funds rate
The rate of interest at which Fed funds are traded. This rate is currently pegged by the Federal Reserve through open-market operations.

fiduciary
A person who has undertaken to act for another person's benefit in a circumstance in which the law imposes a duty of trust; a person having the character or nature of a trustee as to a particular undertaking.

financial asset
An intangible asset held for its monetary benefits; a security.

Financial Times (FT) All-Share Index
UK: A market capitalization-weighted index consisting of approximately 650 companies.

fixed annuity
An insurance contract guaranteeing that the annuitant will receive a specified sum each month, even if the insured outlives his life expectancy.

foreign exchange
Transactions involving the purchase and sale of currencies.

Fortune 500
The leading 500 US companies across all industries tracked by a unit of Fortune Magazine.

forward market
A market in which participants agree to trade some commodity, security, or foreign exchange at a fixed price at some future date.

forward rate
The rate at which forward transactions in some specific maturity are being made, e.g., the dollar price at which Deutschemarks can be bought for delivery three months hence.

funded benefits
That portion of the total benefits, including those not yet vested, estimated as having to be paid under a pension plan that is, as of a given date, covered by funds already accumulated for future payment of benefits.

futures contract
Contracts for the purchase and sale of commodities for delivery some time in the future on an organized exchange and subject to all terms and conditions included in the rules of that exchange.

futures market
A market in which contracts for future delivery of a commodity or a security are bought and sold.

futures
Contracts calling for a cash commodity to be delivered and received at a specified future time, at a specified place and at a specified price.

G

G7
See **Group of Seven**.

GAAP
Generally accepted accounting principles. Hence US GAAP, UK GAAP, etc.

GDP
Gross domestic product (GNP less exports).

gilts
UK: High-quality government debt securities.

GmbH
Gesellschaft mit beschraenkter Haftung. A limited liability company in Germany.

GNP
Gross national product.

go public
To sell shares of what was a close corporation in a public offering.

green
A person, politician, or policy that pursues environmentally friendly aims.

Group of Seven
Seven industrialized nations comprising Canada, France, Germany, Italy, Japan, the United Kingdom and the United States. They hold an annual economic summit in early summer, as well as extraordinary meetings to address economic issues.

guarantor
A person who conditionally promises to pay a creditor if the principal debtor does not.

H

hedge fund
A mutual fund or investment company which, as a regular policy, 'hedges' its market commitments. It does this by holding securities it believes are

likely to increase in value and at the same time is 'short' other securities it believes are likely to decrease in value. The sole objective is capital appreciation.

hedge
To reduce risk, (1) by taking a position in futures equal and opposite to an existing or anticipated cash position or (2) by shorting a security similar to one in which a long position has been established.

I

IFC Emerging Markets Data Base
This first comprehensive database to provide statistics on stock markets in developing countries. The database includes weekly and monthly statistics on nearly 900 stocks in 20 markets. IFC selects stocks based on trading activity, market size and sector diversity, to establish representative indices for stock market performance. *See also* **International Financial Corporation**.

IFC Global (IFCG) index
The name of the IFC index that represents stockmarket performance without taking into account restrictions on foreign investors.

IFC Investable (IFCI) index
The name of the IFC index that takes into account restrictions on foreign investors.

illiquid
Difficult or impossible to turn into cash.

IMRO
UK: Investment Management Regulatory Organization.

incentive compensation
A fee paid to an investment company adviser which is based, wholly or in part, on management performance in relation to specified market indexes.

income statement
A financial report that identifies where money came from and where it went.

income[1]
Money received in the form of dividends, interest, rent, commissions, and salary.

income[2]
Money earned by the principal of a trust.

index[1]
A means of measuring the performance of a financial market through the combined prices of some or all of that market's constituents.

index[2]
To manage assets with the objective of approximating the performance of an index.

insider[1]
Generally, under the securities laws, a person with access to confidential corporate information.

insider[2]
Under SEC reporting requirements, an officer or director of a person holding 10 per cent of the corporation's stock.

interest rate risk
The probability that a share price will be affected when interest rates fluctuate.

interest
Money paid for the use of another's money.

International Financial Corporation (IFC)
IFC was established in 1956 to promote the economic growth of developing member countries through private sector investment. It is owned by the World Bank. IFC pioneered the linkage between developed and emerging countries' capital markets through the use of international investment funds. Over 25 such funds owe their existence to the IFC, including the Korea Fund, Inc., launched in 1984 and listed on the New York Stock Exchange.

intrinsic value
The intrinsic value of an asset is the value that asset ought to have as judged by an investor. Discrepancies between current value and intrinsic value are often the basis of decisions to buy or sell the asset.

inverted market
A futures market where prices for deferred contracts are lower than those for nearby-delivery contracts because of heavy near-term demand for the cash commodity. Normally, prices of deferred contracts are higher, in part reflecting storage costs.

investment return
The combination of yield (interest, dividends, rents, royalties, and other income) and capital gains (or losses) resulting from investing and trading a pension fund's assets.

investment trust
UK: A company that invests its shareholders' contributions in publicly traded securities. They are closed-end investments traded on exchanges in the same way as equities.

issue[1]
To sell a security to its first holders; to deliver commercial paper to its first holder.

issue[2]
A particular group of securities.

J

junk bonds/equities
High-risk bonds/equities that have low ratings or are actually in default.

L

last trading day
The day when trading in an expiring contract ceases, and traders must either liquidate their positions or actually make or accept delivery of the cash commodity. After that, there is no more futures trading for that particular contract month and year.

LBO
Leveraged buy out.

liability[1]
The assignment of financial responsibility for the violation of a legal duty.

liability[2]
A debt; an obligation enforceable in a legal action; a person's claim on another's assets that arises from a transfer of goods or services that has already occurred.

limit move
The maximum that a future price can rise or fall from the previous session's closing price. This limit, set by each exchange, varies from commodity to commodity. Some exchanges have variable limits, whereby the limit is raised automatically if the market moves by the limit for a certain number of consecutive trading sessions.

limited company (Ltd)[1]
UK: A privately-held corporation whose shareholders' liability for the company's debts is limited to their investment in the company's shares.

limited company (Ltd)[2]
UK: Usually an enterprise in the form of a society or trade association whose members' liability is limited by a memorandum to a certain amount that the members commit to contribute on the winding-up of the company.

liquidate
To turn an asset into cash.

listed
Traded on a securities exchange.

load
A charge in the form of a percentage of an investment added to the price of a mutual fund. It is paid to the fund but usually goes to an intermediary who facilitated the transaction.

London interbank offered rate (Libor)
A benchmark rate of interest representing what the most creditworthy banks charge each other for funds. Libors are expressed in various currencies for three- and six-month terms.

long
A trader who has bought futures or options, speculating that prices will rise.

M

manager
A person who manages money for others.

margin call
A demand upon a customer to put up money or securities with the broker. The call is made when a purchase is made; also if a customer's equity in a margin account declines below a minimum standard set by the exchange or by the firm.

margin
The amount paid by the customer when he uses his broker's credit to buy a security. Under Federal Reserve regulations, the initial margin required in the past years has ranged from 50 per cent of the purchase price all the way to 100 per cent.

market capitalization
The total value of a corporation's issued and outstanding common stock which is calculated by multiplying the total number of shares by the price per share.

market price
The last reported price at which the security actually changed hands on a specified date.

market value
The price a willing buyer would pay a willing seller; the market price.

median
The median of a distribution is the value that divides the number of observations in half. If the distribution is normal, the mean and the median will coincide. If the distribution is not normal and has a positive skewness, the mean will exceed the median. If the skewness is negative, the mean will be below the median.

mineral rights
The right to explore and exploit mineral deposits on land that may be separate from the surface ownership of the land.

minority
An ethnic group in the United States that is not considered, by law, to have participated in the benefits of being part of the Western European majority.

money market fund
A mutual fund whose investments are primarily, or exclusively, in short-term debt securities, designed to maximize current income with liquidity and capital preservation.

money market
The market in which short-term debt instruments (bills, commercial paper, bankers' acceptances, etc.) are issued and traded.

Morgan Stanley Capital International
The unit of Morgan Stanley which compiles and monitors some of the leading indices of the world's stock markets. They produce the MSCI World Index, EAFE Index, Asia Pacific and Europe Indices, among others.

mortality rate
Death rate—the proportion of the number of deaths in a specified group to the number living at the beginning of the period in which the deaths occur. Actuaries use mortality tables, which discriminate death rates by age and sex, and sometimes also by occupation or other characteristics. The mortality tables currently being used differ very widely.

multiple correlation
Multiple correlation is a measure of the relationship between one variable (the dependent variable) and two or more other variables (the independent variables) and two or more other variables (the independent variables) simultaneously. It is an extension of simple correlation to include more than one independent variable.

mutual fund
A mutual fund is an investment management company that combines the money of its shareholders and invests it in a wide variety of securities. It provides investors with professional management of funds and a diversification of investments that they would probably not achieve as direct investors in equity markets. Most mutual funds are open-ended, which means that the fund will redeem outstanding shares on request. The number of shares of mutual funds is not fixed, but fluctuates as new shares are sold to investors and outstanding shares are redeemed.

N

Nafta
North American Free Trade Area, comprising USA, Canada and Mexico.

Nasdaq
An automated information network which provides brokers and dealers with price quotations on securities traded over-the-counter. Nasdaq is the acronym for National Association of Securities Dealers Automated Quotations.

nearby contracts
The futures that expire the soonest. Those that expire later are called deferred contracts.

negotiable certificate of deposit
A large-denomination (generally $1m) CD that can be sold but cannot be cashed in before maturity.

net asset value (NAV)
The NAV per share of a portfolio is calculated by dividing the difference between the value of a portfolio's assets and liabilities by the number of shares outstanding.

net income
The amount of money that remains after meeting, or making provisions for, all expenses.

net worth
A figure reached by subtracting the value of all liabilities from the value of all assets. Net worth appears on the bottom right of the balance sheet.

Nikkei 225 Index
Established by the Osaka Exchange, nearly 40 years ago and backed by Japan's foremost business newspaper group, the Nihon Keizei Shimbun, the Nikkei 225 is the index most frequently quoted to describe the movements in Japan's stock market. The 225 stocks selected as the constituents of the index account for roughly 70 per cent in trading volume and 54 per cent in total market value of all stocks listed on the First Section of the Tokyo Stock Exchange. Of the constituents 109 are floor traded and the remaining 116 system traded. The Nikkei Stock Average is calculated every minute as the

arithmetic mean of the last traded prices of the underlying stocks in Tokyo, but unusually is not weighted by market capitalization.

nominal return
The nominal return on an asset is the rate of return in monetary terms, i.e. unadjusted for any change in the price level. The nominal return is contrasted with the real return which is adjusted for changes in the price level.

number of shares traded
Total number of shares traded during the period expressed in millions.

O

OECD
The Organization for Economic Co-operation and Development, an association of 21 nations to promote growth and trade, set up in 1961.

offer
An offerer's proposal stating what he or she is willing to do or not to do in exchange for a specified action or promise by the offeree.

offset
Usually, the liquidation of a long or short futures position by an equal and opposite futures transaction. Open positions can be offset at any time during the life of a futures contract.

OPEC
Organization of Petroleum Exporting Countries. An organization formed in 1961 to administer a common policy for the production and sale of petroleum products. Members are Algeria, Ecuador, Gabon, Indonesia, Iran, Iraq, Kuwait, Libya, Nigeria, Quator, Saudi Arabia, the United Arab Emirates and Venezuela.

open contracts, open interest
The obligation entered into by a party to a futures contract either to buy or to sell the commodity specified. The obligation is 'open' until it is settled by an offsetting transaction or by delivery.

open-end investment company
See **mutual fund**.

opportunity cost
The cost of pursuing one course of action measured in terms of the forgone return offered by the most attractive alternative.

option
A right of buy (call) or sell (put) a fixed amount of a given stock at a specified price within a limited period of time.

OTC
Over-the-counter securities.

over-the-counter (OTC) security
A security usually not listed on a major exchange that trades by means of a computer network linking brokerages.

overbought
A term used to express the opinion that prices have risen too high too fast and so will decline as traders liquidate their positions.

oversold
Like **overbought**, except the opinion is that prices have fallen too far too fast and so probably will rebound.

P

paper
Money market instruments, commercial paper, and other.

participating preferred
A preferred stock which is entitled to its stated dividend and, also, to additional dividends on a specified basis upon payment of dividends on the common stock.

pension assets
The securities and other property purchased with cash contributions to a pension fund, and with investment returns on the fund, and presumably available—upon sale at prevailing market price and so converted into cash—for payment of pension benefits as they fall due.

pension costs
The sum of a pension-sponsoring company's annual contributions to a pension fund over the life of the plan being funded.

pension liabilities
The sum of the obligations to pay stipulated benefits to plan participants over the life of the plan. The nature and measure of such liabilities were a major subject of discussion in this book.

pension-sponsoring organization
A company, or other organization, which established a pension plan, and supplies all or most of the required funding.

plc
UK: public limited company.

point[1]
100 basis points = 1 per cent.

point[2]
One per cent of the face value of a note or bond.

point[3]
In the foreign exchange market, refers to the lowest level at which the currency is priced. Example: 'one point' is the difference between a sterling price of $1.8080 and $1.8082.

political risk
The probability that a company will be affected by political actions.

portfolio management
The management of financial assets for the benefit of another.

portfolio manager
A person (or firm) who, for a fee, assumes responsibility for managing part or all of a client's portfolio; a money manager.

portfolio
A metaphor for an owner's investments.

preferred stock
An equity security that has preference over common stock as to dividends or asset distributions on dissolution of the company.

premium
The amount by which a preferred stock, bond or option may sell above its par value. In the case of a new issue of bonds or stocks, premium is the

amount the market price rises over the original selling price. Also refers to a charge sometimes made when a stock is borrowed to make delivery on a short sale. May refer, also, to redemption price of a bond or preferred stock if it is higher than face value.

price/book value ratio
The P/BV for the index is the total market capitalization divided by the total of the book values of the companies in the index at the end of the period. Book value is the same as 'net worth', which is the difference between total assets and total liabilities.

price/earnings for index
The P/E for the index is the total market capitalization divided by the total earnings of the companies in the index on a trailing 12 months basis.

prime rate
The rate at which banks will lend to their best (prime) customers. The all in cost of a bank loan to a prime credit equals the prime rate plus the cost of the holding compensating balances.

probability distribution
A probability distribution is a distribution of possible outcomes with an indication of the subjective or objective probability of each occurring.

profit-sharing retirement plan
A retirement program to which a percentage of the gross profits of a corporation is contributed each year; the eventual benefits are not predetermined as in the case of a pension plan.

proprietary company (pty.)
Australia, Republic of South Africa (RSA): A private limited company.

proxy statement
A booklet sent by a corporation and accompanied by a proxy describing candidates for election to the board of directors and all other matters to be dealt with at a shareholders' meeting.

proxy
A power of attorney often used to vote shares in a corporation.

prudent man rule
An investment standard. 'A duty to the beneficiary (of a trust)... to make such investments and only such investments as a prudent man would make

of his own property having in view the preservation of the estate and the amount and regularity of the income to be derived.' (Restatement (2d) of Trusts, sec. 227.)

public accountant
Usually a person who has met the same requirements as a CPA but provides advice only to an employer, such as a government agency or a business.

put
A contracted provision requiring repurchase of securities at or after a certain date at a predetermined price.

Q

qualified plans
Retirement plans which meet the requirement of section 401(a), 403(a) or 403(b) of the Internal Revenue Code or the Self-Employed Individuals Tax Retirement Act.

R

rate of exchange
The basis on which the money of one country will be exchanged for that of another.

realized gains and losses
A category on a portfolio manager's or a trustee's report reflecting which assets have been sold and whether they were sold at a profit or a loss.

reasonable man
A judicial fiction who always acts prudently and does the right thing; an expression of the conduct society demands.

regression analysis
Regression or correlation analysis is a statistical technique for estimating the relationship between one variable (dependent variable) and one or more other variables (independent variables).

regression coefficient
A regression coefficient indicates the responsiveness of one variable to changes in another. If the relationship between two variables is described by a straight line, the regression coefficient is the slope of the line. The regression coefficient between rates of return on an asset and rates of return on the market is called the beta coefficient.

reinvestment privilege
A special service offered by most mutual funds and some closed-end investment companies through which dividends from investment income may be automatically invested in additional full and fractional shares. Reinvestment specifics provided by the individual funds.

reinvestment rate[1]
The rate at which an investor assumes interest payments made on a debt security can be reinvested over the life of that security.

reinvestment rate[2]
The rate at which funds from a maturity or sale of a security can be reinvested. Often used in comparison to 'give up' yield.

repurchase agreement (RP or repo)
A holder of securities sells these securities to an investor with an agreement to repurchase them at fixed price on a fixed date. The security 'buyer' in effect lends the 'seller' money for the period of the agreement, and the terms of the agreement are structured to compensate the buyer for this, Dealers use RP extensively to finance their positions.

reserve requirements
The percentages of different types of deposits that member banks are required to hold on deposit at the central bank.

resolution
A statement authorizing an action adopted by a formal vote of a board of directors.

restricted security
A portfolio security not available to the public at large, which requires registration with the Securities and Exchange Commission before it may be sold publicly; a 'private placement'; frequently referred to as 'letter stock'.

return
Profit, usually expressed as a percentage, on an investment in securities or other assets.

revolving line of credit
A bank line of credit on which the customer pays a commitment fee and can take down and repay funds according to his needs. Normally the line involves a form commitment from the bank for a period of several years.

reward-to-variability ratio
The reward-to-variability ratio is the risk premium on an asset per unit of risk as measured by the variability or standard deviation. Sharpe used this measure to rank mutual funds.

RICO
Racketeering Influenced and Corrupt Organizations Act.

rights issue
An offer by a company to its shareholders to purchase additional shares, usually in a fixed ratio to the number of shares currently held.

risk aversion
Risk aversion means riskiness matters and is disliked. A risk averter will hold a portfolio of more than one stock in order to reduce risk for a given expected return. A risk-averse investor will incur additional risk only if he expects a higher rate of return.

risk premium
The risk premium on an asset is the actual return minus the riskless rate of return. In Sharpe's capital asset pricing model, the risk premium for any asset is proportional to its beta—the measure of sensitivity to general market movements.

rollover
Reinvest funds received from a maturing security in a new issue of the same or a similar security.

S

S&P 500
The Standard and Poor's index of 500 leading American companies.

SA[1]
Spain: *Sociedad anonima;* a joint stock company in Spain and other Spanish-speaking countries.

SA[2]
Italy: *Societa anonima;* A joint stock company.

savings and loan association
US: National- or state-chartered institution that accepts savings deposits and invests the bulk of the funds thus received in mortgages.

savings deposits
Interest-bearing deposit at a savings institution that has no specific maturity.

screen[1]
To look for securities or issuers that meet certain defined criteria.

screen[2]
A criterion or group of criteria used to select securities or issuers.

scrip
Shares.

SEC
US: Securities and Exchange Commission.

secondary market
The market in which previously issued securities are traded.

securities
A security is an instrument, issued in bearer or registered form, that is of a type commonly dealt in upon securities exchanges or markets or dealt in as a medium for investment. It is either one of a class or series or by its terms is divisible into a class of series of instruments, and evidences a share, participation, or other interest in property or in enterprise or evidences an obligation of the issuer (UCC, sec 8-102(1)(a)).

serial correlation
Serial correlation measures the degree to which what happens is related to what happened previously. Serial correlation is measured by the simple correlation coefficient between two variables, one being the successive value of the other. Serial correlation can also be measured with lags. For

example, a change in the price of a stock can be serially correlated with the change before the last one as well as with the last one.

share
A unit of ownership in a corporation, mutual fund, or money market mutual fund; stock.

shareholder
The owner of a share, or ownership interest, in a corporation.

short covering
Buying stock to return stock previously borrowed to make delivery on a short sale.

short position
Stocks sold short and not covered as of a particular date. Short position also means the total amount of stock an individual has sold short and has not covered, as of a particular date.

short sale
A person who believes a stock will decline and sells it, despite not actually owning any, is deemed to have made a short sale.

Soc. Anon.
France: *Société Anonyme;* a joint stock company.

social screen
A non-financial criterion or set of criteria applied in the investment decision-making process.

Société d'Investissement à Capital Variable (Sicav)
France/Luxembourg: An open-end investment fund similar to a unit trust in the United Kingdom that is the most common form of collective investment vehicle in France and Luxembourg. It differs from a unit trust in that it is not a product, but a company in its own right, constituted by articles of association and controlled by a board of directors.

specialty manager
An investment manager who handles a portfolio that contributes to diversification away from a core portfolio. For example, if a balanced US portfolio is regarded as a core portfolio, an EAFE or emerging market manager might be seen as a specialty manager. Similarly, one can have 'core' emerg-

ing market managers, and specialty managers who focus on one part of the universe.

spot market
Market for immediate as opposed to future delivery. In the spot market for foreign exchange, settlement is two business days ahead.

spot price
The price at which the physical commodity is selling.

spread^1
Difference between bid and asked prices on a security.

spread^2
Difference between yields on or prices of two securities of differing sorts or differing maturities.

spread^3
In underwriting, difference between price realized by the issuer and price paid by the investor.

standard deviation
The standard deviation is a commonly used to measure of dispersion. It is the square root of the variance. It is based on deviations of observations from the mean and is therefore in the same units as the observations. A measure of relative dispersion is the standard deviation divided by the mean (the coefficient of variation).

sterling
UK: The currency of the United Kingdom. Used in this context, the word has nothing whatever to do with silver.

stock certificate
Evidence of ownership of equity securities; share certificate.

stock dividend
A distribution to shareholders of additional shares of the corporation's own stock.

stock
An ownership share in a corporation.

stockbroker
See **broker**.

stockholder
See **shareholder**.

stop-loss order
An open order given to a brokerage firm to liquidate a position when the market reaches a certain price so as to prevent losses from mounting. Sometimes market price trends are accelerated when concentrations of stop-loss orders are touched off.

subordinated debenture
The claims of holders of this issue rank after those of holders of various other unsecured debts incurred by the issuer.

syndicate
A group of underwriters.

systematic risk
Systematic risk is the volatility of rates of return on stocks or portfolios associated with changes in rates of return on the market as a whole. It can be estimated statistically from the market model. The percentage of total variability that is systematic is given by the coefficient of determination and the degree of responsiveness to market movements is measured by beta.

T

T-bill
See **Treasury bill**.

T-bond
See **Treasury bond**.

tele-diffusion ratio
The number of main telephone lines per 100 people.

thin market
A market in which trading volume is low and in which consequently bid and asked quotes are wide and the liquidity of the instrument traded is low.

thrift institution
US: A savings and loan association, a federal savings bank, or a state-chartered savings bank or industrial bank that accepts deposits and makes loans. Its main banking functions are deposit collection, lending, and servicing checking accounts. Its principal source of funds is deposits, which it uses for residential mortgages, consumer loans, and commercial loans. Its principal source of income from banking activities comes from the interest on loans and fees for its services.

time-weighted rate of return
The time-weighted rate of return is a weighted average of the internal rates of return for sub-periods dated by the contribution or withdrawal of funds from a portfolio. To calculate it, one needs to know the value of the portfolio at the time of each cash inflow or outflow and the dates on which these occur. rates of return on mutual fund shares are time-weighted rates of return.

top-down
A money-management style that begins with an assessment of economic conditions and an ideal asset allocation and then moves toward an ideal allocation of the client's assets.

TOPIX Index
The Tokyo Stock Market for domestic stocks is divided into two layers—the First Section and the Second Section. In general, a newly-listed company's stock is assigned to the Second Section. The First Section contains stocks that have a large market capitalization and are liquid. Stocks in both sections are periodically reviewed with a view to identifying suitable candidates for promotion or relegation. The TOPIX index was launched by the Tokyo Stock Exchange (TSE) in July 1969 as a replacement for the Dow-based formula that the exchange had previously been using. It is a composite index of all stocks listed on the First Section of the TSE. Of the component stocks 149 (44 per cent by weight) are floor traded and 989 are system traded. The index is calculated, each minute, as the arithmetic mean of the last traded prices of the underlying shares in Tokyo, weighted by market capitalization—the method of calculation used for the FT Actuaries indices.

total return
A statistical measure of performance reflecting the result of acceptance of capital gains in shares, plus the result of reinvestment of income dividends.

trading limit
The maximum price movement up or down permitted in one trading session under the rules of an exchange.

Treasury bill (T-bill)
US: A short-term US Treasury obligation, maturing in as little as ninety days after issue, that does not pay interest, but is sold at a discount from its face value.

Treasury bond (T-bond)
US: A bond issued by the US Treasury; any obligation issued by the US Treasury.

trust[1]
A fiduciary relationship created by one person (the creator) in which a second person (the trustee) holds title for the benefit of a third (the beneficiary).

trust[2]
The assured reliance on another's integrity.

trustee
A person who holds, manages, and invests assets for the benefit of a trust's beneficiary.

turnover ratio
The extent to which an investment company's portfolio is turned over during the course of a year. For a closed-end company, the total purchases and sales of securities (other than US government obligations and short-term notes) is divided by two and then divided by average assets. For a mutual fund, a rough calculation can be made by dividing the lesser of portfolio purchases or sales (to eliminate the effects of net sales or redemption of fund shares) by average assets.

U

underwriter
A dealer who purchases new issues from the issuer and distributes them to investors. Underwriting is one function of a investment banker.

unsystematic risk
Unsystematic risk is the variability not explained by general market movements. It is avoidable through diversification. Only inefficient portfolios have unsystematic risk.

V

value/volume of shares traded
Total shares traded during the period. Value is expressed in millions of local currency or US dollars; volume is expressed in millions of shares.

variable-price security
A security, such as stocks or bonds, that sells as a fluctuating, market-determined price.

variable-rate loan
Loan made at an interest rate that fluctuates with the prime.

variance
The variance of a distribution is a measure of variability based on squared deviations of individual observations from the mean value of the distribution. Its square root, the standard deviation, is a commonly used measure of dispersion.

VAT
UK: Value-added tax.

vehicle
A financing or investment option, such as equity or debt.

vested benefits
Those pension benefits, claims to which are inalienable, under terms of particular pension plans and, since enactment of ERISA, under provisions of that law,

volatility
Volatility is that part of total variability due to sensitivity to changes in the market. It is systematic and unavoidable risk. It is measured by the beta coefficient. Efficient portfolios have no additional risk, and volatility is the only source of variability in rates of return.

W

weighting
Weighting is the specification of the relative importance of each of a group of items that are combined. For example, stocks included in indexes may be equally weights or weighted according to value.

withholding tax
Tax withheld at source from interest or dividend generated by an investor in a foreign country.

world market capitalization
The total amount of the various securities issued in the world. The size can differ significantly depending on how it is measured. For example, world market capitalization according to Morgan Stanley Capital International would include only the parts of the world, and each market, that they measure. It excludes smaller companies in many markets, uninvestable parts of some markets and some smaller or investable markets. Others may regard world market capitalization as the total value of all securities in the world, and come up with a much larger figure.

Y

yield curve
A graph showing, for securities, that all expose the investor to the same credit risk; the relationship at a given point in time between yield and current maturity.

yield
Return on an investment in debt. The two components of yield are interest payments and price (depreciation and appreciation).

Appendix A

Withholding tax rates

The following withholding tax tables relate exclusively to US investors in various countries. If you are concerned about withholding taxes in respect of a Japanese, French, British or German investors in their markets, you should confer with your tax accountant or custodian bank. For instance, a US investor in Spain is liable for a net 15 per cent withholding tax on dividends, whereas a British investor in Spain should be exempt. Tax levels depend on double-tax treaties and the degree of reciprocity available between countries. The purpose of showing these rates is mainly to point out that there are often tax consequences of investing overseas and that these are the rates that relate to US investors.

Tax levels and tax treaties change frequently, so these tables should be seen as illustrating the wide differences of taxation between countries, not as an up-to-date tax guide on withholdings. The statistics were compiled with the help of Chase Manhattan Bank's Global Custody group. The information provided by Chase has been abbreviated by the writer, and all error and omissions of data are entirely the writer's.

For specialist advise on individual tax circumstances, the Chase Global Securities Tax Services Group provide a customized hand-holding through the maze of taxation in 46 markets.

		Standard rate (%)	Local withholding tax Reduced to (%)	Tax relief (%)	Notes
Australia	Dividends	0-30	Nil	0-30	(Note 1)
	Interest	10	Nil	10	
Belgium	Dividends	25	Nil	25	(Note 2)
	Interest	10 / 25	Nil	10 / 25	
Canada	Dividends	25	Nil	25	
	Interest	25	Nil	25	
Finland	Dividends	25	15	10	
	Interest	30	Nil	30	
France	Dividends	15			(Note 3)
	Interest	15	Nil	15	
Greece	Dividends	42 / 45	42 / 45	Nil	(Note 4)
	Interest	25	Nil	25	
Indonesia	Dividends	20	15	5	
	Interest	20	15	5	
Japan	Dividends	20	15	5	
	Interest	15-20	10	5-10	
Mexico	Dividends	Nil / 35	Nil / 35	Nil	(Note 5)
	Interest	35	Nil / 15	35 / 20	
Netherlands	Dividends	25	15	10	
	Interest	Nil			
New Zealand	Dividends	30	15	15	
	Interest	15	10	5	
Norway	Dividends	25	15	10	
	Interest	Nil			
Philippines	Dividends	35	25	10	(Note 6)
	Interest	20	10 / 15	10 / 5	
Portugal	Dividends	30	25	5	(Note 7)
	Interest	30	0-25	5-30	
Sweden	Dividends	30	15	15	
	Interest	Nil			
Thailand	Dividends	20	20	Nil	(Note 8)
	Interest	25	Nil / 25	25 / Nil	
USA	Dividends	Nil			(Note 9)
	Interest	Nil			

Figure A.1   US pension trust - tax exempt investor
I: Tax relief can be credited with income payment

Source: Chase Manhattan

Notes on Figure A.1

1. The dividend tax rate varies.

2. Dividends are declared net of the Belgian tax. Therefore, the tax relief equates to 33.33 per cent of the declared dividend. Tax exemption at source is available for certain bonds. In most cases, this requires the investor to convert the bonds into registered form.

3. Exemption at source is available for many bonds.

4. Certain bonds are exempt from Greek withholding tax under local law. The tax treaty provides for exemption, but only for interest on the first 9 per cent per annum return.

5. The tax rates vary.

6. The reduced tax rate on interest varies. The 10 per cent rate generally applies to public bonds.

7. The 30 per cent standard rate comprises a 5 per cent gift tax and a 25 per cent income tax withholding. These combined taxes are often reduced under local incentive legislation to an effective rate of 25 per cent for dividends and 0-25 per cent for interest. A tax treaty is not expected to come into force for some time.

8. Tax exemption on interest from certain bonds is available under local law. No tax treaty is on force currently.

9. Back-up withholding can be avoided provided a completed IRS Form W9 is held by the custodian bank.

		Local withholding tax			Steps to reclaim local tax		
		Standard rate (%)	Reduced to (%)	Tax relief (%)	Investor sign-off needed (1)	IRS sign-off needed (2)	Notes
Austria	Dividends	25	12.5	12.5	No	No	
	Interest	Nil					
Belgium	Dividends	20 / 25	15	5 / 10	No	Yes	
	Interest	10 / 25	10	Nil / 15	No	Yes	
Denmark	Dividends	30	15	15	No	Yes	(Note 3)
	Interest	Nil					
France	Dividends	25	(Note 4)	52.5	No	No	(Note 4)
	Interest	15	Nil	15	No	No	
Germany	Dividends	25	10	15	No	No	(Note 5)
	Interest	Nil / 25	Nil	Nil / 25	No	No	
Ireland	Dividends	Nil					(Note 6)
	Interest	Nil / 27	Nil	Nil / 27	No	No	
Luxembourg	Dividends	15	7.5	7.5	No	Yes	
	Interest	Nil					
Spain	Dividends	25	15	10	Yes	Yes	(Note 7)
	Interest	25	10	15	Yes	Yes	
Switzerland	Dividends	35	15	20	No	No	
	Interest	35	5	30	No	No	
UK	Dividends	Nil	(Note 8)	13.33	Yes	No	(Note 8)
	Interest	25	Nil	25	Yes	Yes	

Figure A.5 US company
II: Tax relief deferred

Source: Chase Manhattan

Notes on Figure A.2

1. If the investor gives the custodian a power of attorney, the custodian can sign tax reclaim forms for the investors in many markets.

2. Certification by the IRS is required where indicated. The reclaim form will then be forwarded to the tax refund office in the market concerned.

3. For dividends, entitlement to refund of the 25 per cent withholding tax, plus refund of 50 per cent tax credit (where applicable), less tax due at 15 per cent of the total of the dividend and the tax credit. In this market, the local tax administration only begins to process dividend tax reclaims after January 15 of the year following dividend payment. For interest, tax exemption is often available at source.

4. For interest, the Italian tax rate is often 12.5 per cent, but can vary from nil to 30 per cent. The US/Italy tax treaty provides for relief where the Italian tax exceeds 15 per cent.

5. A tax treaty came into force recently and provides for relief from Spanish tax withholdings effective 1 January 1991.

6. UK source dividends are generally not subject to UK withholding tax. However, a tax credit (or advance corporation tax) attaches to each dividend. For a 'net' dividend of £75, the tax credit is £25 and the 'gross' dividend is £100. Generally, there is entitlement to a refund of £10 out of the £25 tax credit, equating to 13.33 per cent of the declared dividend. IRS certification is required on the fund's first reclaim.

7. A 3-month ownership test applies to gain the benefit of the tax treaty exemption.

		Local withholding tax standard rate (%)	**Comments**
Argentina	Dividends	20	
	Interest	14.4	
Brazil	Dividends	15	
	Interest		
Chile	Dividends	23.53	
	Interest		
Hong Kong	Dividends	Nil	
	Interest	Nil	
Ireland	Dividends	Nil	
	Interest	30	
Jordan	Dividends	Nil	
	Interest	Nil	
Malaysia	Dividends	Nil	*Dividends are usually declared inclusive of tax credit*
	Interest	20	
Singapore	Dividends	Nil	*Dividends are usually declared inclusive of tax credit*
	Interest	31	
Turkey	Dividends	Nil	
		10.5	

Figure A.3   US pension trust
III: **Tax relief not available**

Source: Chase Manhattan

		\multicolumn{3}{c}{Local withholding tax}	
		Standard rate (%)	Reduced to (%)	Tax relief (%)	Notes
Australia	Dividends	0-30	0-15	0-15	(Note 1)
	Interest	10	10	Nil	
Belgium	Dividends	See D.5			(Note 2)
	Interest	10 / 25	10 / Nil	Nil / 10 / 25	
Canada	Dividends	25	15	10	(Note 3)
	Interest	Nil / 25	Nil / 15	Nil / 25 / 10	
Finland	Dividends	25	15	10	
	Interest	15	Nil	15	
France	Dividends	See D.5			(Note 4)
	Interest	15	Nil	15	
Greece	Dividends	Nil	Nil	Nil	(Note 5)
	Interest	Nil / 10 / 46	Nil	Nil / 10 / 46	
Hungary	Dividends	20	15	5	(Note 6)
	Interest	20	Nil	20	
India	Dividends	20	20	Nil	(Note 7)
	Interest	n/a			
Indonesia	Dividends	20	15	5	
	Interest	20	15	5	
Italy	Dividends	15 / 32.4	15	Nil / 17.4	(Note 8)
	Interest	12.5	12.5	Nil	
Japan	Dividends	20	15	5	(Note 9)
	Interest	15 / 18	10 / 18	5 / Nil	
Mexico	Dividends	Nil / 35	Nil / 15	Nil / 20	(Note 10)
	Interest	Nil / 35	Nil / 15	Nil / 20	
Netherlands	Dividends	25	15	10	
	Interest	Nil			
New Zealand	Dividends	30	15	15	(Note 11)
	Interest	15	2 / 10	13 / 5	
Norway	Dividends	25	15	10	
	Interest	Nil			
Philippines	Dividends	35	25	10	
	Interest	20	10	10	
Portugal	Dividends	30	20 / 25	10 / 5	(Note 12)
	Interest	30	0-25	5-30	
South Korea	Dividends	26.875	15	11.875	(Note 13)
	Interest	21.5	12	9.50	
Spain	Dividends	18			(Note 14)
	Interest	25	Nil	25	
Sweden	Dividends	30	15	15	
	Interest	Nil			
USA	Dividends	Nil			(Note 15)
	Interest	Nil			

Figure A.4 US company - tax exempt investor
I: Tax relief can be credited with income payment

Source: Chase Manhattan

Withholding tax rates   241

Notes on Figure A.4

1. The dividend tax rate varies.

2. Interest derived from bonds issued from 1 March 1990 is subject to 10 per cent withholding tax. Tax exemption at source is available for certain bonds. In most cases, this requires the investor to convert the bonds into registered form.

3. Interest from certain corporate, government and quasi-state bonds is paid without deduction of Canadian tax, under local law. Under US tax treaty, an exemption from Canadian tax extends to interest derived from all government and quasi-state bonds. Other bonds interest (not qualifying for domestic tax exemption) attracts a reduced rate of 15 per cent. Certain qualifying insurance companies can be exempted from Canadian tax on dividends and interest payments.

4. Exemption at source is available for many bonds.

5. For dividends on non-voting preference shares, the standard rate of withholding tax of 35 per cent applies. Local law provides for interest from government bonds to be paid without deduction of Greek tax, and for certain qualifying corporate bonds to be subjected to a reduced 10 per cent tax rate. Exemption from Greek tax on bond interest payments is available under the US tax treaty. However, this only covers the first 9 per cent per annum return. It should be noted that current budget proposals may lead to a change in local tax rates.

6. If an Hungarian company suffers full rates of corporate tax, the applicable rate of withholding tax on dividend income is 10 per cent.

7. The standard rate of withholding tax under local legislation is 20 per cent. The USA/India treaty applies a rate of 25 per cent.

8. Dividends on savings shares are subject to 15 per cent withholding tax.

9. Bond interest payments are subject to a 15 per cent rate of tax. Government and corporate bills, which are discount instruments, are normally taxed at 18 per cent. However, with effect from 1 April 1992, new issues of government bills are exempted from this tax. The Japan/US tax treaty does not extend to tax on discount instruments.

10. For dividends, no tax is payable where the underlying profits have been

subjected to corporate taxation. A treaty between USA and Mexico was signed on 18 September 1992. Interest from government bonds and certain qualifying corporate bonds is paid without deduction of Mexican tax. For other bonds, the standard tax rate of 35 per cent is usually reduced to 10 per cent, where the interest is received by a bank.

11. Foreign investors can elect for qualifying debt instruments to be entered into a levy scheme, in lieu of the withholding tax regime.

12. The 30 per cent standard rate comprises a 5 per cent gift tax and a 25 per cent income tax withholding. These combined taxes are often reduced under local incentive legislation.

13. The standards 26.875 per cent tax rate on dividends comprises 25 per cent withholding tax plus a surcharge of 7.5 per cent of the withholding tax. For bond interest, the standard 21.5 per cent tax rate comprises 20 per cent withholding tax plus a surcharge at 7.5 per cent of the withholding tax.

14. Exemption is available at source on government instruments.

15. Back-up withholding can be avoided, provided a completed IRS Form W9 is held by the custodian.

		Local withholding tax			Steps to reclaim local tax		
		Standard rate (%)	Reduced to (%)	Tax relief (%)	Investor sign-off needed (1)	IRS sign-off needed (2)	Notes
Australia	Dividends	25	12.5	12.5	No	No	
	Interest	Nil					
Belgium	Dividends	1		Tax exemption may be available at source			
	Interest	Nil					
France	Dividends	25		52.5	No	No	(Note 3)
	Interest	15	Nil	15	No	No	
Germany	Dividends	25	10	15	No	No	
	Interest	Nil					
Italy	Dividends	32.4	15	17.4	Yes	Yes	(Note 4)
	Interest	12.5	12.5	Nil			
Luxembourg	Dividends	15	7.5	7.5	No	Yes	
	Interest	Nil					
Spain	Dividends	25	15	10	Yes	Yes	(Note 5)
	Interest	25	10	15	Yes	Yes	
Switzerland	Dividends	35	15	20	No	No	
	Interest	35	5	30	No	No	
UK	Dividends	Nil	(Note 6)	13.33	Yes	Yes	
	Interest	25	Nil (Note 7)	25	Yes	Yes	

Figure A.2   US pension trust
    II: Tax relief deferred

Source: Chase Manhattan

Notes on Figure A.5

1. Provided the investor grants the custodian an appropriate power of attorney, it can sign tax reclaim application forms on behalf of the investor for many countries. Nevertheless, tax reclaim forms still require the investor's signature where noted. Any delay in obtaining the signature will add to the total tax refund period.

2. Thereafter, certification by the IRS is required where indicated. The reclaim form will then be forwarded to the tax refund office in the market concerned.

3. A 20 per cent withholding tax rate applies in the case of dividend on 'AFV' shares. Dividends are usually declared at a rate which is net of Belgian withholding tax. Therefore, the withholding tax equates to 25 per cent of the declared dividend on AFV shares, or 33.33 per cent otherwise. The tax relief equates to 6.25 per cent of the declared dividend on AFV shares, or 13.33 per cent otherwise. Interest derived from bonds issued from 1 March 1990 is subject to 10 per cent withholding tax. See Part I in relation to tax exemption at source on certain bonds.

4. For dividends, entitlement to refund of the 25 per cent withholding tax, plus refund of 25 per cent tax credit (were applicable), less tax due at 15 per cent of the total of the dividend and the tax credit. For interest, tax exemption is often available at source.

5. Tax on bond interest only extends to convertible bonds.

6. Interest from certain government and quasi-state bodies is paid without deduction of Irish tax.

7. Exemption from tax on government instruments is available at source.

8. UK source dividends are generally not subject to UK withholding tax. However, a tax credit (or advance corporation tax) attaches to each dividend. For a 'net' dividend of £75, the tax credit is £25 and the 'gross' dividend is £100. Generally, there is entitlement to a refund of £10 out of the £25 tax credit, equating to 13.33 per cent of the declared dividend. IRS certification is required on the company's first dividend reclaim. However, in the case of mutual funds organized as business trusts, IRS certification is not required for dividend or interest reclaims.

		Local withholding tax standard rate (%)	Comments
Argentina	Dividends	20	*Interest from government bonds and certain corporate bonds is paid without deduction of Argentine tax.*
	Interest	Nil / 14.4	
Brazil	Distribution	15 / 25	*Income distributed by foreign investment funds constituted from resources arising from the conversion of Brazilian foreign debt is subject to 25% Brazilian tax.*
Chile	Distribution	23.53	
China (Shenzen)	Dividends	10	*'B' shares only*
	Interest	n/a	*20% standard rate. 10% rate due to special economic area.*
Colombia	Dividends	12	
	Interest	12	
Hong Kong	Dividends	Nil	
	Interest	Nil	
Jordan	Dividends	Nil	
	Interest	Nil	
Malaysia	Dividends	Nil	*Dividends are usually declared inclusive of a 34% tax credit.*
	Interest	20	
Pakistan	Dividends	16.5	*The standard 16.5% tax rate on dividends comprises withholding tax. For bond interest, the standard tax rates comprise withholding tax at 60% (for banks) or 50% (for other investors), plus a surcharge at 10% of the withholding tax. The surcharge on dividends and bond interest is normally imposed as part of the annual tax return process.*
	Interest	55 / 66	

Figure A.6 US company
III: Tax relief not available

Source: *Chase Manhattan*

Appendix B

The Cadbury Code of Best Practice

(from the Committee on the Financial Aspects of Corporate Governance)

1   **The Board of Directors**

    1.1   The board should meet regularly, retain full and effective control over the company and monitor the executive management.

    1.2   There should be a clearly accepted division of responsibilities at the head of a company, which will ensure a balance of power and authority, such that no one individual has unfettered powers of decision. Where the chairman is also the chief executive, it is essential that there should be a strong and independent element on the board, with a recognized senior member.

    1.3   The board should include non-executive directors of sufficient calibre and number for their views to carry significant weight in the board's decisions.

    1.4   The board should have a formal schedule of matters specifically reserved to it for decision to ensure that the direction and control of the company is firmly in its hands.

    1.5   There should be an agreed procedure for directors in the furtherance of their duties to take independent professional advice if necessary, at the company's expense.

    1.6   All directors should have access to the advice and services of the company secretary, who is responsible to the board for ensuring that board procedures are followed and that applicable rules and regulations are complied with. Any question of the removal of the company secretary should be a matter for the board as a whole.

2 Non-Executive Directors

2.1 Non-executive directors should bring an independent judgement to bear on issues of strategy, performance, resources, including key appointments, and standards of conduct.

2.2 The majority should be independent of management and free from any business or other relationship which could materially interfere with the exercise of their independent judgement, apart from their fees and shareholding. Their fees should reflect the time which they commit to the company.

2.3 Non-executive directors should be appointed for specified terms and reappointment should not be automatic.

2.4 Non-executive directors should be selected through a formal process and both this process and their appointment should be a matter for the board as a whole.

3 Executive Directors

3.1 Director's service contracts should not exceed three years without shareholders' approval.

3.2 There should be full and clear disclosure of directors' total emoluments and those of the chairman and highest-paid UK director, including pension contributions and stock options. Separate figures should be given for salary and performance-related elements and the basis on which performance is measured should be explained.

3.3 Executive directors' pay should be subject to the recommendations of a remuneration committee made up wholly or mainly of non-executive directors.

4 Reporting and Controls

4.1 It is the board's duty to present a balanced and understandable assessment of the company's position.

4.2 The board should ensure that an objective and professional relationship is maintained with the auditors.

4.3 The board should establish an audit committee of at least 3 non-executive directors with written terms of reference which deal clearly with its authority and duties.

4.4 The directors should explain their responsibility for preparing the accounts next to a statement by the auditors about their reporting responsibilities.

4.5 The directors should report on the effectiveness of the company's system of internal control.

4.6. The directors should report that the business is a going concern, with supporting assumptions or qualifications as necessary.

Appendix C

Environmental Declaration

We the undersigned, believe that human welfare, environmental protection and sustainable development depend on the commitment of governments, businesses and individuals. We recognize that the pursuit of economic growth and a healthy environment are inextricably linked. We further recognize that ecological protection and sustainable development are collective responsibilities and must rank among the highest priorities of all business activities, including banking. We will endeavour to ensure that our policies and business actions promote sustainable development: meeting the needs of the present without compromising those of the future.

1. **General Principles of Sustainable Development**

    1.1   We believe that all countries should work towards common environmental goals.

    1.2   We regard sustainable development as a fundamental aspect of sound business management.

    1.3   We believe that progress towards sustainable development can best be achieved by working within the framework of market mechanisms to promote environmental protection. We believe that there is a role for governments to provide the right signals to individuals and businesses, to promote behavioural changes in favour of effective environmental management through the conservation of energy and natural resources, whilst promoting economic growth.

    1.4   We regard a versatile, dynamic financial services sector as an important contributor towards sustainable development.

    1.5   We recognize that sustainable development is a corporate commitment and an integral part of our pursuit of good citizenship. We are moving towards the integration of environmental considerations into internal banking operations and business decisions in a manner which enhances sustainable development.

2 Environmental Management and Banks

2.1 We subscribe to the precautionary approach to environmental management, which strives to anticipate and prevent potential environmental degradation.

2.2 We expect, as part of our normal business practices, that our customers comply with all applicable local, national and international environmental regulations. Beyond compliance, we regard sound environmental practices as one of the key factors demonstrating effective corporate management.

2.3 We recognize that environmental risks should be part of the normal checklist of risk assessment and management. As part of our credit risk assessment, we recommend, when appropriate, environmental impact assessments.

2.4 We will, in our domestic and international operations, endeavour to apply the same standards of environmental risk assessment.

2.5 We look to public institutions to conduct appropriate, up-to-date and comprehensive environmental assessments in ventures with them, and to share the results of those assessments with participating banks.

2.6 We intend to update our management practices, including accounting, marketing, risk assessment, public affairs, employee communications and training, to incorporate relevant developments in environmental management. We encourage banking research in these and related issues.

2.7 We will seek to ensure that in our internal operations we pursue the best practices in environmental management, including energy efficiency, recycling and waste minimization. We will seek to form business relations with suppliers and sub-contractors who follow similarly high environmental standards.

2.8 We support and will develop suitable banking products and services designed to promote environmental protection, where there is a sound business rationale.

Environmental Declaration 255

2.9 We recognize the need to conduct internal environmental reviews on a periodic basis to measure our operational activities against our environmental goals.

3 Public Awareness and Communication

3.1 We will share information with customers, as appropriate, so that they may strengthen their own capacity to reduce environmental risk, and promote sustainable development.

3.2 We will foster openness and dialogue relating to environmental management with all relevant audiences, including governments, clients, employees, shareholders and the public.

3.3 We recommend that banks develop and publish a statement of their environmental policy and periodically report on its implementation.

3.4 We ask the United Nations Environment Programme to assist the industry by providing, within its capacity, relevant information relating to sustainable development.

3.5 We will periodically review the success in implementing this Statement and will revise it as appropriate.

3.6 We encourage other banks to support this Statement.

National Westminster Bank plc, United Kingdom
Royal Bank of Canada, Canada
Deutsche Bank AG, Germany
Hong Kong and Shanghai Banking Corporation, Hong Kong
Westpac Banking Corporation, Australia
Banco do Estado de São Paulo SA, Brazil
Bank Austria, Austria
Bank of Baroda, India
Banky Fampandrosoana Ny Varotra, Madagascar
Credit Suisse, Switzerland
Dresdner Bank AG, Germany
Romanian Commercial Bank SA, Romania
The Royal Bank of Scotland plc, Scotland
The Balkanbank of Bulgaria, Bulgaria

Bank of Philippine Islands
Canadian Imperial Bank of Commerce, Canada
Kenya Commercial Bank, Kenya
Banco Espanol de Credito Banesto, Spain
Bank Handlowy w Warszawie SA, Poland
Bank of Ireland Group, Eire
Commerzbank AG, Germany
Den Danske Bank A/S, Denmark
Landsbanki Islands, Iceland
Swiss Bank Corporation, Switzerland
Arab Bank Ltd, Jordan
Creditanstalt-Bankverein of Austria, Austria
Bank of Nova Scotia, Canada
Kansallis-Osake-Pankki, Finland
Uganda Commercial Bank, Uganda
Komercne Banka, Czech and Slovak Republic

The Royal Bank of Scotland

Corporate Environmental Policy Statement

In recognizing that concern for the environment is an integral and fundamental part of the Bank's corporate strategy, an Environmental Steering Group has been established under the Chairmanship of an Executive Director of the Bank

An environmental review of our operations has been carried out by external consultants.

A programme of improvements resulting from the environmental review is overseen by the Environmental Steering Group which includes Director participation and report twice yearly to the main board of directors.

A Programme of Responsible Energy Management has been established.

Staff are being asked to consider environmental issues carefully when making decisions or when planning and controlling work.

Employees are encouraged to act in accordance with this environmental policy statement and are given appropriate training and education to do so as required.

Another area of priority is minimization of waste at source and facilitating the recycling/re-use of waste material where possible.

The disposal and transport of wastes off-site is carried out with due regard to environmental legislation.

Environmental laws and regulations are monitored closely and implemented to ensure that regulatory requirements are met in full.

Where appropriate, we will inform our suppliers, customers, workforce and the public about the measures we take to protect the environment and seek their co-operation in meeting our objectives.

The Bank subscribes to the concept of "sustainability", i.e. it will, as far as is practical and consistent with its requirements as a business concern, adopt and aim to apply the principle of sustainable development which meets the needs of the present without compromising the abilities of future generations to meet their own needs.

Summary

In light of the foregoing commitment, the Bank's Corporate Environmental Policy Statement may be summarized as follows:

to ensure environmental implications are considered when assessing credit proposals;

to conserve the usage of energy and raw materials;

to endeavour to reduce wastage as far as possible;

to endeavour to recycle materials as far as possible;

to endeavour to avoid pollution of air, land or water;

to improve the working environment;

to observe and, if possible, exceed environmental regulatory standards;

to play a part in community environmental initiatives;

to train employees in good environmental practices;

to use the products and services of suppliers whose environmental policies are compatible with our own.

Appendix D

Representative indices in world markets

Mature markets

Australia:	All Ordinaries, All Mining
Austria:	Credit Aktien
Belgium:	Belgium Lo
Canada:	Metals and Minerals Composite
Denmark:	Copenhagen Stock Exchange
Finland:	HEX General
France:	CAC 40
Germany:	FAZ Aktien, DAX
Hong Kong:	Hang Seng
Italy:	Banca Commercials
Japan:	Nikkei 225, Topix
Netherlands:	CBS Allshare
New Zealand:	CAP 40
Norway:	Oslo Stock Exchange
Singapore:	All Singapore
South Africa:	Johannesburg Stock Exchange Gold Johannesburg Stock Exchange Industrials
Spain:	Madrid Stock Exchange

Sweden: Affärsvärlden General

Switzerland: Swiss Bank Industrials

UK: FT Stock Exchange Industrials
FT Stock Exchange Mid-250

USA: Dow Jones Industrial Average
Standard & Poor's Composite
Nasdaq Composite

Emerging markets

Argentina: General

Brazil: Bovespa

Chile: IPGA General

Greece: Athens Stock Exchange

India: Bombay Stock Exchange

Indonesia: Jakarta Composite

Ireland: ISEQ Overall

Malaysia: Kuala Lumper SE Composite

Mexico: IPC

Philippines: Manila Composite

Portugal: BTA

South Korea: Korea Composite

Taiwan: Weighted Index

Thailand: Bangkok Stock Exchange

Turkey: Istanbul Composite

Appendix E

Some key data providers

USA	UK
Bloomberg L.P.	
499 Park Avenue, 15th Floor New York, NY 10022	City Gate House 39-45 Finsbury Square London EC2A 1PX
212-318-2000	071-330-7500
Datastream International	
299 Park Avenue, 25th Floor New York, NY 10171	58-64 City Road London EC1Y 2AL
212-593-6500	071-250-3000
EXTEL Financial	
Two World Trade Center 18th Floor New York, NY 10048	Fitzroy House 13-17 Epworth Street London EC2A 4DL
212-513-1570	071-251-3333

I/B/E/S Inc.

345 Hudson Street
New York, NY 10014

212-243-3335

47-49 Tooley Street
London SE1 2QT

071-234-5424

Randall-Helms International

19 Center Street
Chatham, New Jersey 07928

201-635-0510

21-26 Garlick Hill
London EC4V 2AU

071-248-6126

Reuters

Reuter America, Inc.
1700 Broadway
New York, NY 10019
212-603-3300

Reuters Ltd.
85 Fleet Street
London EC4P 4AJ
071-510-8379

Index

accounting
    categories of tradition 132
    differences 130-138
Accounting Standards Board
    Draft Statement of Principles 122
active selection 109
ADRs 24, 52, 129-130
    described 186-188
age dependency ratio 71-72
AIMR 171, 173-174
alcohol 162-163
Alliance Trust 13-16
alpha 109
American Depository Receipts
    See ADRs
analysis
    See security analysis
appraised value
    See intrinsic value
Argentina
    country weighting 31, 101
    interest rates 91
    market capitalization 31
    market correlation 46
    market performance 36-37
    settlement 150
Asean 39
aspirational screens 161-162
Association of South East Asian Nations
    See Asean
Australia
    budget deficit/GDP 88
    country weighting 27, 99
    current account 90
    futures contracts 106
    in global equity portfolio 102
    interest rates 90
    market capitalization 28
    market performance 35
    market performance during '87 Crash 44
    pension assets 67-70
    settlement 149-150
Austria
    interest rates 90
    market capitalization 28
    market performance 35
    market performance during '87 Crash 44

    stock options, list of 110
avoidance screens 162
baby boomers 70-71, 73
balance of trade 89
Belgian Congo 4
Belgium
    budget deficit/GDP 88
    current account 90
    interest rates 90
    market capitalization 28
    market performance 35
    market performance during '87 Crash 44
    pension assets 68-70
Benetton 178-179
beta 40, 111, 172
Blairlogie Capital Management 180
Body Shop, The 56-58
bottom-up approach 79
Brazil
    country weighting 31, 101
    GNP 86
    interest rates 91
    market capitalization 31
    market correlation 46
    market performance 36-37
Brussels Stock Exchange 169
Budapest Stock Exchange 36-37
budget deficit 88-89
Buffet, Warren 80
Cadbury Code of Best Practice 159, 249-251
Cammack, Addison 96
Canada
    country weighting 27, 99
    current account 90
    futures contracts 106
    in global equity portfolio 102
    market capitalization 28
    market performance 35
    market performance during '87 Crash 44
    pension assets 67-70
capital
    as factor of production 84-85
Capital Asset Pricing Model 111
    described 42
Capital International Company 27
CAPM
    See Capital Asset Pricing Model

carve-out
    See portfolio, carve-out
cash
    administration 152-153
    use in equity portfolios 143
CDs 74
central value
    See intrinsic value
CERES Principles 164-165
certificates of deposit
    See CDs
CFTC 105-106
Chase Manhattan 149, 154
Chile
    country weighting 31
    interest rates 91
    market capitalization 31
    market correlation 46-47
    market performance 36-37
    settlement 150
China
    country weighting 31
    market capitalization 31
    market performance 36
closed-end funds
    described 184-185
Colombia 30
    country weighting 31
    interest rates 91
    market capitalization 31-32
    market correlation 46-47
    market performance 36-37
commissions, soft 192
Commodity Futures Trading Commission
    See CFTC
concensus estimates 94-95
Copenhagen Stock Exchange 96
corporate governance 159-166
Costa Rica 30
crashes
    See stock markets; crashes
credit ratios 127
currency 139-143
    cross-hedging 141
    forwards 140-141
    hedging 114, 140-143
    options 114, 140-141
    treatment of under US GAAP 136
custody
    global 147-154, 156-157
    reporting 147-148
cyclical turnaround stocks 52-53
Daimler Benz 132-138
data sources 189-193
    listed 261-262

Davidson, Richard 117, 119-120
debt/equity ratio 94, 122
Denmark
    interest rates 90
    market capitalization 28
    market performance 33, 35
    market performance during '87 Crash 44
    pension assets 68-70
    settlement 150
    stock options, list of 110
depreciation 133
developed markets 27-29
    correlations between 41-42
    correlations of 40
    interest rates in 90
    performance of 33-34
    See also MSCIWI Index
dividend yield 92
Domini Social Index (DSI) 166
DVFA 130
EAFE Index 27, 29-30, 32, 42, 74, 82, 98, 100, 140-142, 167-170
    correlation 40-41, 46
    performance of 35-36
economic factors 82-89
Ecuador 30
Edinburgh Investment Trust 16-19, 30
Electrolux 178
emerging markets 27, 29-32, 36-38, 100-101, 105
    correlation 45
    interest rates in 91
    performance of 34-36
Employee Retirement Income Security
    See ERISA
entrepreneur
    as factor of production 85
Environmental Declaration 253-258
environmental investing 161, 163-165
ERISA 23
ERM 116-117
European exchange rate mechanism
    See ERM
factors of production 83-85
fair value
    See intrinsic value
Federal Reserve Bank 58, 81, 142
Finland
    budget deficit/GDP 88
    effect of dollar on markets 115
    HEX Index 96
    interest rates 90
    market capitalization 28
    market performance 35
    performance of market 33
    stock options, list of 110

foreign exchange 153
France
　budget deficit/GDP 88
　country weighting 98-100
　current account 90
　demographics 71-72
　dividend yields 118
　dollar earnings 115
　effect of dollar on markets 115-116
　futures contracts 106
　in global equity portfolio 102
　interest rates 90, 118
　market capitalization 28
　market correlation 41
　market performance 35
　market performance during '87 Crash 44
　money market rate 74
　pension assets 68-71, 73
　stock options, list of 110
Frank Russell 172
futures markets
　contract example 106-107
　rapid implementation by using 105, 107
　stock index contract listing 106
G7 nations 39, 142
GAAP
　German 133, 136-137
　US 133, 136-137
GDP
　ratio to budget deficit 88
　real 85-86
　& telephone line diffusion 65
Generally Accepted Accounting Principles
　See GAAP
German Investment Analysts Association
　See DVFA
Germany
　budget deficit/GDP 88
　country weighting 98-100
　current account 90
　demographics 71-72
　dividend yield 119
　dollar earnings 115
　effect of dollar on markets 115-116
　in global equity portfolio 102
　interest rates 90, 117, 119
　market capitalization 28
　market correlation 41
　market performance 35
　market performance during '87 Crash 44
　money market rate 74
　pension assets 68-70
　stock options, list of 110
Global Custodian 'Roll of Honour' 157
global sector themes 58-65

GNP
　real 85-86
gold
　as investment factor 81
Goodhart's Law 82
goodwill
　treatment under US GAAP 136
governance
　See corporate governance
Graham, Benjamin 79, 92, 122-123, 125, 128
Greece
　country weighting 31
　interest rates 91
　market capitalization 31
　market correlation 46
　market performance 37
gross domestic product
　See GDP
gross national product
　See GNP
growth ratio 126
Hadrian's Wall 3-4
healthcare 162
Henriquez, Billy 43
hidden assets 123
hidden values 123
Hong Kong
　country weighting 99, 114
　futures contracts 106
　in global equity portfolio 102
　interest rates 90
　market capitalization 28
　market performance 35
　market performance during '87 Crash 44
　pension assets 68-70
Hong Kong & Shanghai Banking Corp.
　See HSBC
HSBC 49-50
human rights 162
Hungary 30
　market performance 36-37
IDS 25
IFC 27, 35
　See also IFC Global Index; IFC Investable
　Index; IFCA Index; IFCC Index; IFCL Index
IFC Emerging Markets Index
　See IFC Investable Index
IFC Global Index 29-32, 36, 98
　performance of 37, 74
IFC Investable Index 30-32, 36, 82, 98, 100-101,
167-168, 180
　correlation 46-47
　performance of 37
IFCA Index 27, 168
　correlation 46

IFCC Index
  correlation 46
IFCL Index 27, 168
  correlation 46
IMRO 155, 174
index replication 111
India 30
  country weighting 31
  interest rates 91
  market capitalization 31-32
  market correlation 46
  market performance 37
indicated value
  See intrinsic value
indices
  listed 259-260
Indonesia 30
  country weighting 31
  interest rates 91
  market capitalization 31
  market correlation 47
  market performance 37
inflation 87
  effect of in 1940s 18
infrastructure investing 5
institutional investors
  aims of 39
  types of 39
interest equalization tax 23
interest rates 89-91
international equity investing
  case for 35-36
International Financial Corporation
  See IFC
international investing
  case for 23-25
  early forms of 3-4
international portfolio management 7-8
  early protagonists 9-19
InterSec Research Corporation 171-172
intrinsic value 123, 125
Investment Advisors Act 174
Investment Management Regulatory
  Organization
  See IMRO
investment value
  See intrinsic value
Investment vehicles 177-188
Investor Responsibility Research Center
  See IRRC
Ireland
  market capitalization 28
  market performance 35
  pension assets 68-70
IRRC 162

Italy
  budget deficit/GDP 88
  country weighting 99
  current account 90
  demographics 72
  dollar earnings 115
  effect of dollar on markets 115
  GDP 86
  in global equity portfolio 102
  interest rates 90
  market capitalization 28
  market performance 35
  market performance during '87 Crash 44
  securities lending 155
  settlement 151
James Capel 102
Japan
  bond yields 95
  budget deficit/GDP 88
  country weighting 27, 41, 98-100
  current account 90
  demographics 71-72
  effect of dollar on markets 115-116
  futures contracts 106-108
  in global equity portfolio 102
  inflation 87
  interest rates 90
  market capitalization 28
  market correlation 41, 46
  market performance 35, 40-41
  market performance during '87 Crash 44
  money market rate 74
  pension assets 68-70
  standard deviation of market 40
  top five banks 59
Jordan
  country weighting 31
  interest rates 91
  market capitalization 31
  market performance 37
Kenya 30
key ratios 125-126
Kinki Nippon Railway 123-124
Korea Fund 25
Kyocera Corporation 53-56
labour
  as factor of production 83-84
land
  as factor of production 83
large capitalization stocks 50-52
Livermore, Jesse 52, 105, 109
MacBride Principles 162-163
MacDougall, W.O. 15
Malaysia
  country weighting 31, 99-101

Index 267

Malaysia (cont.)
    in EAFE Index 29
    in global equity portfolio 102
    interest rates 90
    market capitalization 28, 31
    market correlation 46-47
    market performance 35, 37
    market volatility 105
manager, types of
    'style' 170
    country 170
    global 169
    international 170
    regional 170
market correlations 40-45
Markowitz, Harry 41-42
Marshall, Alfred 82
Mexico
    country weighting 31, 99-101
    in global equity portfolio 102
    interest rates 91
    market capitalization 31-32
    market correlation 46
    market performance 36-37
mineral markets 27
Mitsubishi Estate 123-124
monetary factors 89-92
money, weight of 67-75
Morgan Stanley 117
    See also Davidson, Richard; EAFE Index; MSCIWI
Morgan Stanley Capital International World Index
    See MSCIWI
Morocco 30
MSCIWI 24, 27-29, 32-38, 41, 98, 102, 168-169
    performance of 35
multinational companies 177-178
mutual funds 24-25, 73, 170-171
    described 179-183
Nafta 39
Netherlands
    country weighting 99
    current account 90
    dollar earnings 115
    effect of dollar on markets 115-116
    futures contracts 106
    in global equity portfolio 102
    interest rates 90
    market capitalization 28
    market performance 35
    market performance during '87 Crash 44
    money market rate 74
    pension assets 68-70
    stock options, list of 110

network management 149
New York Mercantile Exchange 178
New York Stock Exchange 133, 137, 139
New Zealand
    interest rates 90
    market capitalization 28
    market performance 35
Nigeria
    country weighting 31
    market capitalization 31
Nikkei Index 24, 27, 100
normal value
    See intrinsic value
North American Free Trade Area
    See Nafta
Norway
    effect of dollar on markets 115
    interest rates 90
    market capitalization 28, 32
    market performance 35
    market performance during '87 Crash 44
    pension assets 68-70
    stock options, list of 110
Nowakowski, Chris 98
nuclear power 162
nuclear weapons 162
oil
    as investment factor 81
options
    See stock options, currency optons
Oslo Stock Exchange 96
Pakistan 30
    country weighting 31
    interest rates 91
    market capitalization 31
    market performance 37
passive selection 109
pay-out ratio 126
peer group 169-170
pension assets 67-70
Pension Investment Research Consultants 159-160
pension provisions 133
performance benchmark 167
performance measurement 171
Performance Presentation Standards Committee
    See AIMR
Peru
    country weighting 31
    in IFC Index 30
    market capitalization 31
PFAMCo group of funds 180-182
Philippines
    country weighting 31

Philippines (cont.)
    interest rates 91
    market correlation 47
    market performance 36-37
    settlement 151
Poland 30
    market performance 36
pollution 162
population 70-73
    See also demographics, under specific country entry
portfolio
    carve out 171-172
    construction 105-108
    discretionary 171
    performance measurement 167-174
    standard deviation 42, 47
portfolios
    standard deviation of 42
Portugal
    country weighting 31
    interest rates 91
    market capitalization 31
    market performance 37
price
    ratios 127
    to book value (P/BV) 94, 122
    to cashflow (P/CF) 93-94, 122
    to earnings (P/E) 61, 92-93, 122
profitability ratio 95, 126
Putnam 25
railroads 123-124
    early investment in 10-11, 14, 16-18
railways
    See railroads
ranking of countries 96-97
reasonable value
    See intrinsic value
Rio Earth Summit (1992) 163-164
risk diversification 39-47
risk optimization 121
Russia 30
S&P 500 Index 36, 75, 166
    correlation 40-41
safe-keeping 151-152
SAINTS 10-13
Sandoz 128-130
Scotland
    & global investment 9-10
    See also trusts, Scottish
Scottish American Investment Company
    See SAINTS
SEC 159, 173-174
Securities & Exchange Commission
    See SEC

Securities & Futures Association
    See SFA
securities lending 153-156
security analysis 122-125
    anticipation approach 123
    description function 122
    selective function 122
    value approach 123
settlement 151-152
    See also under specific country entry
SFA 155
Sicav 179
silver
    as investment factor 82
Singapore
    budget deficit/GDP 88
    country weighting 99, 114
    in EAFE Index 29
    in global equity portfolio 102
    interest rates 90
    market capitalization 28
    market performance 35
    market performance during '87 Crash 44
Slepak Principles 162
social investing
    See infrastructure investing
social screening 159-166
Société d'Investissement à Capital Variable
    See Sicav
South Africa 162
    market capitalization 28
South Korea 30
    country weighting 31, 99
    in global equity portfolio 102
    interest rates 91
    market capitalization 31
    market correlation 46
    market performance 37
    See also Korea Fund
Spain
    country weighting 99
    current account 90
    dollar earnings 115
    effect of dollar on markets 115
    in global equity portfolio 102
    interest rates 90
    market capitalization 28
    market performance 33, 35
    market performance during '87 Crash 44
    yield ratio 93
Spain Fund 25
Sri Lanka
    country weighting 31
    in IFC Index 30
    market capitalization 30-31

stability
  measures of 96, 126
standard deviation 172
Statement of Accounting Practices (SSAP) 131-132
stock markets 92
  correlations between 40
  Crash of 1929 45
  Crash of 1987 43-45, 92
  dollar-sensitive 114-116, 140
  history of crashes 43
  performance 33-38
  sector analysis 111-114
  size of 27-32
stock options 107, 109-111
stocks
  high-yield 120
  interest-rate sensitive 116-119, 121
  selection of 109-138
  See also stock selection
Suez Canal 4
Sweden
  Affärsvärlden Index 96
  country weighting 99
  current account 90
  dollar earnings 115
  effect of dollar on markets 115
  in global equity portfolio 102
  interest rates 90
  market capitalization 28
  market performance 35
  market performance during '87 Crash 44
  pension assets 68-70
  stock options, list of 110
Switzerland
  country weighting 99
  current account 90
  dollar earnings 115
  effect of dollar on markets 115-116
  futures contracts 106
  in global equity portfolio 102
  interest rates 90
  market capitalization 28
  market performance 35
  market performance during '87 Crash 44
  money market rate 74
  pension assets
  stock options, list of 110
T. Rowe-Price Fund 25
Taiwan 30
  country weighting 31, 99
  in global equity portfolio 102
  interest rates 91
  market capitalization 31
  market performance 37

Taiwan Fund 25
take-overs 6-7
taxation
  deferred, under US & German GAAP 136
  withholding tax rates 233-247
technical analysis 96
telecommunications
  as global sector theme 60-65
  line diffusion 62-65
  line diffusion and GDP 65
  valuations 60-61
Telefonos de Mexico (Telmex) 101, 121
Templeton Emerging Markets Fund 25
Templeton, John 80
Thailand
  country weighting 31, 99
  in global equity portfolio 102
  interest rates 91
  market capitalization 31
  market correlation 47
  market performance 37
tobacco 162-163
Tokyo Declaration 163
Tokyo Stock Exchange 107
  cost of trading 108
top-down approach 79
  described 81-98, 100-103
Topix Stock Index 107
trusts
  See also closed-end funds
  Scottish 9-19
  UK investment 186-187
Turkey 30
  budget deficit/GDP 88
  country weighting 31
  interest rates 91
  market capitalization 31
  market performance 36-37
  settlement 151
unique investments 53-58
United Kingdom
  budget deficit/GDP 88-89
  country weighting 27, 99-100
  current account 90
  demographics 72
  dividend yield 118
  dollar earnings 115
  effect of dollar on markets 115-116
  futures contracts 106
  gilts 74
  in global equity portfolio 102
  inflation 87
  interest rates 90, 117-118
  market capitalization 28
  market correlation 41, 46

United Kingdom (cont.)
    market performance 35
    market performance during '87 Crash 44
    money market rate 74
    pension assets 68-70
    pension funds 159-160
    securities lending 155
    stock options, list of 110
United States
    budget deficit/GDP 88
    country weighting 27, 32, 98-99
    current account 90
    demographics 72
    effect of dollar on markets 115
    in global equity portfolio 102
    market capitalization 28-29
    market correlation 46
    market performance 35
    market performance during '87 Crash 44
    money market rate 74
    pension assets 68-71
    pension funds 159
    Treasury bonds 68, 74
valuation reporting 148
Venezuela 30
    country weighting 31
    interest rates 91
    market capitalization 31
    market performance 37
Vietnam 30
Volcker, Paul 58, 81, 142
weapons 162
weighting decision 98-102
WM Company 172
World Investment Report (1993) 6
Zimbabwe
    country weighting 31
    market capitalization 31
    market correlation 46

The Publisher....

Probus is a major force on the international business and finance publishing scene. We are committed to publishing the very finest books and information products. Our range of quality books in core business subjects such as investments, banking, the capital markets, accountancy, taxation, property, insurance, sales management, marketing and healthcare, is second to none. We believe that you will find many other titles in our range to be of interest. Are you a writer? If so, please feel free to refer potential publications to us.

You may wish to contact Probus direct at:

Probus Publishing Company	OR	Probus Europe
1925 North Clybourn Avenue		11 Millers Yard
Chicago		Mill Lane
Illinois 60614		Cambridge CB2 1RQ
USA		England
Tel: (312) 868-1100		Tel: (0223) 322018
Tel [Sales]: 1-800-PROBUS-1		Fax: (0223) 61149
Fax: (312) 868-6250		

The World's Futures & Options Markets, Nick Battley (Ed.)
1029pp, Probus Europe, 1994. ISBN 1 55738 513 0

Where in the world can you trade Biotechnology Index options? What are the component stocks of the FT-SE 100 Index? Which is the most heavily-traded of the world's five eurodollar futures contracts? The answers to all these questions—and more—can be found in this fully classified directory, making it **the** essential reference work for everyone with a professional or personal interest in futures and options. This major publication features detailed information on over 550 contracts, categorized by type and listed alphabetically for ease of reference. Of course, in addition to the contracts, the 51 exchanges on which they are traded are covered in full detail.

For those with an appetite for statistics, the appendices contain 7-year historical volume figures, not only for almost every contract, but also for each exchange.

To bring the world of international futures and options directly to your your desk, place an order with your bookseller, or call (0223) 322018 in the UK or (312) 868 1100 in the United States.